WORDS PEOPLE USE

Audrey J. Roth
E. Oliver Camacho

Miami-Dade Junior College

Winthrop Publishers, Inc.
Cambridge, Massachusetts

Cover by Donya Melanson

Contents

3. words about behavior

4. words about work

5. words about cultures

6. words about science

Preface

In *Gulliver's Travels,* Jonathan Swift wrote of Gulliver's voyage to Laputa and his visit to the School of Languages where a group of professors was engaged in abolishing all words. "Since words are only names for things," the Laputians reasoned, "it would be more convenient for all men to carry about with them such things as were necessary to express the particular business they are to discourse on."

Could you picture having to take a computer along with you in the morning if you planned to talk about it during the day? Obviously, the Laputian scheme was folly in Swift's time and would be outrageous in our own. Moreover, it would be poor indeed if language were limited only to words for *things,* for people need words to express *ideas,* too.

As it is, English contains more than 750,000 words, and new ones are constantly being added. It is impossible to learn all these words—and there is really no need for any one person to know them all. But it *is* useful to increase one's personal vocabulary—for reasons ranging from business advancement to better expression of ideas.

Everyone has several vocabularies: for reading and writing, and for speaking and listening. There are words one "knows" and words one "uses"—and many more that would be useful if they were known and used.

The aim of WORDS PEOPLE USE is to increase your vocabulary, and to make available to you many words that will be helpful in both your classes and in day-to-day communication. Some of the words will already be familiar; you can readily define or use them. Others you may recognize. But there are probably many words in this book that will be new to you and these you can most profitably add to your vocabulary.

THE METHOD

It is easy to learn new words in relation to others that have the same or similar word parts. Learning words in subject groups is also a good method. Both ways are used in this book: the words are grouped according to roots—

each unit in the book is a different root—and each chapter is a group of word roots related to the same general subject.

First, each word appears in a context that helps you understand what it means. You write the meaning of the word as you can define it from this context and then check yourself immediately against the summary at the end of the section. Then, there are other exercises within each group that let you work with the word parts (roots and affixes) several times, gaining familiarity with words in reinforcing your new knowledge. There are matching games, true-false exercises, even crossword puzzles for you to fill in. Always the answers are after the exercise for an immediate check. And often you will be asked to write the words you are learning, an activity that helps you remember them.

THE ORGANIZATION

Each chapter in WORDS PEOPLE USE is based on an area of student interest: humanities, technology and business, social science, and natural science. But just as words refuse to be limited by boundaries, these groupings are not limited precisely by either subject matter or other such artificial barriers. A word learned in one chapter may be used in many courses and contexts once it becomes part of your vocabulary.

Words in each chapter are presented in related groups based on Latin or Greek roots. This is partly because words are remembered more easily if they are learned in groups and partly because words with the same root are often in the same area of study. Chapter One explains these ideas in more detail and sets the stage for the rest of the book.

Chapters Two through Six each begin with a pretest: multiple choice questions that require knowledge of those words which appear within the chapter. If you can answer all the pretest questions, you will probably find the vocabulary within that chapter easy to master. If you have trouble with the pretest, a little extra application to studying the words that follow might be useful.

Each chapter consists of several units based on selected vocabulary roots. There are also illustrations of how affixes can expand vocabulary when they are combined with roots. At the end of each chapter there is a posttest of multiple choice questions for you to check your mastery of words within each chapter.

THE EXERCISES

Vocabulary is a working thing, so a vocabulary book must be a working book—one in which you participate. That is the principle on which WORDS PEOPLE USE is built, and there is ample opportunity for you to work with the words in the text.

As we have mentioned, each word root within a chapter is a separate unit. The root is explained and those words which are formed from it appear in a context that gives meaning to the word as well as showing its use. The exercises that follow illustrate several ways of learning the same words: true-false questions, matching exercises, fill-in paragraphs, even crossword puzzles. Always you write or check or in some way actually *work with* the words you are learning. And always the answers are easy to check because they follow each exercise. However, you should keep in mind that in the long run, it will not help you to look at the answers before you do the exercises!

At the end of the book is a general posttest that gives you a chance to demonstrate knowledge of words from throughout the text—and to compare that score with your score on the general pretest at the beginning of the book.

It is hoped that by the time you finish working with this book, instead of carrying *things* with you like the Laputians about whom Jonathan Swift wrote, you will be able to carry with you many new *words*—a vocabulary that enables you to communicate with new ease and assurance on a variety of topics.

A.J.R.
E.O.C.
Miami, Florida

WORDS PEOPLE USE

GENERAL PRETEST

The vocabulary words in this pre-test appear throughout the pages that follow. See how many you already know by choosing the correct completion for each sentence. The number of answers you get correct will indicate your present ability; the post-test at the end of the book will show how much you have been able to improve. The more words you know now, the easier you will find it to learn other words on the following pages, because each word here is related to others in the separate chapters.

DIRECTIONS: In the space next to each number, write the letter that correctly completes the statement.

_____ 1. Jennifer made her biennial trip to Europe in 1970. Her next one will be in
    a. 1971.
    b. 1972.
    c. 1973.
    d. 1974.

_____ 2. If the professor accedes to your request for an A, he would
    a. throw you out of school.
    b. call in the dean.
    c. give you the grade.
    d. give you an F.

_____ 3. When the South formed a separate government from the Union at the time of the Civil War, states joining it drew up formal papers of
    a. secession.
    b. succession.
    c. concession.
    d. intercession.

_____ 4. Because Adolph Hitler was responsible for the slaughter of so many people, he has been accused of
    a. genocide.
    b. regicide.
    c. regimentalism.
    d. patrimony.

_____ 5. Because of the traditional separation of Church and State in the United States, a government unlikely to be accepted is a
    a. theocracy.
    b. technocracy.
    c. bureaucracy.
    d. democracy.

_____ 6. If you were a sculptor looking for a new material, you would be anxious to find one which was
    a. a viaduct.
    b. ductile.
    c. traducible.
    d. inductible.

_____ 7. Someone with macrographia would have to buy a large quantity of
    a. pencils.
    b. pens.
    c. paper.
    d. erasers.

_____ 8. A person with dermographia can "write" on his arm without
    a. using a pen or pencil.
    b. knowing how.
    c. thinking.
    d. being aware of it.

_____ 9. Students often enjoy and profit from classes run as a
    a. colloquium.
    b. colloquial.
    c. elocution.
    d. grandiloquence.

_____10. Someone who behaves spitefully is
    a. malingering.
    b. malicious.
    c. magnanimous.
    d. munificent.

_____11. A mythomaniac has no logical reason for continuously
    a. lying.
    b. drinking.

      c. eating.

      d. talking.

_____12. A xenomaniac would particularly want to at-
tend

      a. his class reunion.

      b. a large, international convention.

      c. a small dinner party at his home.

      d. his office party.

_____13. Neuropathy is concerned with

      a. a pain in a nerve.

      b. an inflammation of a nerve.

      c. any disease of the nervous system.

      d. the surgical cutting of a nerve.

_____14. Persons of the same family share a

      a. nomination.

      b. bimodal.

      c. cognomen.

      d. nominal.

_____15. The city's new center for the performnig arts
was built largely with money from

      a. philanthropists.

      b. philatelists.

      c. philologists.

      d. philoprogenitives.

_____16. People exhibiting the symptoms of xenophobia

      a. are gregarious.

      b. make good public relations men.

      c. should consider medicine as a career.

      d. stay away from strangers.

_____17. Someone with demophobia

      a. feels sick all the time.

      b. socializes well.

      c. prefers to be alone.

      d. is afraid of demons.

_____18. The branch of psychology dealing with the
functional relations between the body and the
mind is called

      a. psychometry.

      b. psychoneurosis.

      c. psychobiology.

      d. psychography.

_____19. A form of therapy that requires the patient to act out situations related to his problem is
    a. psychoanalysis.
    b. psychophysiology.
    c. psychedelic.
    d. psychodrama.

_____20. The government is trying to discourage tobacco addiction by
    a. banning cigarette advertising from TV.
    b. eliminating pesticides.
    c. regularly checking the components of fertilizers.
    d. crop spraying.

_____21. If you want to make a wise decision about which school to enter, you should consider the institution from every
    a. spectacle.
    b. locale.
    c. portent.
    d. aspect.

_____22. When the teapot traveled across the room during a seance, the scientist was convinced he observed
    a. a gadabout.
    b. telepathy.
    c. telekinesis.
    d. a "happening."

_____23. The belief there is only one God is called
    a. ethnocentrism.
    b. monotheism.
    c. polytheism.
    d. anthropomorphism.

_____24. The tape recorder and dictating machine have made unnecessary the job of the
    a. archetype.
    b. arbiter.
    c. scriptwriter.
    d. amanuensis.

_____25. Robert was very embarrassed because he opened the door to the women's lounge rather than the men's lounge

a. advertisingly.
b. avertly.
c. convertedly.
d. inadvertently.

ANSWERS TO PRETEST

1—b; 2—c; 3—a; 4—a; 5—a; 6—b; 7—c; 8—a; 9—a; 10—b; 11—a; 12—b; 13—c; 14—c; 15—a; 16—d; 17—c; 18—c; 19—d; 20—a; 21—d; 22—c; 23—b; 24—d; 25—d.

LAUGH IT OFF

"It's really quite amazing. There are 26 letters and you can make thousands of words with them."

chapter 1

Some Words About Words

DEFINITIONS

What is a *frog*? Is it a four-legged animal that hops? Or a fancy kind of dress fastener? Is it part of a horse's hoof? Or can it hold flowers in an arrangement? A *frog* can be any of these, depending on whether a zoologist, a dressmaker, a blacksmith, or a florist is talking about his work.

In the book *Alice in Wonderland,* Humpty Dumpty boasted to Alice, "When I use a word, it means just what I choose it to mean— neither more nor less." Fortunately, most people have more specific meanings for the words they use than Humpty Dumpty did. Still, some of our more than 750,000 English words often do have more than one meaning, as *frog* does.

Although one word may have several meanings, no two words have precisely the *same* meaning. Even words we call "synonymous" have slight shades and differences of meaning so that infinitely varied expressions are possible and subtle distinctions can be made among ideas and intentions.

English words have two kinds of "meanings": a *denotation* and a *connotation*.

The *denotation* of a word is the generally agreed-upon substance of the idea represented by the letters that make up that word. (Letters have no meaning in themselves but only take on what we call "sense" when used in particular combinations we recognize as words.) This common understanding people have of word meaning is what makes comprehension and communication possible. When you look up the "meaning" of a word in a dictionary, you will find one or more *denotation* or meaning that many people have agreed upon.

Connotation is the attitude or feeling a word arouses in an individual, or the emotional implications of a word. It is highly personal and likely to vary as much as people themselves. "Home," for example, may connote a joyful place filled with the smells of good food and the sound of happy laughter, with loving people and good times. To another person with different childhood memories, "home" might evoke feelings of resentment, memories of quarrels and crowded rooms, of hunger and rats.

6

1970, The Register
and Tribune Syndicate

9-4

"'HOUSE' means it's empty. When people move
in, it's a 'HOME'."

Because connotations give so many and such personal shades of
meaning, when we speak of the "definition of a word" we usually mean
its *denotation*.

The definition of a word must have two qualities in order to be useful:

    1. It must be understandable.

    2. It must set the limits of meaning for the word.

A definition must be in language the reader or listener can understand;
that is, it should be more comprehensible than the word it defines.

It would not help much to learn that a *net* is "any reticulated fabric
decussated at regular intervals, with interstices at the intersections,"
(which is how Samuel Johnson defined the word in his dictionary
completed in 1755) unless you know the meaning of "reticulated,"
"decussated," "interstices," and "intersections." And it is possible that
if you knew all those words, you would already know what a *net* is!

A more recent example of a baffling dictionary definition is to learn
that *runcate* means "pinnately incised." And it probably is not much help
to look up a definition of *synapsis* and discover that it is "the conjugation
of homologous chromosomes . . . during early meiosis" unless you are
studying biology and have already learned the meaning of the words
in the definition.

Another kind of definition not much more understandable than the
word it defines is the one that goes around in a circle. If you do not know

the meaning of *group dynamics* you will probably not learn much by being told, "Well, you know, it's the dynamics of a group." Or, if a dictionary defines *miserly* as "of, like, or befitting a miser," you may still be lost because the definition is not understandable, not more comprehensible than the word it defines.

Lexicographers, the people who compile dictionaries, are well aware of the possibility of their entries not being understandable and usually do their best to guard against confusion. Speakers and writers would do well to be equally cautious.

A definition sets the limits of meaning for a word. "Definition" comes from the Latin *definire* meaning "to set boundaries or limits." So, a definition tells not only what a word *includes* but also what it *excludes*. For example, a *phobia* is a fear. But to say that is what the word means would be to include too much because many fears are not phobias at all. So the definition must tell how *phobia* differs from other fears, or tell what it excludes. The limits are set when the fear is limited to one that is "extremely strong and irrational."

A diagram illustrating the definition of *phobia* might look like this:

For purposes of formal definition, the larger circle is called the *genus* or *class* to which the word being defined belongs. The smaller circle is called the *differens* and tells the special or different characteristics of a word that set it apart from others in its class.

Still another way that a definition sets the limits of meaning for a word is to tell what something *is* (rather than what it is not). To say that a *book* is not edible, not something to write with, not liquid, not wearable, and not a sum of money still fails to tell what a book *is*. So in order to help anyone understand the meaning of a word, the definition should be stated in *positive* terms: A *book* is a volume of printed pages fastened together on one side and encased between protective covers.

SUMMARY

Words have both denotations and connotations.
Definition is usually a denotative meaning.
1. Definitions must be understandable:
    Clear, familiar words should be used.
    A word should not be used in its own definition.
2. A definition sets limits of meaning:
    A word is described by its class.
    It is also differentiated from others in its class.
    It is stated in positive terms.

Finding Definitions: 1. Using Roots and Affixes

People who study languages believe that the hundreds of languages we know today originated from just a few historically related groups called "families." From one of them, Indo-European, has come most of the languages familiar to English-speaking people. The language family split for a number of reasons—geography, natural changes, people moving and coming into contact with new groups—and developed different branches just as a human family splits because of marriages or people moving about and the various branches go their own, though genetically related, ways. Some of the branches of the Indo-European family became Indian dialects and the Slavic languages, including Russian. Other branches of Indo-European led to the development of Greek, Latin, and the Romance Languages (French, Spanish, Italian). Still another branch of Indo-European developed into the Germanic languages.

English is most directly descended from the Germanic branch of languages and more than half of our words come from this source. A smaller number, possibly 35% to 38%, come directly from Latin and Greek, and the remaining approximately 2% come from various other languages.

Besides being generally short and easy to pronounce, Germanic-origin English words can often be put together to form new words.

> *EXAMPLES:* "in" and "to" combine to form *into*
> "stair" and "way" combine to form *stairway*
> "south" and "east" combine to form *southeast*

These Germanic source words, and the combinations they form, are fairly easy and are basic to our language. Much respectable literature has been written using mainly Germanic source words. John Ciardi, a well known contemporary poet, wrote a book of poems for one of his children using only first grade (and therefore mostly Germanic origin) vocabulary words that is amusing even for adults to read. Ernest Hemingway's writing style comes in part from the many Germanic-origin words he used; some of his most famous stories have a vocabulary that a fourth grade child can understand (according to nationally accepted charts and measurements), even though the thought in the stories is on a much higher level.

Many English words come from other branches of Indo-European. Words having to do with philosophy and abstract thought often come from the Latin, and those having to do with science frequently come from the Greek. Longer and more complex words, instead of being formed by joining separate words, as are those of Germanic-origin, are usually made by using *word parts* in *combination* with other word parts.

English words with Latin and Greek origins are, therefore, built on the *root and affix principle*. The word has a root or basis that expresses a central idea. New words are formed, and new meanings developed, by adding affixes: a prefix *before* the root or a suffix *after* it. (Sometimes roots are combined with other roots, in effect making one of them act as an "affix.")

    EXAMPLES: The Latin prefix *ante* means "before"
               The Latin root *ced* means "to go"
               Therefore, the word *antecedent* means "that which goes before."

Definitions: 1) An *antecedent* is a word, phrase or clause to which a pronoun refers; it usually appears before the pronoun.

              2) An *antecedent* is a member of your family who lived at an earlier time.

Roots and affixes can be combined in a number of ways for flexibility. One root can be used with several affixes or one affix can be used with more than one root.

    EXAMPLES: The Latin root word *ced* (*ere*) can be combined with affixes to form additional words such as:
recede—"to go back"
precede—"to go before"

The prefix *ante* can be used with other roots to form additional words such as:
*ante*diluvian—"before the flood" (usually, the one Noah survived)
*ante*bellum—"before the war" (usually, the Civil War between the North and the South)

Greek roots operate in the same way as Latin ones; they combine with affixes or with other roots to make new English words.

    EXAMPLE: bio is a root meaning "life"
              graph is a root meaning "write"
    Therefore, a *biography* is the "written record of a person's life."

Knowledge of roots and affixes offers one of the best ways to determine the meaning of an unfamiliar word—and it is the method you will be practicing throughout this book.

    READ THIS: Cervantes was contemporaneous with Shakespeare.
    NOTE THIS: Contemporaneous is an unfamiliar word. What does it mean?
    THINK THIS: Contemporaneous has three parts, each coming from a Latin source:
              The root is *tempor* from the word "temporis" meaning "time"
              The affixes are *con* meaning "together" and *ous* meaning "full of" or "characterized by"
    CONCLUDE THIS: Contemporaneous means "characterized by a togetherness in time." So the two authors must have lived at the same time.

Obviously, the more roots and affixes you learn, the more words you will be able to recognize or figure out and the larger your vocabulary will become. That increase in word knowledge does not need to be tied to memorizing lists or to remembering isolated bits of information. Rather, you will acquire a most useful skill: the ability to figure out unfamiliar words by applying the principles of word development from roots and affixes.

Finding Definitions: 2. Using Context Clues

A word by itself has little meaning beyond its denotation and connotation. Only when it is put together with other words—put into context—does its full and actual sense become apparent. And the context of a word affects its meaning.

> *EXAMPLES:* Remember to *book* a room at the hotel.
> The police will *book* a criminal suspect immediately.
> Making *book* can be lucrative even though illegal.
> The student knew his teacher like a *book*.
> Anyone caught starting a riot will get the *book* thrown at him.

Obviously, the most familiar denotation of *book* (that is, sheets of paper with writing or printing on them, fastened together along one edge, and enclosed within protective covers) does not apply to the word in any of these sentences. But the context in each sentence does give some clue to its meaning. To *book a room at a hotel* is obviously to do something, especially something involving a location. To *book a criminal suspect,* though it also has to do with an action, suggests a relationship with something unsavory and illegal. To know a *teacher like a book* is a way of making a comparison; the structure of the phrase indicates it is not an activity as the other two examples are. Context, then, is one way to discover meaning.

Sometimes meaning comes from *seeing a word often.* Even if you had never heard the word *farthingale,* but read it repeatedly in books on costumes or in period novels, you would probably discover its meaning before long. (It is a hoop-shaped framework women wore in the 16th and 17th centuries beneath their skirts to make them stand out.)

Meaning is also acquired by *hearing words in context.* No mother is likely to set out to teach her child that *irk* means to annoy, disgust, or tire. But if she says often enough, and with sufficient annoyance or disgust in her voice, "Don't irk me!" any child is bound to learn what the word means and how to use it himself.

Context clues are not all equally apparent. Nor are they always evident at a first, quick glance. "The king walked with regal bearing" and "The housemaid had a regal bearing" show little about the word *regal* except that it probably has something to do with the way a person carries himself. Compare the word, however, in these additional contexts:

The king had a *regal* bearing. As he advanced toward the throne, solemnly yet gracefully, his steps measured, no one in the room needed to see his glittering crown and jeweled scepter to realize that here was a true monarch.

or

Despite years of carrying heavy buckets of water to wash floors and windows, of hearing impatient and spiteful words flung at her, of being subjected to a variety of indignities that would have broken a lesser person, Mary still walked with her body erect and her head unbowed. The housemaid had a *regal* bearing that disconcerted many.

The additional information supplied by other sentences makes the meaning of *regal* readily apparent; the fuller context is the key.

Finding Definitions: 3. Combining Context and Root-Affix Clues

Since context clues are one good way to discover the meaning of words, and root-affix knowledge is another, then combining these methods gives a double-barreled approach to learning new words. And that is the method you can apply in this book. Once you are familiar with the root and affixes of a word, you will find that it appears in a context to help you arrive at its definition by following a few simple steps.

READ THIS: Frank's achluophobia forced him to turn on the lights inside his house at dusk and leave them on until dawn every day.

NOTE THIS: *Achluophobia* is an unfamiliar word. What does it mean?

THINK THIS: ". . . lights on inside his house at dusk and leave them on until dawn." That must mean Frank requires light all night. Probably even when he sleeps. Strange.

". . . forced . . ." It's not just that he feels like turning on lights; he *has* to have them on, and not because of darkness alone.

ALSO, THINK THIS: ". . . achluophobia . . ." The root of that word is *phobia* which means a great fear of

something. However, what does the prefix mean?
What does Frank fear? If he needs lights on all
night long, he must fear lack of light—or, the
DARK!

CONCLUDE THAT: achluophobia means "fear of the dark."

Meaning is thus determined from context clues and from a knowledge of
roots, so the original sentence would be understood to read: "Frank's
achluophobia [fear of the dark] made it necessary for him to keep lights on
inside his house both day and night."

Finding Definitions: 4. Using Dictionaries

The dictionary is probably the most familiar way of finding the denotation
of a word. If you cannot tell from the context what a word means, and if
it does not have a root you are familiar with, the dictionary will give the
meaning you need, as well as other information about a word.

Because the English language changes constantly, it is important to have
a dictionary that comes as close as possible to containing current words.
Therefore, a dictionary of recent date is most useful. (The word *stereo,*
for instance, does not appear in many home dictionaries published fifteen or
twenty years ago.) In the past few years there has been so much interest in
dictionaries that revised editions of many famous ones are available, and
some new ones have been published.

A dictionary does not determine language; the spoken and written
language determines the dictionary. That is, lexicographers do not decide
what a word means. Instead, they gather thousands of examples of how
each word is used, sort out these meanings—often with the aid of computers
—and then record how words are used.

Unabridged dictionaries record all the words and all the "meanings" for
each word that the lexicographer can discover. Consequently, they are very
large books and, although available in libraries, are not often found in private
homes because of their size and weight—and cost.

Abridged dictionaries are probably most familiar for they account for
the overwhelming proportion of dictionary sales. They are shorter versions of
the unabridged dictionary and contain the words and definitions likely to
be of most general interest and usefulness. Although often containing more
than 100,000 entries, abridged dictionaries are not usually much bigger
than a hefty textbook.

Pocket size paperback editions of an abridged dictionary are convenient
to carry to classes and provide quick reference, but their small size limits
the number of entries. More important, size also limits the variety of
information permitted for each entry.

Here is a typical word entry from a popular abridged dictionary *:

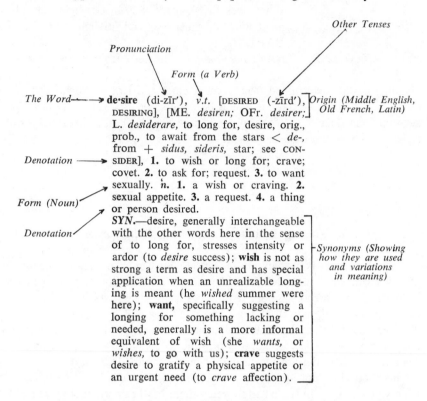

Other Tenses

Pronunciation

Form (a Verb)

The Word ──→ **de·sire** (di-zīr′), *v.t.* [DESIRED (-zīrd′), DESIRING], [ME. *desiren;* OFr. *desirer;* L. *desiderare,* to long for, desire, orig., prob., to await from the stars < *de-*, from + *sidus, sideris,* star; see CON-

Origin (Middle English, Old French, Latin)

Denotation ──→ SIDER], **1.** to wish or long for; crave; covet. **2.** to ask for; request. **3.** to want sexually. *n.* **1.** a wish or craving. **2.** sexual appetite. **3.** a request. **4.** a thing or person desired.

Form (Noun)

Denotation

SYN.—desire, generally interchangeable with the other words here in the sense of to long for, stresses intensity or ardor (to *desire* success); **wish** is not as strong a term as desire and has special application when an unrealizable long-ing is meant (he *wished* summer were here); **want,** specifically suggesting a longing for something lacking or needed, generally is a more informal equivalent of wish (she *wants,* or *wishes,* to go with us); **crave** suggests desire to gratify a physical appetite or an urgent need (to *crave* affection).

Synonyms (Showing how they are used and variations in meaning)

Note that information besides the definition is provided: the pronouncia-tion of the word, its etymology or origin, forms the word might take, and synonyms. (Sometimes there are also other, or different kinds of, entries for words.)

Suppose you need to find out the meaning of the word *forge* in the sentence "Mr. Simmons set to work as soon as he decided to *forge* the Picasso painting." There is no root to guide you to the meaning, and it is difficult to tell from the context exactly what *forge* means. (Buy? Steal? Clean up? Add to?) The dictionary is the next logical place to look for a definition.

In *The Random House Dictionary of the English Language* (College Edition, 1968, p. 518) there are several entries for the word *forge.* They read:

> n. 1. the special fireplace, hearth, or furnace in which metal is heated be-fore shaping. 2. the workshop of a blacksmith; smith.

* *Webster's New World Dictionary of the American Language,* College Edition (1964), p. 397.

Neither of these definitions fits. Besides, *forge* is not used as a noun in the problem sentence. So it is necessary to continue reading the dictionary entry.

> v.t. 3. to form by heating and ham-
> mering; heat into shape.

The painting could hardly be made in such a manner. Further reading is required.

> 4. to form or make in any way. 5.
> to invent (a fictitious story, a lie, etc.).
> 6. to imitate (handwriting, a signa-
> ture, etc.) fraudulently; fabricate a
> forgery.

The painting was certainly made (as in number 4), but that definition would not be relevant because of the context: Mr. Simmons could hardly make a true Picasso painting. Nor could he *invent* a painting in the usual sense of that word.

Therefore, it is safe to conclude that definition number 6—"imitate fraudulently"—is the proper one for *forge* as the word is used in the sample sentence: "Mr. Simmons set to work as soon as he decided to *forge* [imitate fraudulently] the Picasso painting."

In addition to definitions, most dictionaries contain some information about the English language and mechanics, such as grammar and punctuation. Many also have supplementary sections that give the location of colleges and universities, the meaning of people's names, tables of mathematical symbols and formulas, flags of various countries, or lists of foreign words and phrases often used by speakers of English. There is always a general guide to the use of a dictionary contained in it. So, although you may rely on a dictionary primarily for definitions, do not overlook its usefulness for both extensive information on word entries and for other helpful facts.

SUMMARY

Definitions can conveniently be learned in at least four ways:
1. By following the root and affix principle of combining word parts that are common in words of Latin and Greek origin.
2. By examining the context of a word and seeing how it is used with other words in a sentence.
3. By combining context clues and root-affix knowledge.
4. By consulting a dictionary and checking each entry shown for a word until the applicable definition is found.

PRONUNCIATION

Children learn to speak by imitating the sounds they hear and then by associating ideas and objects with the sounds. Later, when they learn to read, they are usually taught to associate symbols (that is, the letters of the alphabet) with sounds. Children also usually discover something about the principles of relationship among sounds rather than just repeating what they hear, so most people can pronounce on sight many words they have never heard.

English is a difficult language to learn because words are not always pronounced the way they look. For instance, *enough* and *bough* ought to have the same ending sound because they look alike. But of course they don't sound alike. The final sound of *enough* is an *uf* as in "huff" and the final sound of *bough* is like the *ow* in "how."

There are also many regional pronunciation differences in the United States; for instance, the word *hill* sounds like "heel" in some areas. People from different English-speaking countries often use different pronunciations for the same word: a *lieutenant* pronounces his rank as *loo–TEN–ant* in the United States but one in Great Britain pronounces his as *LEF–ten–ant.* Time has been responsible for still other pronunciation changes, for about 300 years ago the word "love" rhymed with "move."

Dictionaries show that often more than one pronunciation of a word is common enough to be considered "acceptable," even though there is a tendency toward standardization, just as there is in spelling.

Words have one or more *syllables,* and the rhythm of a language comes from the emphasis or stress on some syllables but not on others in a word. Read aloud the following words:

broken
polite
eating
happy

Listen for the part of each word that you say louder or harder. (*bro*ken, po*lite, eat*ing, *ha*ppy) These are the stressed syllables. People who study language have developed several ways of transferring sounds, including stressed and unstressed syllables, into writing in order to record pronunciation. Sometimes symbols, as well as letters, are used in dictionaries or books to show the sounds of words so they can be repeated accurately.

In this book, a simplified form of showing pronunciation and stressed syllables is used:

1. *Stressed syllables will always be shown in capital letters.*
   EXAMPLE: Incredible will appear as "in–KRED–uh–buhl" to show that the second syllable should receive the voice stress in pronunciation.

2. Every effort is made to *duplicate the actual sounds* of pronunciation and *only standard letters or letter combinations are used.*

EXAMPLES: The long "i" in *isoceles* will be written EYE
The "eu" in *euphony* will be written YOO
The "to" in *autonomy* will be written TAH

Everyone has several vocabularies: one for listening, one for reading, often more than one (depending on level and purpose) for speaking. If vocabulary building is to take place, there ought to be some correlation among these vocabularies, so the sound of a word (from listening) should be related to the ability to reproduce it in speaking. And the ability to recognize a word in print after it has been heard is helpful.

A good way to build vocabulary from this book is to say each word carefully according to the pronunciation key, look at the spelling, and try to learn by sound as well as by meaning. It may also help to read entire sentences aloud to hear how words sound, as well as to see how they look, in context.

Careful and thoughtful listening to words not in this book—in classrooms, lectures, on television, in movies, in conversations—will also help to build vocabulary. In the following chapters, hundreds of *Words People Use* may be familiar to you; many will probably be less familiar, and some will be entirely new. The words on these pages, however, are good starting points for vocabulary improvement.

SUMMARY

Standardized pronunciation is possible because sounds can be recorded in writing.

Say words aloud and listen to their sound carefully in order to learn new words.

In this book, stressed syllables in pronunciation will appear in capital letters.

In this book, standard letters or letter combinations are used to show pronunciation.

chapter 2

Words About Beliefs

PRETEST

DIRECTIONS: In the space next to each number, write the letter that correctly completes the statement.

_____ 1. Some people feel that the enormous expense of conducting a presidential campaign is going to force the United States to become a
   a. bureaucracy.
   b. plutocracy.
   c. theocracy.
   d. autocracy.

_____ 2. Mortimer insisted he had seen a ghost, but because he was known as a liar, the neighbors doubted his
   a. credibility.
   b. cresset.
   c. creel.
   d. credendum.

_____ 3. Laws which prohibit discrimination on the basis of creed are part of the constitutional guarantee of
   a. life.
   b. religious freedom.
   c. equality of action.
   d. guaranteed income.

_____ 4. His perfidy was so apparent to everyone that
   a. the cake fell in the oven.
   b. the teacher gave everyone in the class an A.

    c. the spy was executed.

    d. an affidavit was used to climb the wall.

_____ 5. The country club crowd always invited dozens of young, single men to the "coming out" party of the debs because essentially the older people believed in
    a. endogamy.
    b. exogamy.
    c. digamy.
    d. cernagomy.

_____ 6. A gnostic would most likely be interested in
    a. dancing girls.
    b. student takeover of an administration.
    c. materialism.
    d. spiritual things.

_____ 7. The doctor made a prognosis that
    a. outlined the probable course of the disease.
    b. was a summary of the results of tests already made.
    c. suggested causes of the illness.
    d. ignored the patient altogether.

_____ 8. Views of the inside of concentration camps are likely to appeal to people who delight in
    a. immortality.
    b. amortization.
    c. the morbid.
    d. the mortgage.

_____ 9. If you did not want to bring ignominy upon yourself you would most likely
    a. conduct yourself with dignity in public.
    b. give a good imitation of Tarzan.
    c. give yourself credit for things you had not done.
    d. not respond politely to people in public.

_____10. A bibliophile would also be very likely to be interested in
    a. philology.
    b. philogyny.
    c. seismology.
    d. misogyny.

_____11. "You philanderer!" Mae shouted to Harvey when she discovered he
    a. was making liberal donations to the Philharmonic Symphony.
    b. had no serious intentions toward her.
    c. was forsaking his philatelist friends.
    d changed his mind about letting her borrow his car.

_____12. When Shirley accused Henry of wanting a divorce because he hated marriage, he replied:
    a. "How dare you serve me with extradiction papers."
    b. "I'm no more a misogamist than you are!"
    c. "Stop saying I'm superfluous!"
    d. "Symbolism will get you nowhere."

_____13. Someone who cannot keep his deities straight and accidentally combines them and their attributes has
    a. theocrasy.
    b. theocentrism.
    c. theophany.
    d. theosophy.

_____14. Theodicy is a subject which appears in much literature because it deals with
    a. the form gods take in literary works.
    b. the problem of evil in a world created by a good God.
    c. appearance of gods who talk to men in the early classical literature.
    d. disappearance of documentary evidence about God's works on earth.

_____15. Hester's hostility toward Herbert was subtle rather than
    a. overt.
    b. convertible.
    c. vertical.
    d. reverted.

ANSWERS: 1—b; 2—a; 3—b; 4—c; 5—a; 6—d; 7—a; 8—c; 9—a; 10—a; 11—b; 12—b; 13—a; 14—b; 15—a.

CRAC
KRAS

From the Greek *kratein* meaning "to rule"

MOST groups of people, no matter how small, seem to require a leader. As groups become larger, as governments begin to form in response to need, leaders of government emerge. Words that describe the kind of government and method of leadership have had to evolve in English so that the various kinds of rule can be explained specifically and easily.

The following word parts will be combined with the root in this unit to make new words. Use this list as a reference to find the meaning of words in this unit.

ROOTS AS PREFIXES
tech—art or skill
demo—people
aristo—best
bureau—not witnessed
pluto—wealth
theo—god
mob—a fickle crowd

PREFIX
auto—self

context clues

DIRECTIONS: Pronounce each word in the left hand column and read aloud the sentences in the right hand column. On the basis of context clues in the sentences, fill in the blank space to make a correct definition.

technocracy

tek–NOK–ruh–see

■ Some people believe that if the United States continues to become more gadget-minded and our government and industry continue to become more reliant on machines, all of which need people to fix and run them, we will become a technocracy.

21

■ Although a technocracy may sound like something out of science-fiction, the trend toward training people to run machines makes this possible.

1. A technocracy is _____

_____

democracy

di–MOK–ruh–see

■ As long as some people are denied voting rights on the basis of color or ethnic origin, we cannot have a real democracy.
■ Countries such as Australia that require its citizens to vote have a truer form of democracy than the United States does.

2. Democracy is _____

_____

aristocracy

ar–uh–STOK–ruh–see

■ Aristocracies have fallen when the common people rose up against the ruling class because they felt they were not being represented.
■ Aristocracy is not a representative form of government because those who rule either inherit their position or gain it by extraordinary means not generally available to most people.

3. An aristocracy is _____

_____

autocracy

aw–TOK–ruh–see

■ Autocracy is characteristic of dictatorship.
■ Hitler, although an elected official originally, developed an autocracy that governed every aspect of a German's life.

4. An autocracy is _____

_____

bureaucracy

byou–ROK–ruh–see

- Lower Slobbovia is developing a bureaucracy because of the emphasis on people working in supervisory groups.
- A natural outcome of committees is bureaucracy.

5. A bureaucracy is _____

_____

plutocracy

ploo–TOK–ruh–see

- Even though we no longer have nobility or a strict social class system, a plutocracy is possible.
- Because it becomes increasingly expensive to campaign for public office, a plutocracy may develop.

6. A plutocracy is _____

_____

theocracy

thee–OK–ruh–see

- Strict separation of Church and State makes it impossible for any country to become a theocracy.
- When the church rules the king, the government is actually a theocracy even though it may not be called that.

7. A theocracy is _____

_____

mobocracy

mob–OK–ruh–see

- Mobocracy usually lacks direction and discipline unless intelligent and forceful leaders emerge.
- There is something very unsettling about the idea of mobocracy because the government would have no real leadership or direction.

8. A mobocracy is _____

_____

ANSWERS

1. A <u>technocracy</u> is government by technicians or trained people.
2. <u>Democracy</u> is government of the people.
3. An <u>aristocracy</u> is rule by the nobility or upper class.
4. An <u>autocracy</u> is a government that has absolute power over its citizens.
5. A <u>bureaucracy</u> is government by groups of administrative officials alone.
6. A <u>plutocracy</u> is government by the wealthy.
7. A <u>theocracy</u> is government by a god or his priests.
8. A <u>mobocracy</u> is rule by the mob, or by a large and disorderly crowd.

matching exercise

DIRECTIONS: Write the appropriate letter from the right hand column in the space next to each number so that the numbered words are defined.

———— 1. technocracy   **a.** rule by mob

———— 2. democracy   **b.** government by the wealthy or the rich

———— 3. aristocracy   **c.** government by God or his priests

———— 4. autocracy   **d.** rule by groups of administrative officials

———— 5. bureaucracy   **e.** rule by the nobility or the upper class

———— 6. plutocracy   **f.** a government having absolute power over its citizens

———— 7. theocracy   **g.** rule by technicians

———— 8. mobocracy   **h.** government of and by the people

                        i. rule by those of foreign birth

ANSWERS: 1—g; 2—h; 3—e; 4—f; 5—d; 6—b; 7—c; 8—a.

true-false

DIRECTIONS: Read each sentence carefully and decide whether it is true or false. If it is true, put a T in the space at the right. If it is false, write in an F.

1. A technocracy would provide special training for technicians because they rule the country.   1._____
2. Government by priests is a mobocracy.   2._____
3. Plutocracy refers to a government by groups of administrative officials.   3._____
4. A government by all the people is called a democracy.   4._____
5. In an aristocracy the nobility or upper class rules.   5._____
6. Theocracy means mob rule.   6._____
7. In an autocracy the government has complete power over its citizens.   7._____
8. A government by the wealthy or the rich is a bureaucracy.   8._____

ANSWERS: 1—T; 2—F; 3—F; 4—T; 5—T; 6—F; 7—T; 8—F.

words in use

DIRECTIONS: Read this passage. Then fill in each blank with the appropriate word from among the following choices.

technocracy   aristocracy
mobocracy   democracy
bureaucracy

Formerly the country was an _____; it
                                                    1
was ruled by a king and his nobility. But that was before the government

was overthrown. For a short period after the king was banished there was no real government, but if one were to give it a name he would have had to

have called it a _____, for the mob ruled.
                                  2

Fortunately, this only lasted for a short time; a systematic rule of the

people was conceived, and _____ prevailed.
                                            3

ANSWERS: 1—aristocracy; 2—mobocracy; 3—democracy.

CRED
KRED

From the Latin *credere* meaning "to believe"

WHAT a cultural group believes shapes and directs that culture. Therefore, words built upon the root of "believe" say much about English-speaking people; the fact that it is the basis of words ranging from money to ideas shows the wide range given to beliefs.

The following word parts will be combined with the root in this unit to make new words. Use this list as a reference to find the meaning of words in this unit.

PREFIXES
in—not
dis—not or oppose
ac—to or toward or very

SUFFIXES
ence—act or state or condition
ial—of or pertaining to
ity—state or quality or condition
ous—marked by or given to
ible—able or fit or likely
um—not or oposite of

context
clues

DIRECTIONS: Pronounce each word in the left hand column and read aloud the sentences in the right hand column. On the basis of context clues in the sentences, fill in the blank space to make a correct definition.

credence

KREED–ents

■ It is difficult not to give credence to the observations and statistics of trained sociologists.
■ The report about the Loch Ness monster gained

27

credence when made by reputable scientists and backed by reliable data.

1. Credence means _____

_____

credential

kri–DEN–chuhl

■ A person who can present the proper credentials for a job is often hired over one who cannot provide information about himself or his background.
■ The marvelous meal Maggie made was considered a sufficient credential for her to be hired as cook.

2. Credential means _____

_____

credibility

kred–uh–BIL–uh–tee

■ The witness' credibility was unquestionable and therefore he helped establish the defendant's alibi.
■ The "credibility gap" often spoken of refers to the difference between what is and what people are willing to accept.

3. Credibility is _____

_____

credit

KRED–uht

■ Parents always hope that their children will be honest and therefore a credit to their family.
■ In order to give credit to Montmorency's report of a uranium find, the company had to send out a team of geologists.

4. Credit means _____

_____

creed

KREED

■ One of the foundations of a democratic society is that it permits religious freedom and therefore it can accommodate people of varying creeds.

■ Employers are bound by federal law not to refuse employment to anyone on the basis of race, creed, or color.

5. Creed means _____

_____

credulous

KRED–uh–luhs

■ Many humorous stories are about a naïve person who is so credulous as to accept the most outlandish and exaggerated tales.
■ A credulous person makes a fine audience for someone with a lively imagination.

6. Credulous means _____

_____

incredible

in–KRED–uh–buhl

■ From space reports thus far available, it would be incredible to find life as we know it on Mars.
■ Incredible as it sounds, Shirley really did break the bank at Monte Carlo.

7. Incredible means _____

_____

discredit

dis–KRED–uht

■ The counterspy tried to discredit the report of the spy.
■ The winning jockey was discredited when it was discovered he had attempted to bribe two other jockeys in the race.

8. Discredit means _____

_____

accredited

uh–KRED–uh–ted

■ An accredited physician was always on duty at the camp during the summer.
■ It is always possible to transfer credits from one accredited college to another.

9. Accredited means _____

_____

Words About Beliefs   29

NAME:

credendum

kri–DEN–dum

■ Pronouncements of the Pope become a credendum for his church.
■ Those who believe strongly in a religion also subscribe to its credendum.

10. Credendum means _____

_____

credulity

kri–DYOU–luh–tee

■ You strain my credulity when you ask me to believe you saw little green men get out of a flying saucer on the lawn last night.
■ When Barnum said "There's a sucker born every minute," he was well–aware that the credulity of the public was enormous.

11. Credulity means _____

_____

ANSWERS

1. <u>Credence</u> means belief about the truth of something.
2. <u>Credential</u> means that which provides a basis of confidence about a person.
3. <u>Credibility</u> is believability.
4. <u>Credit</u> means trustworthiness or a reliance on the truth of something.
5. <u>Creed</u> means an authoritative, formulated system, usually of religious beliefs.
6. <u>Credulous</u> means unsuspecting or believing easily.
7. <u>Incredible</u> means too extraordinary to permit belief.
8. <u>Discredit</u> means to deprive of a good reputation.
9. <u>Accredited</u> means to trust or to confer authority on a person or thing.
10. <u>Credendum</u> means a thing to be believed in theology, an article of faith.
11. <u>Credulity</u> means willingness to believe or to trust too readily.

words in use

DIRECTIONS: Read this passage. Then fill in each blank with the appropriate word from among the following choices.

NAME: _____

creed   credulous   discredit
credit   incredible   credendum
credential   credence   credulity

    None of the group would _____
                              1
the mystic even though his _____ was
                              2
_____. He had no _____
          3   4
and could fool none but the _____.
                              5

ANSWERS: 1—discredit or credit; 2—creed or credendum; 3—incredible or credulous; 4—credential or credulity; 5—credulous.

matching exercise

DIRECTIONS: Write the appropriate letter from the right hand column in the space next to each number so that the numbered words are defined.

_____ 1. credence

_____ 2. credential

_____ 3. credibility

_____ 4. credit

_____ 5. creed

_____ 6. credulous

_____ 7. creditable

_____ 8. credendum

_____ 9. discredit

_____10. accredited

a. to deprive of a good reputation

b. too extraordinary to permit belief

c. that which makes a person believable

d. to confer authority on

e. reputable; estimable

f. a belief; particularly, religious belief

g. worthy of belief

h. believes easily; unsuspecting

i. reputation derived from the confidence of others

j. in theology, a thing to be believed

k. that which gives credit

(*more*)

ANSWERS: 1—k; 2—c; 3—g; 4—i; 5—f; 6—h; 7—e; 8—j; 9—a; 10—d.

FID, FIDE
FUHD, FEYED

From the Latin *fidere* meaning "to trust"

SOME words in English, "fidelity," for example, take meaning directly from the Latin source word, and have to do with personal relationships. Interestingly, other words in this group have to do specifically with relationships between people engaged in business together. Obviously, trust and faithfulness in commerce, then, has been an important development in the beliefs of people who use the English language.

The following word parts will be combined with the root in this unit to make new words. Use this list as a reference to find the meaning of words in this unit.

PREFIXES
con—with or together or jointly
af—to or toward or very
in—not
per—through or thoroughly

SUFFIXES
ence—act or state or condition
al—pertaining to
ity—state or quality or condition
ary—belonging to or showing
ant—against or opposite

context
clues

DIRECTIONS: Pronounce each word in the left hand column and read aloud the sentences in the right hand column. On the basis of context clues in the sentences, fill in the blank space to make a correct definition.

confide

kon–FEYED

■ Herkimer realized he could no longer confide in Sally when he discovered that the deep, dark secret he had told her on Saturday night was well–known news at the office on Monday morning.

33

■ You will be able to confide in the doctor because professional custom makes it unnecessary for him to disclose what you say to him even though he testifies in a law court.

1. Confide means _____

_____

confidence

KON–fuh–dents

■ Have confidence that I will catch you if you fall and won't allow you to get hurt.
■ The man accused of murder had such confidence in his lawyer that he was sure he would be judged not guilty.

2. Confidence means _____

_____

affidavit

af–uh–DAY–vuht

■ An affidavit filed with the district attorney was accepted in the court as evidence that John was not even in Chicago on the night of the riot.
■ Since Selma had to be in another state at the time of the trial, before she left she asked to sign an affidavit containing her testimony.

3. An affidavit is _____

_____

infidel

IN–fuh–del

■ "Kill the infidels!" shouted the Moors as they met the Christians in battle.
■ A Buddhist in a Christian country usually is accepted today without question, although in less enlightened times he might be persecuted as an infidel.

4. An infidel is _____

_____

infidelity

in–fuh–DEL–uh–tee

■ Bob indignantly announced that if the company believed he had sold plans for the new Widget to a rival corporation and was therefore guilty of company infidelity, he was ready to resign.

■ Mr. Highes showed great infidelity to his club by leaving it when it was in need of his financial aid.

5. Infidelity means _____

_____

perfidy

PUHR–fuh–dee

■ The perfidy of a soldier who deliberately sells secrets to the enemy is usually punished by trial in a military court.
■ Thomas was so completely perfidious that neither his friends nor his enemies had confidence in him.

6. Perfidy means _____

_____

fidelity

fuh–DEL–uh–tee

■ Perfect fidelity made Janice an excellent employee because she worked late at the office without expecting extra pay and even came in on the weekend if there was work to finish.
■ The king never questioned the fidelity of his chief ministers, so he was very surprised when they revolted.

7. Fidelity means _____

_____

fiducial

fuh–DYOU–shuhl

■ Herbert's fiducial dependence upon his mother made it difficult for him to adjust to going to school when he was old enough for kindergarten.
■ Everyone in the club knew that Montmorency felt he had a fiducial obligation to remain as treasurer once cleared of the suspicion that he had misused funds.

8. Fiducial means _____

_____

fiduciary

fuh–DYOU–she–er–ee

■ Mrs. Smith acted as fiduciary for her daughter, Myrna, when the child inherited six million dollars from a great-aunt.

■ The fiduciary of this property will have to sign papers for the owners before the land can be sold.

9. A fiduciary is _____

_____

confidant

KON–fuh–dant

■ Shirley always wanted to have a confidant but had to settle for the impersonality of a diary as a way of getting troubles out of her mind.
■ The heroine's confidant, who has known of her secret love through all three acts, is usually the girl who ends up with the lead actor's friend at the final curtain of a typical musical.

10. A confidant is _____

_____

ANSWERS

1. *Confide means to trust in someone enough to share secrets or to discuss private affairs.*
2. *Confidence means a firm belief or trust; assurance.*
3. *An affidavit is a written statement made on oath.*
4. *An infidel is a person who does not believe in a particular religion, especially the prevailing one.*
5. *Infidelity means a lack of faith, truth or loyalty usually toward another person.*
6. *Perfidy means treachery or the deliberate betrayal of trust.*
7. *Fidelity means faithful devotion to one's duty or obligations.*
8. *Fiducial means based on a firm belief or faith.*
9. *A fiduciary is a person who holds something in trust for another such as the guardian of a minor or of property.*
10. *A confidant is a close, trusted friend.*

fill in the blanks

DIRECTIONS: Fill in the blank in each sentence with the appropriate word from among the following choices.

confide   infidel
confidence   fiducial

affidavit   infidelity
confidant   perfidy
fiduciary   fidelity

1. To trust someone enough to share secrets with him is to

   _____ in him.

2. A close, trusted friend is a _____.

3. A _____ is someone who holds something

   in trust for another.

4. Treachery or deliberate betrayal is called _____.

5. It is _____ if it is based on firm belief or

   faith.

6. _____ means faithful devotion to one's duty.

7. _____ implies assurance.

8. A written statement made on an oath is an _____.

9. A person who does not believe in the established religion of an area is

   considered an _____.

10. If you are disloyal or lack faith you are guilty of _____.

ANSWERS: 1—confide;   2—confidant;   3—fiduciary;   4—perfidy;   5—fiducial;
6—fidelity; 7—confidence; 8—affidavit; 9—infidel; 10—infidelity.

true-false

DIRECTIONS: Read each sentence carefully and decide whether it is true or
false. If it is true, put a T in the space at the right. If it is false, write in an F.

1. Confide means to trust in someone enough to share secrets or
   to discuss private affairs.   1._____

2. Confidence means a firm belief or trust; assurance. 2._____
3. An affidavit is a lack of faith. 3._____
4. An infidel means the killing of infants. 4._____
5. Perfidy is devotion to one's duty. 5._____
6. Fiducial means based on a firm belief or faith. 6._____
7. Fidelity means unfaithfulness. 7._____
8. A fiduciary is a person who holds something in trust for another such as a guardian for a minor child. 8._____
9. A confidant is a close, trusted friend. 9._____
10. Infidelity means trust and loyalty. 10._____

ANSWERS: 1—T; 2—T; 3—F; 4—F; 5—F; 6—T; 7—F; 8—T; 9—T; 10—F.

GAM
GAM

From the Greek *gamos* meaning "marriage"

THAT marriage is a basic belief of English-speaking peoples is obvious from the several words which have been developed to describe different kinds of marriage—or lack of marriage. This group contains words pertaining to the condition of having one or more spouses, separately or simultaneously, and even words for marrying inside or out of a particular group.

The following word parts will be combined with the root in this unit to make new words. Use this list as a reference to find the meaning of words in this unit.

PREFIXES

mono—one or alone
bi—two
mis—wrong or bad
di—two
tri—three

poly—many
cern—to mingle
exo—outside of
endo—within

context

clues

DIRECTIONS: Pronounce each word in the left hand column and read aloud the sentences in the right hand column. On the basis of context clues in the sentences, fill in the blank space to make a correct definition.

monogamy

muh–NOG–uh–mee

■ In countries where divorce is impossible people are forced into monogamy.
■ Monogamy has traditionally been the mode of marital life in the United States, but that custom has also led to looser divorce laws.

1. Monogamy is _____

_____

bigamy

BIG–uh–mee

- A real-life bigamist was reported in the paper recently because, like the movie character, he was discovered to have wives and children living in two separate cities.
- Neither wife of the bigamist knew of the existence of the other woman.

2. Bigamy is _____

_____

misogamy

muh–SOG–uh–mee

- Marcia's misogamy was traced, by her psychiatrist, to unhappy memories of her parents' marriage.
- Wilson never went out with girls because he was a misogamist who feared that a girl would trap him into marriage.

3. Misogamy is _____

_____

digamy

DIG–uh–mee

- Many cases of digamy are reported in the society columns of the newspaper; the name of the previous spouse is often included.
- The somewhat unusual custom of a wife killing herself in order to be buried with her husband would make digamy impossible.

4. Digamy means _____

_____

trigamist

TRIG–uh–muhst

- The sheik was permitted four wives, but while looking for the last one, he was only a trigamist.
- John figured that three is better than two, so he became a trigamist.

5. A trigamist is _____

_____

polygamy

puh–LIG–uh–mee

- Some Mormon sects still practice polygamy because the many children that result from such a union are desirable.

■ If you plan on becoming a polygamist, better be prepared to pay the usual household bills several times over and to settle the inevitable arguments.

6. Polygamy means _____

_____

cernogamy

ser–NOG–uh–mee

■ The development of communes and devotion to more than one person outside the self has led to a rise of cernogamy in such communities.
■ Bob and Carol and Ted and Alice were close friends, but they were not cernogamous.

7. Cernogamy means _____

_____

exogamy

ek–SOG–uh–mee

■ Because incest is not permitted in this society, marriages must be exogamous.
■ Now that interracial marriages are becoming more frequent in the United States, the disapproval against exogamy is decreasing.

8. Exogamy means _____

_____

endogamy

en–DOG–uh–mee

■ The prince will have to be endogamous because only another member of royalty will be considered a suitable wife for him.
■ Endogamy is so preferred by certain religions that marrying outside the church is cause for expulsion from it.

9. Endogamy means _____

_____

ANSWERS

1. *Monogamy is one marriage during a lifetime.*
2. *Bigamy is marriage to a second person while still legally married to another.*

3. _Misogamy_ is hatred of marriage.
4. _Digamy_ means a legal second marriage after the termination of the first one.
5. A _trigamist_ is one who has three spouses at the same time.
6. _Polygamy_ means having more than one mate at the same time.
7. _Cernogamy_ means two or more men and two or more women married to each other; group marriage.
8. _Exogamy_ means marriage outside a particular group.
9. _Endogamy_ means marriage within a certain group.

true-false

DIRECTIONS: Read each sentence carefully and decide whether it is true or false. If it is true, put a T in the space at the right. If it is false, write in an F.

1. Monogamy is the practice of being married to only one person at a time.   1._____
2. Bigamy is marriage to a second person while being still legally married to another.   2._____
3. Love of marriage is called misogamy.   3._____
4. Digamy means dignity or the absence of shame.   4._____
5. A trigamist is one who has three spouses at the same time.   5._____
6. Polygamy means having one mate at a time.   6._____
7. Cernogamy refers to group marriages.   7._____
8. Marriage within a particular group is called exogamy.   8._____
9. Endogamy means marriage outside a particular group.   9._____

ANSWERS: 1—T; 2—T; 3—F; 4—F; 5—T; 6—F; 7—T; 8—F; 9—F.

matching exercise

DIRECTIONS: Write the appropriate letter from the right hand column in the space next to each number so that the numbered words are defined.

_____ 1. monogamy   **a.** marriage outside of a particular group

_____ 2. bigamy   **b.** having more than one mate at the same time

_____ 3. misogamy   **c.** marriage within a certain group

_____ 4. digamy   **d.** group marriage; two or more men and two or more women married to each other

_____ 5. trigamist   **e.** marriage to a second person while still legally married to another

_____ 6. polygamy   **f.** hatred of marriage

_____ 7. cernogamy   **g.** a legal second marriage after the termination of the first one

_____ 8. exogamy   **h.** love of marriage

_____ 9. endogamy   **i.** one who has three spouses at the same time

     j. one marriage during a lifetime

ANSWERS: 1—j; 2—e; 3—f; 4—g; 5—i; 6—b; 7—d; 8—a; 9—c.

words in use

DIRECTIONS: Fill in the blanks in each sentence with the appropriate word from among the choices directly below.

monogamy	digamy
bigamy	cernogamy
misogamy	endogamy
polygamy	exogamy

In the United States you can be legally tried for the crime of

_____ if you marry more than one
     1

person at a time. The reason for this is that our culture practices

————————————————. However you may marry a second time
                    2

if your previous marriage has been dissolved legally or by death. This

practice is called ————————————————.
                            3

ANSWERS: 1—bigamy; 2—monogamy; 3—digamy.

GNOSIS
NO-sis

From the Greek *gnosis* meaning "knowledge" or *gno* meaning "to know"

THE "g" in this root is usually a silent letter. However, when the root appears following a prefix, the "g" is usually heard as a "hard" sound. Although one word is the same as the root ("gnosis," meaning mystical knowledge), most words developed from "knowing" use a prefix to form specific meanings.

The following word parts will be combined with the root in this unit to make new words. Use this list as a reference to find the meaning of words in this unit.

PREFIXES
pro—according to or before
dia—through
i—no

SUFFIXES
ic—dealing with
ant—doing or showing
logy—study or science of
ate—cause
ive—quality of

context
clues

DIRECTIONS: Pronounce each word in the left hand column and read aloud the sentences in the right hand column. On the basis of context clues in the sentences, fill in the blank space to make a correct definition.

gnostic

NOS–tik

■ A religious gnostic would not put much store in the beliefs a man held.
■ "Give me books and more books so I may have learning and more learning," said the gnostic, "for it is from this source I derive my knowledge that will lead to salvation."

1. A gnostic is _____

_____

NAME: _____

agnostic

ag–NOS–tik

■ Henry became an agnostic when he decided that he could never really learn about God.
■ Agnostics have not rejected religious beliefs in the same way that atheists have; they just question teachings about a God.

2. An agnostic is _____

_____

cognizant

KOG–nuh–zuhnt

■ You should be cognizant of the possibility of further student uprisings and do your research paper before the library is occupied and shut off from your use.
■ If parents were cognizant of their children's problems more quickly, there might be fewer school failures and dropouts.

3. Cognizant means _____

_____

prognosis

prog–NO–suhs

■ The doctor studied the X-rays and finally said, "The prognosis for a full recovery is excellent."
■ Dr. Watkins shook his head regretfully and said, "The diagnosis is cancer and the prognosis is six to twelve months to live."

4. Prognosis means _____

_____

gnosiology

NO–se–ol–uh–jee

■ If you study gnosiology, you will have to take courses on the psychology of learning.
■ The function of the different senses—seeing, hearing, touching, etc.—contribute to an understanding of gnosiology.

5. Gnosiology is _____

_____

diagnosis

deye–ig–NO–suhs

■ I can make a diagnosis of your reading problem and then let you work in the reading lab to overcome the difficulties.

■ A dentist can make a diagnosis about which teeth have cavities by looking at an X-ray.

6. Diagnosis is _____

_____

diagnostician

deye–ig–nos–TISH–uhn

■ A famous diagnostician was called in all the way from London to consult on this most unusual and baffling case.
■ Diagnosticians are now using computers to help them make judgments based on past experience with various symptoms and diseases.

7. A diagnostician is _____

_____

gnosis

NO–suhs

■ The gnosis of Madame Mantague was well–known for she was said to have direct knowledge from higher powers.
■ The high priest was believed to have magical powers based on gnosis.

8. Gnosis means _____

_____

ignorant

IG–nuh–rant

■ An ignorant person makes statements about things he knows nothing about and then expects to be believed and to have his directions followed.
■ If you are ignorant of a subject, go to the library and read about it.

9. Ignorant means _____

_____

ignorance

IG–nuh–ruhnts

■ Ignorance is not bliss; it's stupidity.
■ Ignorance of the law is no excuse for breaking a law, according to lawyers and judges.

10. Ignorance means _____

_____

Words About Beliefs   47

ignoramus

ig–nuh–RAY–muhs

■ A true ignoramus is one who never even tries to learn anything.

■ In this age of mass communication and high literacy, the only excuse a person has for being an ignoramus is his own laziness.

11. An ignoramus is _____

_____

ignore

ig–NOUHR

■ Myrna was tired of being ignored by the movie talent scouts, so she accepted an offer to be the Playmate for March.

■ One sure way to be ignored is to talk too much so that people seldom know when you have something important to contribute and when you're just chattering.

12. Ignore means _____

_____

prognosticate

prog–NOS–tuh–kate

■ Consult a crystal ball if you hope to prognosticate the outcome of the football game.

■ To prognosticate questions on the final exam is easy if you just review your notes from the term.

13. Prognosticate means _____

_____

cognitive

KOG–nuht–iv

■ Some questions on the test are in the cognitive domain and are easy to spot because they call only for a good memorization of the textbook.

■ Morris admired his friend's cognitive ability that made studying easy and quick.

14. Cognitive means _____

_____

cognoscenti

kon–yo–SHENT–ee

■ It seemed that all the cognoscenti in town assembled to admire the paintings on display opening night at the new art gallery.

■ If the cognoscenti approve of your play, you are sure to have a success because they will spread the word and publish reviews that will make everyone want to see the show.

15. Cognoscenti are _____

_____

ANSWERS

1. *A gnostic is one who holds the theory that knowledge rather than belief is the way to salvation.*
2. *An agnostic is one who holds that certain things about the essential nature of the universe are unknown and unknowable.*
3. *Cognizant means aware.*
4. *Prognosis means an opinion of the probable results, usually of a disease.*
5. *Gnosiology is the science of cognition or of apprehending.*
6. *Diagnosis is to determine the cause or identity of a problem.*
7. *A diagnostician is one who specializes in making diagnoses.*
8. *Gnosis means superior wisdom of mysteries or spiritual truth.*
9. *Ignorant means having no knowledge.*
10. *Ignorance means no knowing.*
11. *An ignoramus is one who knows nothing.*
12. *Ignore means to refuse to take notice.*
13. *Prognosticate means to foretell the future.*
14. *Cognitive means the power of knowing or apprehending.*
15. *Cognoscenti are those with superior knowledge in a field, especially in the fine arts.*

true-false

DIRECTIONS: Read each sentence carefully and decide whether it is true or false. If it is true, put a T in the space at the right. If it is false, write in an F.

1. A gnostic is a person who does not believe in God. 1._____
2. An agnostic is the theory that knowledge is the way to salvation. 2._____

3. If you are aware of people around you, you are cognizant of them. 3._____
4. Prognosis is a disease. 4._____
5. A medical diagnosis is made to determine the cause or identity of a problem. 5._____
6. To prognosticate is to foretell the future. 6._____
7. Cognitive is the science of apprehending. 7._____
8. Ignorance indicates the lack of knowledge. 8._____
9. Superior wisdom of mysteries or spiritual truth is called gnosis. 9._____
10. The word "ignore" indicates that a person has a superior knowledge in a field, especially in the fine arts. 10._____

ANSWERS: 1—F; 2—F; 3—T; 4—F; 5—T; 6—T; 7—F; 8—T; 9—T; 10—F.

fill in the blanks

DIRECTIONS: Fill in the blank in each sentence with the appropriate word from among the following choices.

ignorance	cognitive
diagnosis	prognosis
prognosticate	gnosiology
agnostic	gnostic
gnosis	cognizant

1. A _____ believes that knowledge rather

than belief is the way to salvation.

2. An _____ is one who holds that certain

things about the essential nature of the universe are unknown and

unknowable.

3. If you are _____ it means you are using all

your senses to be aware.

4. The prediction of probable results, usually of a disease, is called

   a _____.

5. The science of cognition or of apprehending is _____.

6. A _____ is made to determine the cause

   or identity of a problem.

7. The superior wisdom of mysteries or spiritual truth is

   _____.

8. _____ means not knowing.

9. To _____ is to foretell the future.

10. Someone with the power of knowing or apprehending is

    _____.

ANSWERS: 1—gnostic; 2—agnostic; 3—cognizant; 4—prognosis; 5—gnosiology; 6—diagnosis; 7—gnosis; 8—ignorance; 9—prognosticate; 10—cognitive.

scrambled

words

DIRECTIONS: Unscramble the following words. They are defined in parentheses.

1. gosins: _____

   (refers to superior wisdom of mysteries or spiritual truth)

2. gostinc: _____

   (a theory that knowledge rather than belief is the way to salvation)

3. tincagos: _____

   (certain things about the nature of the universe are unknown and unknowable)

4. pogosirns: _____

    (refers to the prediction of probable results usually
    of a disease)

5. vecigonit: _____

    (it means the power of knowing or apprehending)

ANSWERS: 1—gnosis; 2—gnostic; 3—agnostic; 4—prognosis; 5—cognitive.

MORS, MORI
MORS, MORuh

From the Latin *mortalis* meaning "death" and *morir* meaning "to die"

BELIEFS and customs about death are part of every society. Interestingly, they seem to be repeated in otherwise varied cultures and in different ages. The English words that communicate ideas about death are also closely related, though their range of implication is wide.

The following word parts will be combined with the root in this unit to make new words. Use this list as a reference to find the meaning of words in this unit.

PREFIX
im—not

ROOT
gage—pledge

SUFFIXES
fy—pertaining to
id—marked by or showing
al—of or belonging to
ous—marked by or given to
ician—director or manager
ary—engaged in or performing
ize—make

context
clues

DIRECTIONS: Pronounce each word in the left hand column and read aloud the sentences in the right hand column. On the basis of context clues in the sentences, fill in the blank space to make a correct definition.

immortal

im–MORT–uhl

■ Napoleon is an immortal figure among military men and in the history of France.
■ According to Homer, the immortals in the Greek pantheon cavorted in heaven and looked down upon the people taking part in the Trojan War.

1. Immortal means _____

_____

morgue

MORG

■ The morgue is a scary place to many people who prefer not to be in the presence of dead bodies.
■ The police report indicated that the body would remain in the morgue until the next of kin could be notified to come and identify it.

2. A morgue is _____

_____

mortify

MOR–tuh–feye

■ If you want to really mortify Silas, just mention the fact that his wife used to be a strip-teaser.
■ The skier was mortified when he fell while coming out of the starting gate for the giant slalom.

3. Mortify means _____

_____

morbid

MOR–buhd

■ Get out and have fun again even though you have had a death in the family; it is no use being morbid because you must go on living.
■ Did you see the morbid photograph of the victims of the automobile accident?

4. Morbid means _____

_____

moribund

MOR–uh–buhnd

■ Certain dialects are moribund because the people who use them are fast dying out.
■ The patient was moribund so it was time to send for a priest to administer the last rites of the church.

5. Moribund means _____

_____

mortal

MORT–l

■ Man constantly seeks new ways of prolonging life, even though he knows he is only mortal.
■ Ponce de Leon searched for the Fountain of Youth, yet discovered that he was only mortal

and that there was no magic fountain to prolong life.

6. Mortal means _____

_____

mortgage

MOR–gij

■ You can get a mortgage on the house in order
to buy it, but the interest rate is going up so
you'd better do it quickly.
■ Winston signed a mortgage on the downtown
property before he found out that he could have
sold it for several million dollars.

7. A mortgage is _____

_____

mortician

mor–TISH–uhn

■ The mortician will arrange everything for the
funeral.
■ Jessica Mitford, in her book *The American
Way of Death,* takes morticians to task for
charging high fees for fancy coffins and unnecessary frills on funerals.

8. A mortician is _____

_____

mortiferous

mor–TIF–uhr–uhs

■ A mortiferous gas was responsible for killing
the sheep.
■ Before you do that chemistry experiment, check
it again and be sure it will not be mortiferous.

9. Mortiferous means _____

_____

mortuary

MOR–chuh–wer–ee

■ An ambulance brought the body to the mortuary and the family followed in its own car
in order to make a casket selection.
■ Mr. Morgan, the mortician, did not feel the
mortuary was a morbid place because it was
only a temporary stopping place for his clients.

10. A mortuary is _____

_____

amortize

AM–uhr–teyez

■ You can amortize this loan on the car by monthly payments over a three-year period.
■ If you plan to amortize this portion of the investment loan, you will have to make payments more regularly.

11. Amortize means _____

_____

ANSWERS

1. *Immortal* means not subject to death or having eternal fame.
2. A *morgue* is a place where unidentified bodies or victims who die in accidents are temporarily held for identification, claim, or investigation.
3. *Mortify* means shame, humiliation, or wounded pride.
4. *Morbid* means gruesome or relating to disease or psychologically unhealthy.
5. *Moribund* means at point of death or approaching an end.
6. *Mortal* means liable or subject to death.
7. A *mortgage* is a temporary and conditional pledge of property to a creditor as security against a debt.
8. A *mortician* is a funeral director or undertaker.
9. *Mortiferous* means bringing or producing death; deadly.
10. A *mortuary* is a place where dead bodies are prepared or kept before burial or cremation.
11. *Amortize* means to liquidate a debt by payments.

fill in the blanks

DIRECTIONS: Fill in the blank in each sentence with the appropriate word from among the following choices.

immortal   mortal
morgue   mortgage
mortify   mortician
morbid   mortiferous
moribund   mortuary

1. A _____ is a place where dead bodies are

prepared or kept before burial or cremation.

2. A _____ is the funeral director or

undertaker at whose establishment the body was kept before burial.

3. A temporary and conditional pledge of property to a creditor as security against a debt is a _____.

4. "All men are _____", is a famous syllogistic premise because all men are liable or subject to death.

5. Cancer of the lung is considered a _____ illness.

6. _____ means not subject to death or having eternal fame.

7. To bring shame to a man or to humiliate him is to _____ him.

8. To be at the point of death is to be _____.

9. _____ means gruesome or relating to disease or to be psychologically unhealthy.

10. The bodies of unidentified victims of accidents are temporarily held for identification at the _____.

ANSWERS: 1—mortuary; 2—mortician; 3—mortgage; 4—mortal; 5—mortiferous; 6—immortal; 7—mortify; 8—moribund; 9—morbid; 10—morgue.

matching exercise

DIRECTIONS: Write the appropriate letter from the right hand column in the space next to each number so that the numbered words are defined.

_____ 1. immortal   **a.** bringing or producing death; deadly

_____ 2. mortal   **b.** a temporary pledge of property to a creditor as security against debt

_____ 3. morgue   **c.** gruesome or relating to disease

(*more*)

_____ 4. mortgage

_____ 5. mortify

_____ 6. mortician

_____ 7. morbid

_____ 8. mortiferous

_____ 9. moribund

_____10. mortuary

d. a funeral director or undertaker

e. not subject to death; having eternal fame

f. a place where unidentified bodies are temporarily held for identification

g. to cause someone shame or humiliation

h. to be at the point of death

i. a place where dead bodies are prepared for burial or cremation

j. to liquidate a debt by payments

k. liable to or subject to death

ANSWERS: 1—e; 2—k; 3—f; 4—b; 5—g; 6—d; 7—c; 8—a; 9—h; 10—i.

scrambled

words

DIRECTIONS: Unscramble the following words. They are defined in parentheses.

1. gumore: _____

   (a place where unidentified bodies are held for identification)

2. bundimor: _____

   (at the point of death; dying)

3. yorramut: _____

   (a place where dead bodies are prepared for burial or cremation)

4. latorm: _____

   (liable or subject to death)

5. rfitomy: _____

   (it means shame, humiliation or wounded pride)

ANSWERS: 1—morgue; 2—moribund; 3—mortuary; 4—mortal; 5—mortify.

NOM
NOM

From the Latin *nomen* meaning "name"

EVERY time someone asks, "What's your name?" he is using a word similar to the Latin root that means "name." The word not only indicates what a person is called, but also is used to "name someone to a position" or to "name words for a special use" or to "name that which has something in common." Some of these special kinds of names are words in this section.

Two French expressions are often used in English:

nom de plume meaning a pen name or name other than his own under which someone writes and publishes.

nom de guerre (literally, "name of war") meaning an assumed name or pseudonym.

The following word parts will be combined with the root in this unit to make new words. Use this list as a reference to find the meaning of words in this unit.

PREFIXES
de—from or down or completely
co—with or together
i—not
a—on or in or towards
pseudo—false or fictitious

SUFFIXES
ate—office or office-holder
ot—doer or agent
al—of or belonging to
tion—the act of
ee—one who receives action

context

clues

DIRECTIONS: Pronounce each word in the left hand column and read aloud the sentences in the right hand column. On the basis of context clues in the sentences, fill in the blank space to make a correct definition.

nominate

NOM–uh–nate

■ If you decide to nominate Jasper for the presidency, be sure he was born in the United States because that is one of the qualifications for office.

59

■ Nora nominated Noreen for treasurer of the Ladies' Club because Noreen had a reputation for never overdrawing her bank account.

1. Nominate means _____

_____

denominator

di–NOM–uh–nate–or

■ The only common denominator between Chuck and Winthrop was that both loved girls with blue eyes.
■ Herkimer decided that the denominator he shared with Millicent was their love of skiing.

2. A denominator is _____

_____

cognomen

kog–NO–muhn

■ The cognomen Rockefeller is shared by several men in public life; David, Nelson, Winthrop, Laurence, and John D. IV.
■ Smith is one of the most common cognomen in the telephone book of any large city.

3. A cognomen is _____

_____

nominal

NOM–uhn–l

■ The nominal head of state is the king, but in actuality the prime minister controls the government.
■ Sociologists agree that although the man is the nominal head of the household in the United States, women rule the homes.

4. Nominal means _____

_____

denomination

di–nom–uh–NAY–shuhn

■ All members of the Methodist denomination will meet Saturday to plan their new church on Main Street.
■ One denomination that seems to have more privileges than others is the senior class.

5. A denomination is _____

_____

nomenclature

NO–muhn–klay–chuhr

- The nomenclature medical students learn enables them to sound terribly intelligent, though outsiders may not know they are simply naming the bones of the foot.
- Printers are easier to deal with if you learn the nomenclature of their profession than if you do not understand their terminology.

6. Nomenclature means _____

_____

nominee

nom–uh–NEE

- The party nominee for postmaster decided to withdraw before the election.
- In a classic hoax many years ago, one nominee for college homecoming queen turned out to be a cow entered by the agriculture students.

7. Nominee means _____

_____

ignominy

IG–nuh–min–ee

- Richard went off into the wilderness and became a hermit because he could no longer bear the ignominy he brought upon his family by spying for a foreign nation.
- The football team felt their defeat was an ignominy when the score reached 77–0.

8. Ignominy means _____

_____

agnomen

ag–NO–muhn

- Sylvester often embarrassed his girl-friend when he called her in public by the private agnomen of "Sweetie-Pie Sweetums."
- "Red" is an agnomen often given to people with red hair.

9. An agnomen is _____

_____

pseudonym

SOO–duh–nim

- Register at the hotel under a pseudonym if you do not wish to be disturbed by people from the office wanting to talk business over the phone.

■ Robert Taylor would be using his own name rather than a pseudonym if he signed a check with the name Spangler Arlington Brugh.

10. A pseudonym is _____

_____

ANSWERS

1. _Nominate_ means to propose someone for elective office.
2. A _denominator_ is something shared or held in common.
3. A _cognomen_ is a last name or family name.
4. _Nominal_ means in name only; not in actuality.
5. A _denomination_ is a class or kind of persons or things having a specific name.
6. _Nomenclature_ means names or terms special to a particular study or business.
7. _Nominee_ means one nominated for a post or office.
8. _Ignominy_ means disgrace or dishonor.
9. An _agnomen_ is a nickname.
10. A _pseudonym_ is a false name.

matching exercise

DIRECTIONS: Write the appropriate letter from the right hand column in the space next to each number so that the numbered words are defined.

_____ 1. nominate   **a.** a nickname

_____ 2. denominator   **b.** one nominated for a post or office

_____ 3. cognomen   **c.** a false name

_____ 4. nominal   **d.** disgrace or dishonor

_____ 5. denomination   **e.** to propose someone for elective office

_____ 6. nomenclature   **f.** a last name or family name

_____ 7. nominee   **g.** something shared or held in common

_____ 8. ignominy   **h.** a class or kind of person or thing having a specific name

_____ 9. agnomen   **i.** in name only; not in actuality

_____ 10. pseudonym   **j.** a letter of credit

k. names or terms special to a particular study or business

ANSWERS: 1—e; 2—g; 3—f; 4—i; 5—h; 6—k; 7—b; 8—d; 9—a; 10—c.

fill in the blanks

DIRECTIONS: Fill in the blank in each sentence with the appropriate word from among the following choices.

pseudonym
agnomen
nominee
nomenclature
denomination

ignominy
nominal
nominate
cognomen
denominator

1. To _____ means to propose someone for

   elective office.

2. A _____ is something shared or held

   in common.

3. Another term for your last name is a _____.

4. _____ means in name only.

5. A class or kind of persons or things having a specific name is referred

   to as a _____.

6. _____ means names or terms special to a

   particular study or business.

7. A person who is nominated for a post or office is called a

   _____.

8. One who is disgraced or dishonored suffers _____.

9. An _____ is a nickname.

10. A false name is a _____.

ANSWERS: 1—nominate;   2—denominator;   3—cognomen;   4—nominal;   5—denomination;   6—nomenclature;   7—nominee;   8—ignominy;   9—agnomen;   10—pseudonym.

crossword puzzle

ACROSS

4—a last name or family name
5—it means in name only

DOWN

1—disgrace; dishonor
2—a nickname
3—to propose someone for elective office

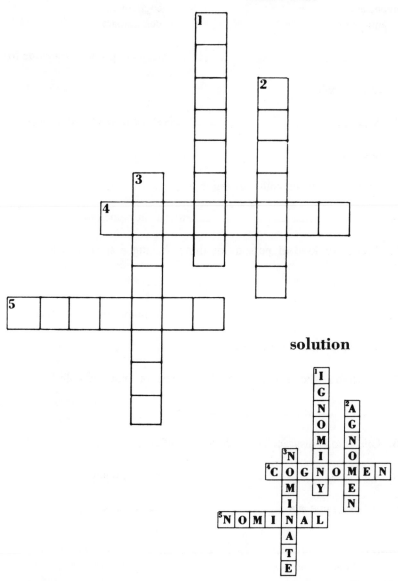

solution

PHILO
FEYE-lo

From the Greek *philos* meaning "loving"

"PHIL" is a variation of this root and means "loving", "friendly", "lover", or "friend of", as in the words *anglophile* (meaning "lover of English things") and *bibliophile* (meaning "lover of books"). It is appropriate that this root forms the basis of many English words, and our culture could probably do with more acceptance of the concept in the word rather than with more words formed from the root.

> PHILADELPHIA is called the "city of brotherly love," a name derived from the root "philo."

> PHILATELY—stamp collecting—is a combination of *phil* and *ateleia;* the latter part of the word means "freedom from taxes" and comes from the fact that when someone receives a letter with a stamp on it, the charges for the stamp and delivery have already been paid.

The following word parts will be combined with the root in this unit to make new words. Use this list as a reference to find the meaning of words in this unit.

ROOTS AS AFFIXES
tech—art or craft
anthro(po)—man or human
and(ros)—man
hellens—Greek
math—mathematics
gen—birth
polemic—war or dispute
logy—word or discourse
harmonic—harmony

PREFIX
pro—before or in behalf of

SUFFIXES
ately—tax or product
gym—woman
ist—doer or believer
tive—quality or condition of

65

context
clues

DIRECTIONS: Pronounce each word in the left hand column and read aloud the sentences in the right hand column. On the basis of context clues in the sentences, fill in the blank space to make a correct definition.

philotechnic

fil–o–TEK–nik

- Anyone who collected books and paintings, often went to concerts, and studied sculpture deserves to be called a philotechnician.
- Some people think we would have more philotechnic people in this country if the schools would stress music, painting and literature more.

1. Philotechnic means _____

_____

philanthropy

fil–AN–thruh–pee

- Children who give contributions to church collections are more likely to grow up with a sense of philanthropy than those who do not.
- It is possible that today philanthropy is encouraged more by high taxes than by a desire to help the less fortunate.

2. Philanthropy means _____

_____

philander

fuh–LAN–der

- Missy stopped dating Manny, because when she heard about all his other girlfriends, she decided he was nothing but a philanderer.
- Philandering may be fun, but it seldom leads to marriage.

3. Philander means _____

_____

philately

fuh–LAT–uh–lee

- Philatelists value highly stamps which are inadvertently misprinted.
- Philately is a good hobby for parents to introduce to their children if the adults plan a trip and will be writing home to the youngsters.

4. Philately means _____

_____

philter

FIL–tuhr

- In fiction, if not in fact, anyone who doubted his ability to attract a member of the opposite sex could always give the other person a philter.
- Part of the humor of *A Midsummer Night's Dream* comes from one character drinking a philter which carries with it the provision that the first person seen upon her awakening will be the object of her affection, and that person turns out to have the head of an ass.

5. A philter is _____

_____

philalethist

fil–al–LEE–thist

- In its broadest interpretation, anyone who studies and reads and is sincere about wanting to learn could be called a philalethist.
- "The truth shall make you free" could be the slogan of philalethists.

6. A philalethist is _____

_____

philhellenism

fil–HEL–en–ism

- Philhellenists flock to Greece, drawn by their attraction to the country which was the foundation for much of Western culture.
- Despite unpopular governments, philhellenism draws many tourists who overlook current politics in their search for past glories.

7. Philhellenism means _____

_____

philogynist

fil–LOJ–uhn–ist

- Heterosexual men are also philogynists.
- Montmorency's philogyny got him into a number of embarrassing situations when he forgot which woman he had made a date with or what excuse he gave to one he could not meet.

8. A philogynist is _____

_____

philomath

FIL–o–math

- A philomath does not limit his learning to mathematics, although the word seems to indicate he does.

■ People who continually study and take courses are often philomaths.

9. A philomath is _____

philopolemic

fil–uh–PO–lem–ik

■ Mercenary soldiers are often philopolemics who crave the adventure and glory they think war can bring them.
■ Peace-loving nations should be sure never to allow philopolemics to rule them.

10. A philopolemic is _____

philoprogenitive

fil–uh–pruh–JEN–uh–tiv

■ Many people feel that welfare payments should be denied the philoprogenitive unless they practice birth control.
■ At various times in cultural history, large families were less a matter of philoprogenitivity and more a matter of having enough help on a farm or of being sure the family name was carried on.

11. Philoprogenitive means _____

philology

fi–LOL–uh–jee

■ Philologists have a field day whenever a new manuscript that was believed lost is discovered.
■ Philology has enabled us to know more about ancient people and to understand their beliefs and thoughts because information comes directly from the people themselves in the form of their written records.

12. Philology means _____

philharmonic

fil–har–MON–ik

■ So many orchestras use the term "philharmonic" as part of their title because it best describes the attitude both of the musicians and of the people they play for.

■ Phil loved the local philharmonic because he enjoyed the harmony apparent in the orchestrations.

13. Philharmonic means _____

_____

ANSWERS

1. *Philotechnic* means love of the arts.
2. *Philanthropy* means affection for mankind, especially by making donations that will help others.
3. *Philander* means to make love without serious intentions.
4. *Philately* means one who loves stamps and therefore collects them.
5. A *philter* is a love potion.
6. A *philalethist* is one who loves truth.
7. *Philhellenism* means love of Greece.
8. A *philogynist* is a lover of women.
9. A *philomath* is a lover of learning.
10. A *philopolemic* is a lover of war.
11. *Philoprogenitive* means loving to have children or prolific.
12. *Philology* means love of learning and literature or the study of written records.
13. *Philharmonic* means music–loving.

matching exercise

DIRECTIONS: Write the appropriate letter from the right hand column in the space next to each number so that the numbered words are defined.

_____ 1. philotechnic   **a.** loves to have children

_____ 2. philanthrope   **b.** lover of war

_____ 3. philander   **c.** lover of learning

_____ 4. philatelist   **d.** one who loves truth

_____ 5. philalethist   **e.** love potion

_____ 6. philhellenist   **f.** a lover of women

_____ 7. philogynist   **g.** love of the arts

_____ 8. philomath   **h.** to make love triflingly

(*more*)

_____ 9. philopolemic

_____10. philogenitive

i. self love

j. a lover of mankind

k. a lover of Greece

l. a stamp collector

ANSWERS: 1—g; 2—j; 3—h; 4—l; 5—d; 6—k; 7—f; 8—c; 9—b; 10—a.

fill in the blanks

DIRECTIONS: Fill in the blank in each sentence with the appropriate word from among the following choices.

philotechnic

philanderer

philter

philhellenism

philomath

philoprogenitive

philharmonic

philanthropy

philately

philalethist

philogynist

philopolemic

philology

1. A genuine love for the arts is _____

   expression.

2. A _____ loves all mankind.

3. A man who gives a woman the impression he loves her but doesn't care

   and then goes on to another is a _____.

4. Some of the world's great personalities have been _____

   _____ and indirectly have amassed great wealth by collecting

   stamps.

5. All prominent religions and philosophies praise the _____

   _____ for he sincerely loves the truth.

6. A _____ is one who loves Greece and

   all things Greek.

7. An extreme fondness or love of women would identify a man as a

   _____.

8. If you would like to have children, you can be called

   _____.

9. Some interpreters of history say that Hitler's insistence on

   continuing World War II after all was lost was due to his

   _____ personality.

10. An individual who has accumulated an unusual amount of knowledge

    is probably a _____.

ANSWERS: 1—philotechnic; 2—philanthrope; 3—philanderer; 4—philatelist; 5—philalethist; 6—philhellenist; 7—philogynist; 8—philoprogenitive; 9—philopolemic; 10—philomath.

words in use

DIRECTIONS: Fill in the blank in each sentence with the appropriate word from among the following choices.

philotechnic	philhellenist
philanthrope	philoprogenitive
philander	philopolemic
philatelist	philomath
philogynist	philalethist

Frank a _____ had extreme love for his
                         1

fellow man. He would have to be considered a _____
                                             2

as well for he loved Greece and all its art forms. Some people had

called him a _____ for with his huge
                  3

storehouse of energy he never stopped trying to learn new things.

_____(pl.) respected him highly because
                4

amidst all of his many interests he managed to find time for his

valuable stamp collection.

ANSWERS: 1—philanthrope; 2—philhellenist; 3—philomath; 4—philatelist.

affixes at work

DIRECTIONS: Add your own words to the blanks at the bottom of the
diagram.

philatel**ist**

_____

art**ist**
(one who practices art)

_____

dent**ist**
(one who practices dentistry)

_____

pian**ist**
(a piano player)

_____

antagon**ist**
(one who opposes another)

_____

opportun**ist**
(one who takes advantage of every circumstance)

_____

moral**ist**
(one concerned with regulating the morals of others)

_____

theor**ist**
(one who theorizes)

_____

_____

Suffix: *ist* means "one who does or makes a practice of"

THEO
THEE-o

From the Greek *theos* meaning "god"

ALL cultures seem to have had some representation of god or gods, beings higher than man toward which he looked for help, explanation, and assurance. The present Western concept of God is sophisticated and abstract in relation to the primitive one that was primarily an explanation of natural phenomena.

The following word parts will be combined with the root in this unit to make new words. Use this list as a reference to find the meaning of words in this unit.

ROOTS AS AFFIXES
centri—center
crac—to rule
crasy—mixture
crat—supporter of
dicy—justice
gony—generation
logy—word or discourse
morph—form or shape
phany—to appear
sophy—wise

PREFIXES
mono—one or sole
a—not or without
poly—many

SUFFIXES
ism—act or state of
ic—pertaining to or belonging to
ist—one who does or makes

context
clues

DIRECTIONS: Pronounce each word in the left hand column and read aloud the sentences in the right hand column. On the basis of context clues in the sentences, fill in the blank space to make a correct definition.

theocentric

thee–uh–SEN–trik

- A theocentric person is likely to spend much of his time in church or reading about religion.
- Although many ancient societies were theocentric, they still managed to carry on the day-to-day activities that made them economically independent.

1. Theocentric means _____

_____

theocracy

thee–OK–ruh–see

- The American belief in separation of Church and State would not permit this country to become a theocracy.
- Although some countries have "state religions" they are not theocracies because the religious representatives have no real governmental power.

2. Theocracy is _____

_____

theocrasy

thee–OK–ruh–see

- It is possible that monotheism was prompted, in part, by a culture which had so many gods that theocrasy developed.
- An unlettered person can either believe in theocrasy or, because his mind is not exposed to other forms of learning, can maintain a differentiation among his gods.

3. Theocrasy means _____

_____

theocrat

THEE–uh–krat

- The Pharaohs of ancient Egypt were theocrats because they were believed to be descended from the gods.
- The Japanese as recently as World War II believed their Emperor a theocrat, but the country has since become more democratic and recognizes that Hirohito is only a mortal.

4. A theocrat is _____

_____

theodicy

thee–OD–uh–see

- Many philosophers in the age of reason attempted to reconcile the goodness of God with the evil they saw around them and thus wrote on the subject of theodicy.
- Theodicy is a problem to which people often address themselves when they need reconciliation between their beliefs and what they see around them in the world.

5. Theodicy means _____

_____

theogony

thee–OG–uh–nee

- An example of theogony is the story of Athena who is supposed to have sprung from the forehead of Zeus.
- The theogony of the early Greeks accounted for the parentage of Zeus and his sister-wife Hera as well as for the brothers of Zeus by indicating that all were sprung from a race of giants.

6. Theogony means _____

_____

theologian

thee–uh–LO–juhn

- Ministers are also theologians.
- A book on religion would be a good gift for a theologian because it would fit in with his interests.

7. A theologian is _____

_____

theology

thee–OL–uh–jee

- Until fairly recently, the study of philosophy automatically meant the study of theology.
- Theology, philosophy, and psychology are among the courses taken by young men who wish to become priests, ministers, and rabbis.

8. Theology means _____

_____

theomorphic

thee–uh–MOR–fik

- A fundamental biblical belief is that man is theomorphic.
- In Greek mythology and epic poetry the gods often appear in the form of men, the opposite of theomorphism.

9. Theomorphic means _____

_____

theophany

thee–OF–uh–nee

- Theophany was an ordinary occurrence to the heroes of the *Iliad* and the *Odyssey* who often conversed with the gods or received direct aid from them in battle.

Words About Beliefs   **75**

■ Reports of theophany today are rare and require extensive documentation before anyone accepts the manifestation as truly being that of God.

10. Theophany means _____

_____

theosophy

thee–OS–uh–fee

■ The latter parts of Dante's *Divine Comedy* in which the author approaches the final spheres before gazing into the fountain of light eternal are tinged with theosophy.
■ Theosophy is recognized by many as a religious cult and there is an organization of its adherents called the Theosophical Society.

11. Theosophy means _____

_____

monotheism

mon–uh–THEE–iz–um

■ The Judaeo-Christian tradition is monotheistic.
■ In *The Oresteian Trilogy* of Aeschulus it is easy to trace the development of thought from polytheism to the beginnings of monotheism.

12. Monotheism means _____

_____

polytheism

pol–i–THEE–iz–um

■ When the Romans "appropriated" the gods of the Greeks, they helped to prolong the belief in polytheism.
■ The polytheism of India makes it possible to direct prayers to the god which appears most likely to fulfill them.

13. Polytheism means _____

_____

atheist

A–thee–ist

■ Mrs. Wilson objected to the recitation of a daily prayer in school because she was an atheist.
■ Atheists in Center City united to protest the display of a cross on the courthouse because their tax money was being used to support a religious belief contrary to their thought.

14. An atheist is _____

_____

NAME: _____

ANSWERS

1. *Theocentric* means having God as the focus of interest.
2. *Theocracy* is a form of government in which God, a deity, (or his priests) is recognized as the civic ruler.
3. *Theocrasy* means a mingling of the attributes of several deities into one.
4. A *theocrat* is a person who rules as a divine king or representative of God or another deity.
5. *Theodicy* means the vindication of the goodness of God despite the existence of evil.
6. *Theogony* means an account of the origin of gods.
7. A *theologian* is a person versed in the study of God.
8. *Theology* means the study of God and his relation to the universe.
9. *Theomorphic* means having the form or likeness of God.
10. *Theophany* means the appearance of God or of a god to man.
11. *Theosophy* means a form of thought claiming a mystical insight into the divine nature.
12. *Monotheism* means a belief in a single God.
13. *Polytheism* means the belief in several gods.
14. An *atheist* is one who has no belief in God or in deities.

fill in the blanks

DIRECTIONS: Fill in the blank in each sentence with the appropriate word from among the following choices.

theocentric	theocracy
theocrasy	theocrat
theodicy	theogony
theologian	theology
theomorphic	theophany
theosophy	monotheism
polytheistic	atheist

1. A person whose every action, thought and desire is dedicated to God

   is properly called a _____.

2. A state of _____ is attained by many

   Yogis when they reach the apex of their contemplation.

3. The often-heard question, "If God is good, how can he permit so much

evil in the world?" is the basic one of _____.

4. Most clergymen are interested in studies which speculate on the origin

    of deities, even though the _____ might

    not be one of their own belief.

5. A whole system of study concerns God and his dealings with human

    beings; it is called _____.

6. Some of the world's great religions have a _____

    concept and believe that man is formed or shaped in the image of God.

7. Examples of _____ are offered by every

    religion for a physical manifestation of God to human beings seems to

    have been at the beginning of all of the great faiths.

8. Archaeologists know that the ancient Greeks had a

    _____ religion because they discovered

    statues of a variety of gods the people worshipped.

9. Most people believe in a supreme being but the _____

    _____ does not.

10. _____ is the basis of the true mystic's

    belief in God.

*ANSWERS: 1—theocentric; 2—theocrasy; 3—theodicy; 4—theogony; 5—the-
ology; 6—theomorphic; 7—theophany; 8—polytheistic; 9—atheist; 10—theosophy.*

word comprehension

DIRECTIONS: Read the paragraph. Then put a check next to
each word in the list below that is described in the paragraph.

When confronted by an individual who does not believe
that God exists, a specialist in theology could not offer mystical
insight as proof to the skeptic. This type of a person can only

be convinced if God were to make a personal appearance to him. Perhaps then he, too, might be interested in the defense of God against evil.

_____ 1. theocentric

_____ 2. theocrasy

_____ 3. theodicy

_____ 4. theogony

_____ 5. theologian

_____ 6. theomorphic

_____ 7. theopathy

_____ 8. theophany

_____ 9. theosophy

_____10. atheist

ANSWERS: 3; 5; 8; 9; 10.

affixes at work

DIRECTIONS: Add your own words to the blanks at the bottom of the diagram.

theo(entric)

centralize
(concentrate power in the center)

centrifugal
(force acting away from the center)

centripetal
(force acting toward the center)

helio**centric**
(with the sun as a center)

ego**centric**
(self-centered)

Root as Prefix or Suffix: *centr* or *centri* or *centro* means "center" or "of the center"

(mono)theism

monologue
(dramatic sketch performed by one actor)

monograph
(written account of a single thing)

monarch
(only ruler)

monocarpic
(bearing but once and dying)

monochrome
(with a single color)

monolingual
(knowing or using only one language)

mononuclear
(having only one nucleus)

Prefix: *mono* means "one," "sole," or "alone"

VERT

VERT

From the Latin *vertere* meaning "to turn"

IT is possible to turn around people's actions, a river's course, a product's location, a person's personality, and even one's beliefs. In fact, the variations in words built on the root meaning "to turn" run from "advertising" to "perversity". In many of the words, the idea of turning is worked in so subtly that their origin is not immediately evident. But the fact that the words which follow are only a portion of those available indicates how many different "turns" our language has.

The following word parts will be combined with the root in this unit to make new words. Use this list as a reference to find the meaning of words in this unit.

PREFIXES
con—with or together
intro—within or towards
per—through or thoroughly
in—not
ad—to
ex—out of
re—back or again
di—away from
sub—under or beneath
a—not or without
contro—against
ambi—around or both

SUFFIXES
ent—doing or showing
a—belonging to or of
ise—to cause or become

context

clues

DIRECTIONS: Pronounce each word in the left hand column and read aloud the sentences in the right hand column. On the basis of context clues in the sentences, fill in the blank space to make a correct definition.

81

convert

kuhn–VERT

- For hundreds of years men looked for a substance they could convert into gold by some magical or chemical means.
- You can convert your insurance policy into cash within a stated period of time.

    1. Convert means _____

_____

introvert

IN–truh–vert

- An introvert usually prefers to be by himself rather than to be with people who might intrude on his thoughts.
- Herbert proved to be such an extreme introvert that no girl would go out with him a second time because he always seemed lost in his own thoughts and was so hard to talk to.

    2. An introvert is _____

_____

perverse

per–VERS

- Rudy is so perverse he'd disagree with anything you said just for the sake of an argument.
- It takes a perverse person to express such contrary opinions every time a discussion starts.

    3. Perverse means _____

_____

pervert

per–VERT

- The purpose of this course is to teach you about geography; do not pervert it by talking about the people you met on vacation trips.
- Montmorency found it easy to pervert the purpose of the funds allocated for research and use them for personal gain.

    4. Pervert means _____

_____

inadvertent

in–uhd–VERT–nt

- I took a left turn inadvertently and ended up on Z street instead of on A street.
- The new soldier inadvertently fired a red flare instead of a green one with the result that the troops retreated rather than advanced.

5. Inadvertent means _____

_____

extrovert

EKS–truh–vert

■ Mary is friendly and outgoing; a real extrovert.
■ Henry was such an extrovert that as soon as he got with the Boy Scouts he forgot all his own problems.

6. An extrovert is _____

_____

vertical

VER–ti–kl

■ The windows on each floor of the building are set above each other; a vertical line drawn from the first to the tenth floors will show that they are perfectly aligned.
■ The vertical take-off ability of the helicopter makes it useful in areas where there isn't enough room for an airplane landing strip.

7. Vertical means _____

_____

revert

ri–VERT

■ The mice that had been transformed into horses to pull Cinderella's coach reverted to their original state when the clock struck twelve.
■ In the movie *Charley,* the main character was a mentally retarded man who gained great intelligence by taking a drug, but reverted to his original state when the effects of the drug wore off.

8. Revert means _____

_____

advert

ad–VERT

■ If you advert to her changed hair color, be sure you are complimentary or else keep quiet.
■ Wilbur may want to advert to his ability as a basketball player when he has an interview with the admissions officer of the college.

9. Advert means to _____

_____

advertise

AD–ver–teyez

- Anyone with home–crafted items to sell can advertise them without cost in the campus newspaper.
- Advertise your better mousetrap so the public will know it is available.

10. Advertise means to _____

_____

divert

duh–VERT

- Divert the stream at this point so you can build the bridge over dry land; then permit the stream to revert to its actual course.
- The strip-teaser diverted the attention of customers while her partner, the pickpocket, took away their money.

11. Divert means to _____

_____

subvert

sub–VERT

- If you intend to subvert the student senate, you first must be elected to that body or you will never have the opportunity to overthrow those in it with whom you disagree.
- FBI men manage to infiltrate the rackets and thus subvert the power of the men who control them.

12. Subvert means to _____

_____

overt

O–vert

- Hubert's overt show of affection to Cornelia led them to kiss in the halls between classes and to hold hands when walking.
- The only overt sign of his duel was a scar along the right cheek; the experience, however, left him more cowardly than ever.

13. Overt means _____

_____

avert

uh–VERT

- Medical students watching their first autopsy often avert their eyes when the cadaver is exposed to view.
- Workers managed to avert the catastrophe of

the flood by building a dike of sandbags to hold
back the water.

14. Avert means _____

_____

controvert

kon–truh–VERT

- If you controvert my statements one more time,
  I'll see that you never get elected again because
  I can no longer stand your disagreements!
- Nobody could controvert the evidence supplied
  by the witnesses, so the bank robber was con-
  victed.

15. Controvert means _____

_____

ambivert

AM–bi–vert

- Henry is an ambivert because he is able to
  strike a happy medium between being forever
  quiet and forever talking.
- To be an ambivert would seem desirable, but
  not everyone's personality allows him to be
  outgoing sometimes and reticent at others.

16. Ambivert means _____

_____

ANSWERS

1. *Convert means to change into a different form.*
2. *An introvert is someone who has an inward turn of mind; self-concern.*
3. *Perverse means contrary.*
4. *Pervert means to turn away or to lead astray.*
5. *Inadvertent means unexpected.*
6. *An extrovert is someone whose interests are directed outside of himself.*
7. *Vertical means upright or perpendicular to the horizon.*
8. *Revert means to return or turn back.*
9. *Advert means to turn attention to; to remark or comment about.*
10. *Advertise means to call attention to a product or service.*
11. *Divert means to turn aside or away from.*
12. *Subvert means to overthrow or to cause the downfall of someone or some-
    thing.*
13. *Overt means open to view or knowledge; not secret.*
14. *Avert means to turn away or aside.*
15. *Controvert means to oppose or argue against.*
16. *Ambivert means a personality type between an introvert and an extrovert.*

fill in the blanks

DIRECTIONS: Fill in the blank in each sentence with the appropriate word from among the following choices.

ambivert	inadvertent
convert	advertise
controvert	revert
introvert	advert
pervert	divert
invert	subvert
extrovert	vertical
avert	

1. To _____ attention is to turn aside

   one's concentration from one person or thing to another.

2. To overthrow or cause the downfall of an organized group is to

   _____ it.

3. If you turned something upside down you would _____

   _____ it.

4. A person who is an _____ has interests

   directed outside of himself.

5. If you turn your attention to something you _____

   to it.

6. _____ means to return or turn back.

7. When you change a sow's ear into a silk purse you _____

   _____ it.

8. You can usually _____ failure in an

   examination by preparing ahead of time for the test.

9. If a person's personality is turned inward, he is said to be

   an _____ .

NAME: _____

10. To _____ an idea is to lead it so far from

the original that it is almost unrecognizable.

ANSWERS: 1—divert; 2—subvert; 3—invert; 4—extrovert; 5—advert; 6—revert; 7—convert; 8—avert; 9—introvert; 10—pervert.

matching exercise

DIRECTIONS: Write the appropriate letter from the right hand column in the space next to each number so that the numbered words are defined.

_____ 1. convert

_____ 2. introvert

_____ 3. pervert

_____ 4. extrovert

_____ 5. invert

_____ 6. revert

_____ 7. advert

_____ 8. divert

_____ 9. subvert

_____10. avert

a. to turn away or lead astray

b. to turn inward, especially one's mind

c. to avoid

d. to change into something of a different form

e. return or turn back

f. to turn attention to; to refer

g. interests directed outside the self

h. to turn upside down

i. to overthrow or cause the downfall of

j. not secret

k. to turn aside

ANSWERS: 1—d; 2—b; 3—a; 4—g; 5—h; 6—e; 7—f; 8—k; 9—i; 10—c.

words in use

DIRECTIONS: Read the following paragraph. Then fill in each blank with the appropriate word from among the following choices.

inadvertent

convert

revert

subvert

extrovert

converter

divert

vertigo

(*more*)

The general had an outgoing personality and was considered an

_____ by most people. He said he would try
1

to _____ his medical troops into combat
2

soldiers and this might make his forces strong enough to

_____ the enemy's attack. He made certain
3

of cooperation by saying that anyone trying to _____
4

the idea would be shot.

ANSWERS: 1—extrovert; 2—convert; 3—divert; 4—subvert.

PEANUTS ®

By Charles M. Schulz

affixes at work

DIRECTIONS: Add your own words to the blanks at the bottom of the diagram.

convert

concentric
(having a common center)

concern
(to relate to; to distress)

concert
(agreement in design or plan)

concede
(to grant as a right)

concise
(brief and to the point)

concur
(to come together; agree)

condemn
(to pronounce guilty)

condominium
(individual ownership of a unit in an apartment building)

Prefix: *con* means "with," "together," or "jointly"

POSTTEST

DIRECTIONS: In the space next to each number, write the letter that correctly completes the statement.

_____ 1. Violent overthrow of a government with no consideration of an alternate form of government leads to
   a. theocracy.
   b. plutocracy.
   c. mobocracy.
   d. aristocracy.

_____ 2. When a foreign ambassador presents his credentials to the president of the U.S., he is literally
   a. presenting his country's request for foreign aid.
   b. presenting papers which enable the president to have confidence in him as a governmental representative.
   c. asking for credit to be extended in order to establish a favorable balance of trade between two countries.
   d. asking that his beliefs be respected.

_____ 3. A fairly frequent cause for divorce is
   a. infidelity.
   b. fiduciariness.
   c. confidences.
   d. infidels.

_____ 4. A wealthy and sincere Moslem man who believed in following tradition would probably not be
   a. a misogamist.
   b. a monogamist.
   c. a cernagomist.
   d. a gnosis.

_____ 5. Someone who knows nothing and doesn't care to learn is called an
   a. agnostic.
   b. cognoscenti.
   c. ignoramus.
   d. prognosis.

_____ 6. If a diagnosis revealed you needed work on coherence, you would most likely
     a. pay the doctor and take your medicine.
     b. reject help in mechanics.
     c. work to improve your writing.
     d. thank the nurse and make another appointment.

_____ 7. Among the first people to call the family of the deceased was the
     a. caterer.
     b. mortician.
     c. tinker.
     d. shoemaker.

_____ 8. The sign announcing "Nondenominational Church Services" served as an invitation to
     a. only Methodists.
     b. agnostics.
     c. everyone interested.
     d. only non-Christians.

_____ 9. Mr. McDuff insisted he was a philalethist because he
     a. had an eye for pretty girls.
     b. didn't believe in God.
     c. said he loved truth.
     d. was enamored of Alethia.

_____10. The philharmonic patrons settled down to an evening of
     a. watching movies.
     b. listening to music.
     c. sampling the new wines.
     d. enjoying the fashion show.

_____11. Montmorency was branded a philogynist because he
     a. liked to swim in the nude.
     b. often did gymnastics at home.
     c. had a great many girlfriends.
     d. liked exotic foods.

_____12. When archaeologists discovered statues of their gods in every room of the houses they unearthed, on most pieces of pottery, on the walls of every temple, and even lining the streets,

they concluded that the people whose culture
they were working with were probably
   a. theatrical.
   b. theocentric.
   c. thematic.
   d. centripetal.

_____13. One who refuses to believe in God as a creator
and ruler of the universe is
   a. an agnostic.
   b. an atheist.
   c. asocial.
   d. antipathetic.

_____14. Government by a priestly group or class is
called
   a. religiosity.
   b. theocracy.
   c. monarchy.
   d. prestocracy.

_____15. Students often seek to divert a teacher from his
planned lessons by
   a. asking for clarification of a point just
      made.
   b. bringing in something unrelated.
   c. listening carefully.
   d. taking notes.

*ANSWERS: 1—c; 2—b; 3—a; 4—b; 5—c; 6—c; 7—b; 8—c; 9—c; 10—b;
11—c; 12—b; 13—b; 14—b; 15—b.*

chapter 3

Words About Behavior

PRETEST

DIRECTIONS: In the space next to each number, write the letter that correctly completes the statement.

_____ 1. An example of a herbivorous animal is
   a. a whale.
   b. a dog.
   c. a giraffe.
   d. a lion.

_____ 2. If the landlord decided to revoke your lease you would
   a. have to look for another place to live.
   b. be happy and pick out the colors for the new paint job.
   c. sign the petition without question.
   d. check the television reception in the house or apartment.

_____ 3. A dipsomaniac has an irrational craving for
   a. books.
   b. money.
   c. alcohol.
   d. sweets.

_____ 4. A narcomaniac has an irrational enthusiasm for
   a. narcissuses.
   b. drugs.
   c. night life.
   d. condiments.

_____ 5. If you defer to the person behind you in line at the movies you would
   a. offer him candy.
   b. try to take off your shoes while waiting.
   c. let him purchase his ticket before you get yours.
   d. detail your troubles to him.

_____ 6. An ambivert is most likely to be
      a. able to write with either hand.
      b. bitter because of the vicissitudes of life.
      c. one who suffers from frequent headaches.
      d. a well-adjusted person.

_____ 7. An example of malapropos conduct at a wedding would be to
      a. kiss the bride and congratulate the groom.
      b. toast the bride's former boyfriend.
      c. drink a toast to the newlyweds.
      d. shake hands with the best man.

_____ 8. A person with agorophobia will not enjoy
      a. roughing it on the prairie.
      b. a movie.
      c. wearing an angora sweater.
      d. a new car.

_____ 9. An acrophobe is
      a. a crossword puzzle fan.
      b. a gourmet.
      c. afraid of heights.
      d. afraid of open spaces.

_____10. When the end man in a minstrel show wants to tell a joke that requires a straight man, he usually calls, "Mr. _____!"
      a. Tardiloquence.
      b. Electrician.
      c. Elocutioner.
      d. Interlocutor.

_____11. If you want your handwriting analyzed, you must submit a
      a. species.
      b. specimen.
      c. speculum.
      d. speculator.

_____12. In children's stories, a malediction is usually pronounced by
      a. the good fairy.
      b. the innocent children.
      c. the witch.
      d. the prince.

ANSWERS TO PRETEST
1—c; 2—a; 3—c; 4—b; 5—c; 6—d; 7—b; 8—a; 9—c; 10—d; 11—b; 12—c.

DIC, DICT
DIK, DIKT

From the Latin *-dicere* meaning "to say" or "to speak"

TALKING is probably our principle way of communicating; it is hard to go for even a few hours without voicing, thinking, encountering, or acting in some way that is not related to the root word DIC or DICT. Our language, then, contains a variety of words with this root.

The following word parts will be combined with the root in this unit to make new words. Use this list as a reference to find the meaning of words in this unit.

PREFIXES
contra—against
male—bad or ill
bene—good
in—not
ab—from or away
pre—before

SUFFIXES
ation—the act of
or—doer or agent
ial—of or belonging to
ate—office or officeholder
(t)ive—belonging to or tending to

ROOTS AS AFFIXES
phone—sound or voice
ver—truth

context
clues

DIRECTIONS: Pronounce each word in the left hand column and read aloud the sentences in the right hand column. On the basis of context clues in the sentences, fill in the blank space to make a correct definition.

dictation

dik–TA–shun

- If you learn to take dictation, you can record in your notebook exactly what the teacher says during class lectures.
- Myrtle gave dictation to Betsy, her secretary, who wrote it in her notebook.

1. Dictation is _____

_____

diction

DIK–shun

- Girls who want to work for the telephone company must have clear diction.
- Radio and television announcers study diction so they can be clearly understood by all their listeners.

2. Diction means _____

_____

dictaphone

DIK–tuh–fone

- The dictaphone is a convenient device for busy executives to use on their way to work; their secretaries can then transcribe the letters without having to take them from direct dictation.
- A tape recorder is a kind of dictaphone.

3. A dictaphone is _____

_____

dictatorial

dik–tuh–TOR–ee–ul

- Teachers with a dictatorial manner are not likely to be popular with students who want to practice self-discovery.
- The dictatorial tone of Frank's letter left doubt as to who was running the office.

4. Dictatorial means _____

_____

dictum

DIK–tum

- When the General issues a dictum, the privates had better pay attention to it.
- The dictum of the state road department called for immediate purchase of land for the new highway.

5. Dictum means _____

_____

contradict

kon–truh–DIKT

- Children are usually taught not to contradict their elders by denying the accuracy of what they are told.
- The weather turned warm and sunny, a contradiction of the forecast heard that morning on the radio.

6. Contradict means _____

_____

malediction

mal–uh–DIK–shun

- The witch pronounced a malediction against the beautiful baby saying it would grow up to be a bumblebee.
- A malediction consisting of four-letter words usually called "unprintable" succeeded in unnerving the tightrope walker.

7. A malediction is _____

_____

benediction

ben–uh–DIK–shun

- The benediction pronounced at the end of the religious service is designed to give the congregants hope for the future.
- A clergyman is usually asked to say the benediction at the beginning of a graduation ceremony.

8. Benediction means _____

_____

indicate

IN–duh–kate

- Please indicate your preference for carrying a sign, waving a banner, or leading catcalls at the political rally tonight.
- If you do not indicate the time that you want to take a class, we will enroll you at an hour that is convenient for the teacher.

9: Indicate means _____

_____

indicative

in–DIK–uh–tiv

- Ronald hoped that Margie's unwillingness to sit next to him at the game was not indicative of her whole attitude toward him.
- There is an old saying that cold hands are indicative of a warm heart.

10. Indicative means _____

_____

abdicate

AB–duh–kate

- If you refuse to vote, you abdicate your responsibility as a citizen with control of his own government.

■ The king decided to abdicate the throne in order to marry the woman he loved.

11. Abdicate means _____

_____

predict

pri–DIKT

■ Fortune-tellers say they can predict the future.
■ It is risky to try to predict the outcome of horse races.

12. Predict means _____

_____

verdict

VER–dikt

■ Every time you buy a piece of clothing you pass a verdict on its use or appearance by deciding to make the purchase.
■ The verdict of the jury forced Horace to be put behind bars for ten years.

13. Verdict means _____

_____

ANSWERS

1. *Dictation* is to say words to be written down by another person.
2. *Diction* is clear, correct, and effective speech.
3. A *dictaphone* is an instrument for recording speech.
4. *Dictatorial* means overbearing.
5. *Dictum* means an authoritative statement.
6. *Contradict* means to oppose or deny something by voicing objections.
7. A *malediction* is a curse.
8. *Benediction* means a blessing.
9. *Indicate* means to show, tell, or point out.
10. *Indicative* means that which suggests an action or event.
11. *Abdicate* means to renounce, as a throne or a high office.
12. *Predict* means forecast.
13. *Verdict* means a judgment or opinion.

words in use

DIRECTIONS: Read the following paragraph. Then fill in each blank with the appropriate word from among the following choices.

diction
dictum
contradict
abdicate
verdict

dictation
dictaphone
indicative
malediction

When the king heard of the witch's curse, he was so afraid of her

_____ that he decided he should
1

_____. Accordingly, he issued an official
2

_____ reflecting his _____.
3   4

ANSWERS: 1—malediction; 2—abdicate; 3—dictum; 4—verdict.

matching exercise

DIRECTIONS: Write the appropriate letter from the right hand column in the space next to each number so that the numbered words are defined.

_____ 1. diction

_____ 2. verdict

_____ 3. dictum

_____ 4. malediction

_____ 5. abdicate

_____ 6. benediction

_____ 7. dictaphone

_____ 8. contradict

_____ 9. dictation

_____10. indicative

a. an instrument for recording speech

b. to oppose something; to deny

c. a judgment or opinion

d. a curse, a bad saying

e. a blessing

f. that which suggests an action or an event

g. saying or speaking

h. an authoritative statement

i. to renounce, as a throne or a high office

j. stating words to be written by another

k. to exasperate, to burden

l. severe lassitude

ANSWERS: 1—g; 2—c; 3—h; 4—d; 5—i; 6—e; 7—a; 8—b; 9—j; 10—f.

Words About Behavior   **99**

crossword puzzle

ACROSS

3—to renounce
4—to deny
5—a judgment

DOWN

1—an authoritative statement
2—that which suggests

solution

FER

FER

From the Latin *ferre* meaning to "bear" or "carry"

BEARING or carrying—news, packages, ideas, emotions—is basic to the way people behave. So it is not surprising that this root forms the basis of many words that convey various kinds of carrying.

The following word parts will be combined with the root in this unit to make new words. Use this list as a reference to find the meaning of words in this unit.

PREFIXES
trans—across or through
re—back or again
in—not
de—from or down
con—with or together
pre—before

SUFFIXES
ile—suitable for or likely
ence—act or state or condition

context

clues

DIRECTIONS: Pronounce each word in the left hand column and read aloud the sentences in the right hand column. On the basis of context clues in the sentences, fill in the blank space to make a correct definition.

transfer

trans–FER

■ Be sure to transfer the lunch from the car to the boat before you unhitch the trailer for launching.
■ You can usually transfer credits from one ac-credited school to another.

1. Transfer means _____

_____

refer

ruh–FER

■ Refer to your list of course requirements if you are not sure which classes to take next term.
■ A dictionary definition that refers you to another definition is frustrating and time–consuming.

2. Refer means _____

_____

infer

in–FER

■ The police gathered ten pages of facts about the behavior of the prisoner on the night of the riot but left it to the judge to infer whether or not he was guilty as charged.
■ Cynthia has had such success in her career so far that Max inferred she would be a good client for him to manage.

3. Infer means _____

_____

defer

di–FER

■ Children do not always defer to their parents' wishes.
■ Protocol requires that a congressman defer to a justice of the Supreme Court when they are together at social events.

4. Defer means _____

_____

confer

kon–FER

■ Sam decided to confer with his boss and ask for a raise.
■ One successful way to prepare for a test is to confer with a classmate and try to determine what questions the teacher is likely to ask.

5. Confer means _____

_____

prefer

pri–FER

■ You might prefer to order tutti-frutti instead of mocha-polka ice cream.
■ George prefers to spend his time studying instead of going out with girls.

6. Prefer means _____

_____

fertile

FUR–tl

■ Anyone with a fertile imagination can easily find ten uses for a straight pin.
■ Soil conservationists have discovered many methods of keeping soil fertile even though several crops a year are planted on the same ground.

7. Fertile means _____

_____

suffer

SUF–er

■ People who believe in euthanasia or mercy killings often give as a reason for their belief a reluctance to allow people to suffer for a long time without hope of relief.
■ Matilda would not suffer such discomfort if she didn't wear such a tight girdle.

8. Suffer means _____

_____

reference

REF–uh–rents

■ Look up the proper reference in the library in order to collect information for your term paper.
■ I will supply you with good references if you want to look for another job.

9. Reference means _____

_____

ANSWERS

1. *Transfer means to convey from one person or place to another.*
2. *Refer means to look back at something.*
3. *Infer means to derive from facts.*
4. *Defer means to have courteous regard for a person.*
5. *Confer means to exchange ideas.*
6. *Prefer means to choose one before another, to give priority.*
7. *Fertile means capable of breeding or of growing and developing.*
8. *Suffer means to undergo or to bear up under pain or sorrow.*
9. *Reference means the direction of attention.*

matching exercise

DIRECTIONS: Write the appropriate letter from the right hand column in the space next to each number so that the numbered words are defined.

_____ 1. refer   **a.** to convey from one person or place to another

_____ 2. reference   **b.** to have courteous regard

_____ 3. infer   **c.** to bear up under pain, sorrow, etc.

_____ 4. fertile   **d.** to look back at something

_____ 5. defer   **e.** to derive from facts

_____ 6. confer   **f.** capable of breeding; carrying pollen

_____ 7. prefer   **g.** to choose above another, to give priority

_____ 8. transfer   **h.** to exchange ideas

_____ 9. suffer   **i.** to refer; to classify within a general group; look back

ANSWERS: 1—d; 2—i; 3—e; 4—f; 5—b; 6—h; 7—g; 8—a; 9—c.

true-false

DIRECTIONS: Read each sentence carefully and decide whether it is true or false. If it is true, place a T for true in the space at the right. If it is false, write in an F.

1. To convey from one person or place to another is to defer.   1._____
2. To give priority is to prefer.   2._____
3. An efferent nerve would carry messages inward.   3._____

4. One might confer to exchange ideas.   4._____
5. Afferent means to carry outward.   5._____
6. If you wished to put something off you would infer it.   6._____
7. To bear up under pain is to suffer.   7._____
8. Fertile refers to breeding.   8._____
9. To classify within a general group is to transfer.   9._____

ANSWERS: 1—F; 2—T; 3—F; 4—T; 5—F; 6—F; 7—T; 8—T; 9—F.

fill in the blanks

DIRECTIONS: Fill in the blank in each sentence with the appropriate word from among the following choices.

refer	transfer
inference	reference
defer	confer
prefer	suffer
fertile	

1. To hand a package from one person to another is to

   _____ it.

2. Whenever we exchange ideas we _____

   with each other.

3. Young people should _____ to an aged

   person if both want to go through a door at the same time.

4. Most people _____ to be healthy rather

   than sick.

ANSWERS: 1—transfer; 2—confer; 3—defer; 4—prefer.

Words About Behavior   **105**

"*Tell me more about this kleptomaniac tendency, Mrs. Henderson.*"

LOC, LOQ
LOK

From the Latin *loqui* meaning "to speak"

THERE are so many different kinds of speech that there needs to be many words to describe the act: to oneself, too much, with others, badly, and many more. Some of these words are in the following section.

The following word parts will be combined with the root in this unit to make new words. Use this list as a reference to find the meaning of words in this unit.

PREFIXES
col—with or together
soli—alone
al—pertaining to
e—out of or off
inter—among or between
grand—great

SUFFIXES
ism—act of or condition
tion—act or condition of
ity—quality or state
ious—full of
ence—act or condition
ent—doing or showing
y—full of

ROOT AS AFFIX
ventri—belly

context
clues

DIRECTIONS: Pronounce each word in the left hand column and read aloud the sentences in the right hand column. On the basis of context clues in the sentences, fill in the blank space to make a correct definition.

colloquial

ka–LO–kwi–al

■ One can be said to speak a language well when he is able to use colloquial expressions rather than rely only on the artificial and formalized patterns of speech.
■ Most people would feel awkward if they could not resort to colloquial speech as a change from formal speech.

1. Colloquial means _____

_____

ventriloquism

ven–TRIL–uh–kwisum

■ It is always fun for children to hear a ventriloquist because his dummy generally makes him the butt of jokes.
■ Ventriloquism is an art that comes in handy if you want to make people think you are in a different part of the room from where you actually are.

2. Ventriloquism is _____

_____

soliloquy

suh–LIL–uh–kwi

■ Hamlet's most famous soliloquy begins "To be or not to be", though he has several other speeches in the play when he is alone on the stage.
■ The stage is not required for a soliloquy; anyone may soliloquize at home when he is alone.

3. A soliloquy is _____

_____

loquacity

low–KWAS–uh–tee

■ Jennifer's loquacity got her into trouble because she had so many opportunities to say the wrong thing.
■ A senator's loquacity is useful during a Senate filibuster.

4. Loquacity is _____

_____

loquacious

low–KWAY–shus

■ A truly loquacious person will often ruin a good movie for you because of his continual talk.
■ Women are supposed to be more loquacious than men, but this is not necessarily true.

5. Loquacious means _____

_____

allocution

AL–uh–ku–shun

■ Many people who are not accustomed to speaking in public tend toward allocution when they have a chance to make a speech, especially when they want to impress an audience with the "rightness" of their statements.

■ Sylvester was so tired of all the allocution at the meeting that he suddenly raised his hand to challenge the speaker on auto safety.

6. Allocution means _____

_____

eloquence

EL–uh–kwents

■ The senator was known for his eloquence, for his choice of exact words, and for his ability to quote scriptural passages.
■ If eloquence were a requisite for the job, Marsha could talk anyone into hiring her.

7. Eloquence is _____

_____

eloquent

EL–uh–kwant

■ Eloquent speakers acquire their skill by studying words so they can choose the right ones on speaking engagements.
■ The visiting speaker made such an eloquent plea for aid to the underprivileged that everyone in the audience was immediately anxious to contribute money to this cause.

8. Eloquent means _____

_____

elocution

el–uh–KYOU–shun

■ Mrs. Smith's children used to take elocution lessons because she hoped the study would prepare them all to be relaxed when they had to give speeches in class.
■ Most college speech classes try to teach a form of elocution that is natural and informal.

9. Elocution means _____

_____

interlocution

IN–ter–low–KYOU–shun

■ At least two people are required for interlocution.
■ The interlocution following the student's presentation of his paper made it evident that everyone in the class had become interested in the subject.

10. Interlocution is _____

_____

interlocutor

IN–ter–LOK–yoo–ter

- The interlocutor at a minstrel show has to sit in the middle because he feeds lines to the two end men.
- An interlocutor appeared as if from nowhere and began to question Charlie.

11. An interlocutor is _____

_____

grandiloquent

gran–DIL–uh–kwant

- Henry made such a grandiloquent speech that it left his listeners marveling that such a small man could make such pompous statements.
- "Too bad," Sidney murmured, "that Sylvester's ideas are not as grandiloquent as his speech."

12. Grandiloquent means _____

_____

colloquy

KOL–a–kwi

- If a teacher is willing to engage in colloquy with a student, he may get the student to be open enough to find out about the effectiveness of his teaching.
- A colloquy at second base among the baseman, the umpire, and the runner resulted in the runner being declared out and the baseman being sent to the showers.

13. Colloquy means _____

_____

colloquium

kuh–LOK–wee–um

- Many educators feel that a colloquium in the classroom is an ideal way of helping students explore a subject.
- The president of Widget Manufacturing called together his ten vice presidents for a colloquium to discuss reasons for production delays.

14. A colloquium is _____

_____

NAME: _____

ANSWERS

1. *Colloquial* means ordinary or familiar conversation.
2. *Ventriloquism* is the art of throwing one's voice or making it seem to come from another source.
3. A *soliloquy* is talking to oneself while (or as if) alone.
4. *Loquacity* is talking too much.
5. *Loquacious* means talkative.
6. *Allocution* means a formal speech, especially one not open to discussion.
7. *Eloquence* is speaking with fluency, force, and effectiveness.
8. *Eloquent* means expressive and moving.
9. *Elocution* is the study and practice of public speaking.
10. *Interlocution* is conversation.
11. An *interlocutor* is someone who participates in a dialogue. (In minstrel shows, a man who acts as announcer and plays straight man to the men sitting on either end of the row.)
12. *Grandiloquent* means pompousness, especially in speech or tone.
13. *Colloquy* means a dialogue or conversational exchange.
14. A *colloquium* is an informal conference or group discussion.

true-false

DIRECTIONS: Read each sentence carefully and decide whether it is true or false. If it is true, put a T in the answer space at the right. If it is false, write in an F.

1. A loquacious person talks very little.   1._____
2. Fluent, forceful speech is eloquent speech.   2._____
3. Colloquy means a conversation or a conference.   3._____
4. The informal speech that is generally used is colloquial speech.   4._____
5. An individual who speaks with pompous eloquence is grandiloquent.   5._____
6. A seminar, if it has several lecturers, is a colloquium.   6._____
7. When a person can speak so that his voice seems to come from another source he practices ventriloquism.   7._____
8. The Gettysburg Address is an example of allocution.   8._____
9. A synonym for conversation is interlocution.   9._____
10. A soliloquy really means talking to someone else.   10._____

ANSWERS: 1—F; 2—T; 3—T; 4—T; 5—T; 6—T; 7—T; 8—T; 9—T; 10—F.

words in use

DIRECTIONS: Fill in the blanks with the correct words from among the following choices.

grandiloquence   pauciloquy
eloquent   colloquium
ventriloquism   loquacious
colloquial   interlocutor

The _____ man excelled in
                    1

_____. One of his main problems was
                  2

_____ and he frequently exhibited this even
             3

in _____ speech. He certainly would have been
              4

a bad selection for a lecturer at any _____
                                            5

because he was really too _____ to hold an
                              6

audience for any length of time.

ANSWERS: 1—loquacious; 2—ventriloquism; 3—grandiloquence; 4—colloquial; 5—colloquium; 6—loquacious.

MANIA
MAY-nee-uh

From the Latin *-mania,* extreme frenzy or unusual mental excitement; also from the Greek *manikos,* insane

IN ADDITION to being the root of many words describing an extreme manifestation of what otherwise would be normal activity, "mania" is also a word describing a behavior. Thus, any irrational, excessive concentration on a single idea or thought with a compulsion to act out that thought continuously is called a *mania.*

The following word parts will be combined with the root in this unit to make new words. Use this list as a reference to find the meaning of words in this unit.

ROOTS AS AFFIXES

klep—thief
pyro—fire
megalo—large or great
dipso—thirst
narco—stupefy, or make numb
xeno—stranger

theo—god
nymph—young woman
gyn—woman
myth—story
graph—word or write
phago—eating
logo—word

context
clues

DIRECTIONS: Pronounce each word in the left hand column and read aloud the sentences in the right hand column. On the basis of context clues in the sentences, fill in the blank space to make a correct definition.

kleptomania

KLEP–toe–MAY–nee–uh

■ Mrs. Willoby's husband continually had to explain her kleptomania to department store detectives.

113

■ It is difficult to tell whether a person stealing merchandise is a kleptomaniac or a thief.

1. Kleptomania is _____

_____

pyromania

PIE–roe–MAY–nee–uh

■ Entire blocks of buildings have been burned out because of the actions of a single pyromaniac.
■ It is sometimes said facetiously that the emperor Nero, who fiddled while Rome burned, was actually afflicted with pyromania.

2. Pyromania is _____

_____

megalomania

MEG–uh–loe–MAY–
nee–uh

■ Megalomania has led many men to become dictators.
■ Sylvester tried to be the leader of everything the senior class did, thus giving vent to his megalomania.

3. Megalomania is _____

_____

dipsomania

DIP–so–MAY–nee–uh

■ Dipsomania can be an expensive illness for an individual, although distillers might find it profitable.
■ A true dipsomaniac will drink anything containing alcohol.

4. Dipsomania is _____

_____

narcomania

NAR–ko–MAY–nee–uh

■ One who wants to withdraw from the normal world might try morphine and thus become a narcomaniac.
■ Prolonged use of drugs, even under medical supervision, sometimes results in narcomania.

5. Narcomania is _____

_____

xenomania

ZE–no–MAY–nee–uh

- Someone afflicted with xenomania would look for foreign labels in any piece of clothing he considered buying.
- A "buy American" campaign would make a xenomaniac most uncomfortable.

6. Xenomania is _____

_____

theomania

THEE–o–MAY–nee–uh

- Frequent church attendance alone does not make a theomaniac.
- In theomania, God may be used as a substitute for normal personal relationships.

7. Theomania is _____

_____

nymphomania

NIM–foe–MAY–nee–uh

- Myrtle did not realize she had nymphomania, even though she constantly lusted for men.
- No school board would knowingly hire a nymphomaniac to teach young children.

8. Nymphomania is _____

_____

gynecomania

GEYE–nuh–ko–MAY–
   nee–uh

- Gynecomania interferes with a man's ability to earn a living because the disorder prevents him from keeping any job where women also work.
- The prisoner, who was arrested for molesting women, was diagnosed as a gynecomaniac by the psychiatrist.

9. Gynecomania is _____

_____

mythomania

MITH–o–MAY–nee–uh

- James did not steal the money, yet his mytho-mania caused him to lie and say he did.
- Mythomaniacs make good storytellers because they are not concerned with the truth of situations they describe.

10. Mythomania is _____

_____

graphomania

GRAF–o–MAY–nee–uh

■ Wilson had graphomania so he was always writing notes to himself, stories, conversations he heard, even doodles.

■ Mary's graphomania forced her to carry a pencil with her wherever she went and she wrote on anything handy: paper, books, fences, even bathroom walls.

11. Graphomania is _____

_____

phagomania

FAG–o–MAY–nee–uh

■ Sylvia's weight increased from 125 to 250 pounds before she admitted to herself that her phagomania rather than a physical disability was the reason for her food craving.

■ Mr. Morris carried snacks with him because his phagomania was so acute he could never satisfy his appetite.

12. Phagomania is _____

_____

logomania

LOW–go–MAY–nee–uh

■ Few of the people who knew Sylvester understood that he walked around mumbling constantly because he suffered from logomania.

■ Everybody who talks a great deal should not be diagnosed as a logomaniac by people not qualified to make such judgments.

13. Logomania is _____

_____

ANSWERS

1. _Kleptomania_ is a compulsion to steal.
2. _Pyromania_ is the need to set fires continually.
3. _Megalomania_ is obsession with the idea of one's own greatness.
4. _Dipsomania_ is an insatiable desire for alcoholic beverages.
5. _Narcomania_ is an unnatural craving for drugs.
6. _Xenomania_ is an extreme need for foreign things.
7. _Theomania_ is an unnatural overindulgence in religion.
8. _Nymphomania_ is a woman's excessive compulsion for sexual relations with men.

9. *Gynecomania is a man's unnatural compulsion for sexual relations with women.*
10. *Mythomania is a psychological need for continuous lying.*
11. *Graphomania is a compulsion to write.*
12. *Phagomania is a compulsion to eat.*
13. *Logomania is a compulsion to speak.*

matching exercise

DIRECTIONS: Write the appropriate letter from the right hand column in the space next to each number so that the numbered words are defined.

———————— 1. kleptomania   **a.** compulsion for alcohol

———————— 2. pyromania   **b.** compulsion to wash

———————— 3. megalomania   **c.** compulsion to set fires

———————— 4. dipsomania   **d.** compulsion toward religion

———————— 5. narcomania   **e.** compulsion to assault women

———————— 6. xenomania   **f.** compulsion of woman for sexual ex-
                                      periences

———————— 7. theomania   **g.** compulsion for foreign things

———————— 8. nymphomania   **h.** compulsion for drugs

———————— 9. gynecomania   **i.** compulsion to lie

————————10. mythomania   **j.** compulsion to steal

                                 k. compulsion to speak

                                 l. compulsion to be great and powerful

                                 m. compulsion to wander

                                 n. compulsion to eat

ANSWERS: 1—j; 2—c; 3—l; 4—a; 5—h; 6—g; 7—d; 8—f; 9—e; 10—i.

words in use

DIRECTIONS: Read the following passage. Then match the appropriate symptoms with the mania described by writing its definition in the blank space next to each word.

NAME: _____

A.

Dr. Simms thought the case very interesting. At first the patient exhibited many symptoms such as excessive eating and talking. But they were of short duration and gave way to other symptoms: continuous praying and then ceaseless writing. Dr. Simms finally decided that the man was simply a malingerer trying to avoid the draft.

1. graphomania: _____

2. theomania: _____

3. phagomania: _____

4. logomania: _____

B.

The psychologist had an unusual party. He invited all his patients. The one with xenomania preferred not to attend, but the party was a success anyway. The mythomaniac and the logomaniac spent a great deal of time together, and the phagomaniac was at the buffet table all evening.

1. xenomaniac: _____

2. mythomaniac: _____

3. logomaniac: _____

4. phagomaniac: _____

ANSWERS: A: 1—compulsion to write; 2—compulsion to pray; 3—compulsion to eat; 4—compulsion to talk.

B: 1—obsessed by foreign things; 2—compulsion to lie, or tell stories; 3—compulsion to talk; 4—compulsion to eat.

PHOBIA
FOE-beh-uh

From the Latin *-phobus,* fearing, and the Greek *-phobos*

EVERYONE has some fears. When a fear is so strong it makes a person act in unusual ways, and when it is not founded on reasons thoughtfully considered or intellectually arrived at, it becomes the subject of special study and requires a special name. Thus, any fear which is *extremely strong* and is *irrational* is called a *phobia.*

The following word parts will be combined with the root in this unit to make new words. Use this list as a reference to find the meaning of words in this unit.

ROOTS AS AFFIXES

zoo—animal
graph—write or word
agora—large open space
demo—the people
pyro—fire

xeno—stranger
hematri—blood
miso—uncleanliness
claust—a closed-in place
ryp—dirt

PREFIX
acro—highest point

context
clues

DIRECTIONS: Pronounce each word in the left hand column and read aloud the sentences in the right hand column. On the basis of context clues in the sentences, fill in the blank space to make a correct definition.

zoophobia

ZOE–uh–FOE–beh–uh

- The animals frightened the zoophobe so much that he fainted.
- Tommy's mother refused to allow him to keep a pet because she has zoophobia.

1. Zoophobia is _____

_____

agoraphobia

uh–GOR–uh–FOE–
    beh–uh

■ So severe was his agoraphobia that he could not even bear to listen to songs about the prairie.
■ The bride's agoraphobia forced the groom to cancel honeymoon plans for a cross-country drive.

2. Agoraphobia is _____

_____

demophobia

DEM–uh–FOE–beh–uh

■ For a moment the psychologist thought that he, too, had succumbed to demophobia, for he felt the crowd would suffocate him.
■ Television has been a wonderful invention for demophobic baseball and football fans.

3. Demophobia is _____

_____

acrophobia

AK–ruh–FOE–beh–uh

■ An acrobat who developed acrophobia would no longer be able to perform on a trapeze or high wire.
■ The true acrophobe will not live or work on the upper stories of a tall building.

4. Acrophobia is _____

_____

graphophobia

GRAF–uh–FOE–beh–uh

■ Because the man suffered from graphophobia, he began trembling as soon as he touched the pen.
■ Anyone who shows symptoms of graphophobia would have a hard time doing term papers for college courses.

5. Graphophobia is _____

_____

pyrophobia

PIE–roe–FOE–beh–uh

■ The pyrophobe ran from the room when the host struck a match for a guest's cigarette.
■ You could never get a pyrophobic man to work for the fire department.

6. Pyrophobia is _____

_____

xenophobia

ZEE–no–FOE–beh–uh

■ Ever since John developed xenophobia he has refused to trust anyone he has not known for many years.
■ The thought of meeting new people is scary to a xenophobe.

7. Xenophobia is _____

_____

hematriphobia

HUH–mat–ruh–FOE–
beh–uh

■ The very thought of blood nauseated the hematriphobe.
■ The only job available to Sally, a hematriphobe, is at the blood bank, so she has been out of work for two weeks.

8. Hematriphobia is _____

_____

misophobia

MIS–uh–FOE–beh–uh

■ Mr. Simpson was forced to leave his job at the laundry when he developed misophobia.
■ Someone suffering from misophobia will refuse to shake hands with another person.

9. Misophobia is _____

_____

claustrophobia

CLAWS–tro–FOE–beh–uh

■ Harold's claustrophobia kept him from ever entering an elevator.
■ An air raid shelter would be a frightening place for a claustrophobe.

10. Claustrophobia is _____

_____

rypophobia

reye–po–FOE–beh–uh

■ Constant handwashing and bathing are often symptoms of rypophobia.
■ Constance's rypophobia caused her to keep away from the outdoors and especially from parks, gardens, and open fields.

11. Rypophobia is _____

_____

ANSWERS

1. *Zoophobia is a fear of animals.*
2. *Agoraphobia is a fear of open spaces.*
3. *Demophobia is a fear of crowds.*
4. *Acrophobia is a fear of heights.*
5. *Graphophobia is a fear of writing.*
6. *Pyrophobia is a fear of fire.*
7. *Xenophobia is a fear of strangers.*
8. *Hematriphobia is a fear of blood.*
9. *Misophobia is a fear of contamination.*
10. *Claustrophobia is a fear of closed spaces.*
11. *Rypophobia is a fear of dirt.*

words in use

DIRECTIONS: Read the following paragraph. Then answer the multiple choice questions by circling the letter that indicates correct completion of the statement.

A.

The doctor's initial diagnosis indicated strong symptoms of agoraphobia. Further study, however, indicated two other conclusions were possible: demophobia or rypophobia. Both were rejected when the patient manifested additional symptoms that clearly pointed to misophobia.

1. The doctor first thought his patient had a fear of
   a. contamination.
   b. blood.
   c. crowds.
   d. open spaces.

2. Before the doctor arrived at his final diagnosis, he suspected the patient feared dirt as well as
   a. blood.
   b. crowds.
   c. mirrors.
   d. nudity.

3. The final diagnosis was fear of
   a. feathers.
   b. contamination.
   c. crowds.
   d. writing.

4. Not mentioned in the paragraph was the fear of
   a. crowds.
   b. contamination.
   c. blood.
   d. dirt.

ANSWERS: A. 1—d; 2—b; 3—b; 4—c.

B.

DIRECTIONS: Read the poem. Then fill in the blank spaces to tell why each person at the tea party acted the way he did.

The claustrophobe and the misophobe had both come to tea,
The two had told the xenophobe that he could have his free,
While the xenophobe would not accept all that company.
The misophobe could not touch the cup that held his tea,
And the claustrophobe asked that his be served out on the balcony.

1. claustrophobe _____

2. misophobe _____

3. xenophobe _____

ANSWERS: B. 1—because he was afraid of closed places; 2—because he feared the cup was contaminated; 3—because he feared strangers or people he didn't already know.

matching exercise

DIRECTIONS: Write the appropriate letter from the right hand column in the space next to each number so that the numbered words are defined.

_____ 1. claustrophobia   **a.** fears animals

_____ 2. graphophobia   **b.** fears smothering

_____ 3. xenophobia   **c.** fears darkness

_____ 4. agoraphobia   **d.** fears people

(more)

_____ 5. misophobia   **e.** fears fire

_____ 6. demophobia   **f.** fears automobiles

_____ 7. hematriphobia   **g.** fears electricity

_____ 8. pyrophobia   **h.** fears heights

_____ 9. zoophobia   **i.** fears blood

_____10. acrophobia   **j.** fears writing

                                             k. fears closed places

                                             l. fears open spaces

                                             m. fears strangers

                                             n. fears contamination

                                             o. fears crowds

ANSWERS: 1—k; 2—j; 3—m; 4—l; 5—n; 6—o; 7—i; 8—e; 9—a; 10—h.

FAMILY CIRCUS

"Our Daddy said you have a phobia. Can we see it?"

SPEC
SPEK

From the Latin *spectare* meaning "to look at" or "to see"

You have undoubtedly been a *spectator* at a *spectacle*. Perhaps you have also told someone about a *spectacular* thing you saw. The terms describing the person and what was seen all come from the same Latin root; so do many other words that enable us to discuss the many ways of looking at how people behave.

The following word parts will be combined with the root in this unit to make new words. Use this list as a reference to find the meaning of words in this unit.

PREFIXES
in—not or opposing
re—back or again
a—on or in or at
dis—not or oppose
de—away from or down
sus—under or beneath

SUFFIXES
or—doer or agent
ate—office or office holder
tion—act or condition of
able—able to or capable of

context
clues

DIRECTIONS: Pronounce each word in the left hand column and read aloud the sentences in the right hand column. On the basis of context clues in the sentences, fill in the blank space to make a correct definition.

species

SPEE–shez

■ Among most species of birds, the males have the bright-colored plumage.
■ Jacques Cousteau discovered a strange species of fish that had remained almost unchanged since pre-historic times.

1. Species means _____

_____

specimen

SPES–uh–men

- Collecting specimens of local rocks can be the beginning of an interesting hobby.
- The skilled scientist slid the slithery specimen onto the microscope slide.

2. A specimen is _____

_____

spectacle

SPEK–tuh–kl

- If you lie on the floor of the drugstore, kick and scream, and shout "bad" words, you will succeed in creating a spectacle of yourself.
- The spectacle of 22 brawny men running over a field chasing a ball every Sunday afternoon is something millions of people enjoy.

3. A spectacle is _____

_____

spectator

SPEK–tay–ter

- Basketball attracts more paying spectators than does any other sport.
- Dozens watched, but not one spectator came to the aid of the man being robbed and beaten by thugs.

4. A spectator is _____

_____

speculate

SPEK–yoo–LATE

- One may speculate on what fantastic future space explorations are in store now that several seemingly impossible feats have been accomplished.
- Hilda hesitated to speculate about what would have happened if she had failed the test.

5. To speculate is to _____

_____

speculator

SPEK–yoo–LAY–ter

- Speculators are always ready to invest in gold and uranium stocks in the hope that they can get rich quickly.

■ Reputable stock market brokers do not encourage investments from speculators who cannot afford to lose their money.

6. A speculator is _____

_____

inspect

in–SPEKT

■ A man who inspects airplanes must watch the products carefully because any defect he overlooks can cause a serious accident.
■ If you inspect the cards carefully, you will see that each ace has a slight nick in one corner.

7. Inspect means _____

_____

respect

ruh–SPEKT

■ Many adults complain that children today have no respect for their parents.
■ It is a mark of respect to take off one's hat when the flag passes by in a parade.

8. Respect means _____

_____

respectable

ruh–SPEK–tuh–bl

■ Respectable hotels seldom allow people without baggage to register.
■ No respectable suburbanite is seen outdoors on Saturday unless he is pushing a lawnmower.

9. Respectable means _____

_____

aspect

AS–pekt

■ After examining every aspect of the situation, we decided the enemy did not look very well prepared and we would attack at dawn.
■ Father assumed such a terrifying aspect when I told him we wanted to get married that I dared not look him in the face.

10. Aspect means _____

_____

disrespect

DIS–ruh–SPEKT

■ Despite changes in manners and customs, it is still considered a mark of disrespect for a gentleman to remain seated when a lady enters the room.
■ Children sometimes misbehave out of need for attention rather than out of disrespect for their parents.

11. Disrespect means _____

_____

despicable

DES–pik–uh–bl

■ The villain in the movie was such a despicable character that he even took candy away from little children.
■ Dan did a dastardly, despicable deed when he faced a dilemma demanding deering-do or death.

12. Despicable means _____

_____

suspect

suh–SPEKT

■ The murder suspect was quizzed by the police but they failed to discover anything that could connect him to the crime.
■ Students are often asked to report to teachers anyone they suspect of cheating on an exam.

13. Suspect means _____

_____

ANSWERS

1. *Species means a class or group of individuals having some common characteristics or qualities.*
2. *A specimen is a part of something taken as typical of the whole.*
3. *A spectacle is something impressive; a public show or display.*
4. *A spectator is a person who looks on; an observer.*
5. *To speculate is to engage in thought or to engage in a business transaction involving a high risk and the chance of large gains.*
6. *A speculator is one who takes a risk in a business transaction.*
7. *Inspect means to look at closely and critically.*
8. *Respect means admiration for a person or deference to someone.*
9. *Respectable means worthy; of good social reputation.*

10. *Aspect* means the appearance of something to the eye or mind.
11. *Disrespect* means discourtesy, rudeness; lack of respect.
12. *Despicable* means contemptible or deserving to be despised.
13. *Suspect* means to believe to be guilty with insufficient proof.

matching exercise

DIRECTIONS: Write the appropriate letter from the right hand column in the space next to each number so that the numbered words are defined.

_____ 1. species

_____ 2. specimen

_____ 3. spectacle

_____ 4. speculate

_____ 5. inspect

_____ 6. aspect

_____ 7. suspect

_____ 8. disrespect

_____ 9. spectator

_____ 10. respectable

a. to distrust

b. the lack of respect; discourtesy

c. a class of individuals having common attributes and a common name

d. to look at closely; to examine

e. a position in which something may be regarded

f. an item or part of a typical thing

g. to think

h. worthy of honor or esteem

i. correct in character or behavior

j. an eye-catching or public display

k. an onlooker

ANSWERS: 1—c; 2—f; 3—j; 4—g; 5—d; 6—e; 7—a; 8—b; 9—k; 10—h.

words in use

DIRECTIONS: Read the following passage. Then fill in each blank with the appropriate word from among the following choices.

aspect
species
speculate
respectable
specimen

disrespect
inspect
respect
spectator
suspect

NAME: _____

Every _____ in the biology lab
                    1

took a close look at the _____. It was of a rare
                                    2

_____ of animal, and one could only
            3

_____ upon its value to science. Its discoverer
            4

was treated with proper _____.
                                5

ANSWERS: 1—spectator; 2—specimen; 3—species; 4—speculate; 5—respect.

true-false

DIRECTIONS: Read each sentence carefully and decide whether it is true or false. If it is true, put a T in the answer space at the right. If it is false, write in an F.

1. A species is a glass that enlarges things.   1._____
2. To distrust someone is to suspect him.   2._____
3. To examine is the same as to inspect.   3._____
4. Speculate means to write.   4._____
5. Aspect refers to an onlooker.   5._____
6. A lack of courtesy indicates disrespect.   6._____
7. Correct character or behavior is properly termed specimen.   7._____
8. A spectacle is an eye-catching or public display.   8._____
9. A spectator is one who assumes a business risk.   9._____
10. If you respect a man you feel he is worthy of honor or esteem. 10._____

ANSWERS: 1—F; 2—T; 3—T; 4—F; 5—F; 6—T; 7—F; 8—T; 9—F; 10—T.

VOC
VOK

From the Latin *vox* meaning "voice"

Vox POPULI is the Latin term meaning "the voice of the people" and it was on this basis of general opinion that many decisions were made. In our own time, the "voice" that is heard in the root VOC describes many kinds of behavior besides group agreement.

The names of the tools of language itself—voice and vocabulary—are among the modern derivatives from this Latin root.

The following word parts will be combined with the root in this unit to make new words. Use this list as a reference to find the meaning of words in this unit.

PREFIXES
ad—to
a—on or in or at
pro—before or in behalf of
re—back or again
in—not
e—out of or off or from
con—with or together

SUFFIXES
ate—office or office–holder
tion—action or condition of
al—of or belonging to
tive—belonging to or tending to
ous—marked by or given to
ize—to cause or become

ROOTS AS AFFIXES
equi—equal to
fer—carry or bear

context
clues

DIRECTIONS: Pronounce each word in the left hand column and read aloud the sentences in the right hand column. On the basis of context clues in the sentences, fill in the blank space to make a correct definition.

advocate

AD–vuh–kate

■ In her speeches, Cynthia, a leader in the Women's Freedom Movement, often advocated that women throw away their girdles and bras.

131

■ If you advocate the abolishment of grades, you ought to make your beliefs known.

1. To advocate is to _____

_____

avocation

av–uh–KA–shun

■ Flying is Mr. Johnson's vocation, but stamp collecting is his avocation.
■ I found several books showing how an avocation can be turned into a money-making part time job or even full time work.

2. Avocation means _____

_____

equivocal

i–KWIV–uh–kl

■ The politician's equivocal speech left his listeners in doubt as to whether he was for or against a raise in taxes.
■ Myron decided that because of the equivocal wording of the material he had to edit, readers would not know the author's true point of view.

3. Equivocal means _____

_____

equivocate

i–KWIV–uh–KATE

■ If a policeman stops you and asks questions, you had better not equivocate but should give direct answers.
■ The student who equivocates on an essay test is often presumed to be deliberately confusing because he does not know the right answer.

4. Equivocate means _____

_____

provocative

pruh–VOK–uh–tiv

■ Humphrey made such a provocative speech that everyone in the audience immediately left to sign up for work on the slum clearance project.
■ At Simpson's provocative suggestion, Brunhilde followed him into the kitchen and took out the cook book so she could start making eggs Benedict.

5. Provocative means _____

_____

vociferous

vo–SIF–er–us

■ "If you were not so vociferous," Hilda complained, "you could quiet down enough for people to be able to listen to you."
■ The rioting students were so vociferous the administration could not separate their demands from the name-calling that went on.

6. Vociferous means _____

_____

vocation

vo–KA–shun

■ Anyone who decides to become a clergyman chooses a worthy vocation.
■ The school gave vocational training in order to produce more residents capable of handling jobs required by local industry.

7. A vocation is _____

_____

revoke

ruh–VOK

■ The state has the power to revoke your driver's license if you get involved in too many accidents.
■ When the city decided to revoke its prohibition about swimming at Lucifer's Dam, children flocked to the site.

8. Revoke means _____

_____

invocation

in–vuh–KA–shun

■ It is customary for a clergyman to give an invocation at the beginning of dinners and graduation exercises.
■ Ancient people used to have their priests invoke the blessing of the gods before any major undertaking, like war.

9. An invocation is _____

_____

evoke

i–VOK

- It is possible to evoke the feeling of an early movie by letting the actors move jerkily and by using a strobe light on them.
- The rooms evoked jeers and catcalls because the students were so dissatisfied with them.

10. Evoke means _____

_____

convocation

KON–vuh–KA–shun

- A convocation ceremony often precedes a college or high school graduation.
- A convocation of cardinals is called to name a new pope.

11. Convocation means _____

_____

vocalize

VO–kl–eyez

- Singers usually vocalize in their dressing rooms before going on stage for a performance.
- Nobody will ever know you are dissatisfied with the dinner unless you vocalize your opinion.

12. Vocalize means _____

_____

ANSWERS

1. To advocate is to plead in favor of someone or something.
2. Avocation means a hobby.
3. Equivocal means of uncertain significance; of doubtful nature or character.
4. Equivocate means to use ambiguous terms in order to deceive.
5. Provocative means to excite to action.
6. Vociferous means crying out noisily.
7. A vocation is one's work or career.
8. Revoke means to recall or take back.
9. An invocation is a calling on for favor or protection.
10. Evoke means to call up, produce or suggest.
11. Convocation means a calling together or assembling by summons.
12. Vocalize means to make a sound with the voice; to utter or to sing.

matching exercise

DIRECTIONS: Write the appropriate letter from the right hand column in the space next to each number so that the numbered words are defined.

———— 1. advocate

———— 2. avocation

———— 3. convocation

———— 4. equivocation

———— 5. provocative

———— 6. vociferous

———— 7. vocation

———— 8. revocation

———— 9. invocation

————10. evocation

a. one's work or career

b. the calling on for aid or protection

c. produced or performed by the voice

d. to plead in favor of someone or something

e. a hobby

f. to excite to action

g. call forth

h. to use ambiguous terms in order to deceive

i. assembling by summons

j. a recall; an annulment

k. loud speech

ANSWERS: 1—d; 2—e; 3—i; 4—h; 5—f; 6—k; 7—a; 8—j; 9—b; 10—g.

true-false

DIRECTIONS: Read each sentence carefully and decide whether it is true or false. If it is true, put a T in the space at the right. If it is false, write in an F.

1. Advocate is to add numbers.   1.————
2. An avocation is a hobby.   2.————
3. A convocation is a list of the things you own.   3.————
4. Equivocation is sometimes difficult to understand.   4.————

Words About Behavior   **135**

5. Anything provocative might excite or stimulate a person into action.   5._____
6. Vociferous means talkative.   6._____
7. Vocation means a trip.   7._____
8. A return from a vacation is a revocation.   8._____
9. Invocation refers to the use of ambiguous terms in order to deceive.   9._____
10. An evocation means the work one does to earn a living.   10._____

ANSWERS: 1—F; 2—T; 3—F; 4—T; 5—T; 6—F; 7—F; 8—F; 9—F; 10—F.

scrambled

words

DIRECTIONS: Unscramble the following words. They are defined in parentheses.

1. atecodav: _____
   (it means to plead in favor of someone or something)

2. novotica: _____
   (it means one's work or career)

3. taverinoco: _____
   (a recall; an annulment)

4. equitecova: _____
   (to use ambiguous terms in order to deceive)

5. viforecuso: _____
   (loud speech)

ANSWERS: 1—advocate; 2—vocation; 3—revocation; 4—equivocate; 5—vociferous.

affixes at work

DIRECTIONS: Add your own words to the blanks at the bottom of the diagram.

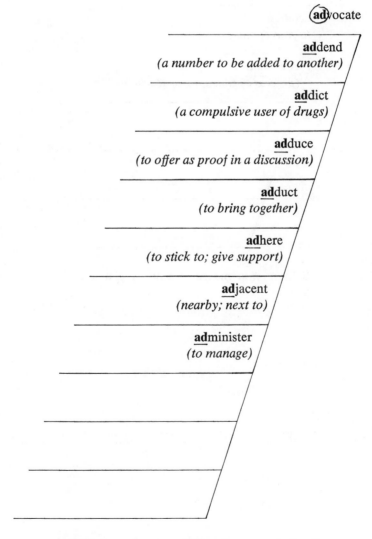

advocate

addend
(a number to be added to another)

addict
(a compulsive user of drugs)

adduce
(to offer as proof in a discussion)

adduct
(to bring together)

adhere
(to stick to; give support)

adjacent
(nearby; next to)

administer
(to manage)

Prefix: *ad* means "toward, to, or before"

avocation

natation
(the action or art of swimming)

generation
(average time span between birth of parents and their offspring)

justification
(act or process of being justified)

lactation
(to secrete milk)

education
(process of educating or teaching)

Suffix: *tion* means "action or state of"

VOR
VOR

From the Latin *vorare* meaning "to devour"

EATING habits and preferences vary widely so that animals have physically developed to handle their requirements. The tooth structure shows this readily: sharp teeth for meat-eaters, flat teeth for grain-eaters.

The root VOR is combined with a number of prefixes to describe the eating habits of animals, and because there are so many variations of behavior, there are many words.

The following word parts will be combined with the root in this unit to make new words. Use this list as a reference to find the meaning of words in this unit.

ROOTS AS AFFIXES
carn—flesh
herb—plant
frug—fruit
gran—grain
gram—grain or seed
phyt—plant
pisc—fish

PREFIX
omni—all

SUFFIX
ous—marked by or given to or filled with

context
clues

DIRECTIONS: Pronounce each word in the left hand column and read aloud the sentences in the right hand column. On the basis of context clues in the sentences, fill in the blank space to make a correct definition.

voracious

vo–RA–shus

■ Mortimer had such a voracious appetite that he often raided Sally's refrigerator when he went to call for her.

■ After seeing Susie push her way to the head of the luncheon line every day, the other girls in the typing pool decided she was fat because she was voracious.

1. Voracious means _____

_____

omnivorous

om–NIV–er–us

■ Man is an omnivorous animal deriving life-giving food from plant as well as from animal life.
■ Neither your garden nor the small animals in it are safe from the hungry omnivorous animals.

2. Omnivorous means _____

_____

carnivorous

kar–NIV–uh–rus

■ My sister fed chicken to the starfish because she read it was a carnivorous animal.
■ Do not leave left-over meat within the reach of a carnivorous pet if you plan to eat the meat yourself at another time.

3. Carnivorous means _____

_____

herbivorous

her–BIV–er–us

■ Some of the largest, fiercest-looking animals that would seem to thrive on meat are actually herbivorous.
■ Sam made vegetable-burgers his main diet item because he had herbivorous eating habits.

4. Herbivorous means _____

_____

frugivorous

froo–JIV–uh–rus

■ Some breeds of monkeys are frugivorous and therefore love bananas.
■ Although fruit is good for you to eat, humans could not really live on a frugivorous diet without some supplements.

5. Frugivorous means _____

_____

granivorous

gruh–NIV–er–us

- Farmers take advantage of the granivorous nature of mice and put traps or poison in their grain storage bins to rid themselves of this costly pest.
- Birds in captivity are often granivorous, yet they enjoy a change in their diet when owners fed them a bit of lettuce.

6. Granivorous means _____

_____

graminivorous

GRAM–uh–NIV–er–us

- Cows are graminivorous so they must graze in fields where natural food is available to them.
- It is said that people turn graminivorous when deprived of the plants (i.e., fruits and vegetables) they normally eat.

7. Graminivorous means _____

_____

phytivorous

FEYE–tiv–uh–rus

- The giraffe has such a long neck because he is phytivorous and must reach the high branches of trees in order to survive.
- If you want your decorative foliage trees to look attractive and full-leaved, you must spray frequently and kill the phytivorous insects that destroy the leaves.

8. Phytivorous means _____

_____

piscivorous

puh–SIV–er–us

- Whales are not piscivorous animals; they eat smaller and more primitive forms of sea life.
- Fish that prey upon other fish are piscivorous.

9. Piscivorous means _____

_____

insectivore

in–SEK–ti–vor

- Frogs are insectivores and therefore useful residents of gardens.
- A popular sports car bumper strip used to read "I am an insectivore," but so few people under-

stood it that the strip was changed to read "I eat harmful insects."

10. An insectivore is _____

_____

ANSWERS

1. *Voracious means very greedy or eager to eat.*
2. *Omnivorous means an animal that feeds on both plants and animals.*
3. *Carnivorous means a meat-eating animal.*
4. *Herbivorous means a plant-eating animal.*
5. *Frugivorous means a fruit-eating animal.*
6. *Granivorous means a seed- or grain-eating animal.*
7. *Graminivorous means a grass-eating animal.*
8. *Phytivorous means feeding on the leaves of plants.*
9. *Piscivorous means fish-eating.*
10. *An insectivore is an animal that feeds on insects.*

words in use

DIRECTIONS: Read the following passage. Then fill in each blank with the appropriate word from among the following choices.

carnivorous   insectivore
herbivorous   piscivorous
voracious   frugivorous
omnivorous

Frank was definitely _____ because he
                             1

could eat anything. His pet wildcat was _____,
                                              2

but his trained seal was _____. All three of
                               3

them were _____ eaters, so he always had big
4

grocery bills. Frank also kept a strange plant in his house. It was called a

"venus flytrap," and it was an _____.
5

ANSWERS: 1—omnivorous; 2—carnivorous; 3—piscivorous; 4—voracious; 5—insectivore.

matching exercise

DIRECTIONS: Write the appropriate letter from the right hand column in the space next to each number so that the numbered words are defined.

_____ 1. omnivorous   **a.** feeds on insects

_____ 2. piscivorous   **b.** a meat-eating animal

_____ 3. voracious   **c.** feeding on grass

_____ 4. herbivorous   **d.** feeding on the leaves of plants

_____ 5. frugivorous   **e.** fish eating

_____ 6. granivorous   **f.** very greedy or eager to eat

_____ 7. phytivorous   **g.** feeding on fruit

_____ 8. graminivorous   **h.** feeding on seeds or grain

_____ 9. insectivore   **i.** feeds on birds

_____ 10. carnivorous   **j.** it feeds on paper

     k. a plant-eating animal

     l. an animal that feeds on both plants and animals

ANSWERS: 1—l; 2—e; 3—f; 4—k; 5—g; 6—h; 7—d; 8—c; 9—a; 10—b.

crossword puzzle

ACROSS

2—feeding on grass
4—greedy or eager to eat
5—a meat–eater

DOWN

1—feeds on both plants and animals
3—feeds on fish

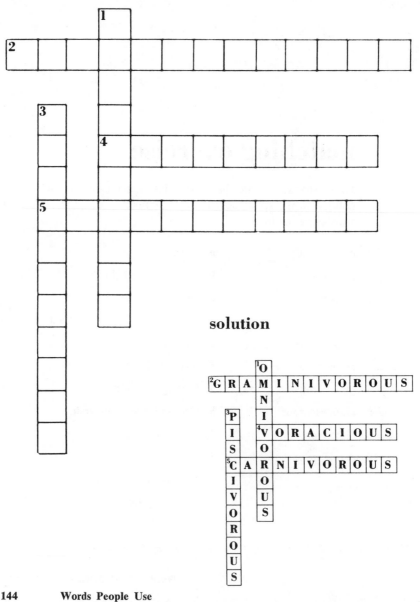

solution

POSTTEST

DIRECTIONS: In the space next to each number, write the letter that correctly completes the statement.

_____ 1. If you were voracious you would probably
   a. send out for another flower arrangement.
   b. have high food bills.
   c. have to keep away from the zoo.
   d. drive carefully.

_____ 2. Herkimer Jones decided to appear as advocate of Junie Juniper; that is, he was to be her
   a. butler.
   b. physician.
   c. lawyer.
   d. insurance adjuster.

_____ 3. A megalomaniac is overly concerned with
   a. megaphones.
   b. men.
   c. himself.
   d. women.

_____ 4. Given the choice of the four listed below, the nymphomaniacal person requires
   a. men.
   b. women.
   c. dogs.
   d. fish.

_____ 5. The ability to make inferences depends on
   a. enough people.
   b. gathering related facts.
   c. fast talking.
   d. easy transportation.

_____ 6. Someone who maladministers is likely to
   a. be a hypocritical minister.
   b. act out his fears reluctantly.
   c. be untrustworthy to hire as manager of a drugstore.
   d. be the first in a class to complete his term paper.

_____ 7. A mayor judged guilty of malfeasance would be most likely to have
   a. gone hunting on July 4.
   b. made fun of the baboons at the zoo.
   c. taken personal vacations on funds set aside for waste disposal improvement facilities.
   d. failed to show up for opening ceremonies of the new freeway.

_____ 8. Someone who has pyrophobia would probably not have to defend himself against a charge of
   a. arson.
   b. slander.
   c. petty larceny.
   d. homicide.

_____ 9. If you really wanted to impress a formal gathering of important people you might draw yourself up, take a firm stand at the microphone and try
   a. a soliloquy.
   b. an allocution.
   c. an interlocutor.
   d. loquacity.

_____ 10. If you call a person loquacious, you mean he is
   a. too locally oriented.
   b. too talkative.
   c. not sufficiently talkative.
   d. loco or crazy.

_____ 11. If you are a respectful person, you can demonstrate this characteristic by
   a. groveling before royalty.
   b. rising when a much older person enters a living room in which you are a guest.
   c. going horseback riding regularly.
   d. brushing teeth twice a day and visiting your dentist twice a year.

_____ 12. People who invest heavily in the cotton market with the expectation of making a quick profit are called
   a. speculators.
   b. expectorants.

NAME: _____

        c. inspectors.
        d. despicable.

_____13. You should learn to take dictation so you
        a. will be able to stand up well under criticism.
        b. can handle power tools effectively.
        c. take notes in class.
        d. construct a learning environment.

ANSWERS: 1—b; 2—c; 3—c; 4—a; 5—b; 6—c; 7—c; 8—a; 9—b; 10—b; 11—b; 12—a; 13—c.

chapter 4

Words About Work

PRETEST

DIRECTIONS: In the space next to each number, write the letter that correctly completes the statement.

_____ 1. Which is the most probable ending to the following sentence? After Wanda was abducted, her family received a message
   a. telling how she baked a cake.
   b. asking for ransom.
   c. from the registrar that she passed all her courses.
   d. that the dress fit perfectly.

_____ 2. The ad for a factotum went unanswered because
   a. factories aren't cheap to purchase.
   b. they are seldom manufactured today.
   c. people tend to specialize rather than to do a variety of jobs well.
   d. this wingless species became extinct in the 18th century.

_____ 3. People who are factious
   a. are likely to argue a lot.
   b. always try to be funny.

    c. are sure to smile a great deal.

    d. have an uncontrollable urge to sun them-
selves.

_____ 4. The choice of a site for the new hydroelectric
plant had to be
    a. in the mountains.
    b. on a level plain or plateau.
    c. next to water.
    d. on a main highway or rail line.

_____ 5. Some older people who are annoyed at "hip-
pies" who refuse to bathe speak scathingly of
them as people who must have
    a. hydrophobia.
    b. hydrafoils.
    c. hydrocephalus.
    d. dehydrated.

_____ 6. Hire an amaneunsis if you want to
    a. learn how to garden.
    b. write a letter.
    c. fix the plumbing.
    d. paint a picture.

_____ 7. In order to classify blood types you would have
to study
    a. metrology.
    b. meteorology.
    c. cetology.
    d. hematology.

_____ 8. An organization that wanted to control the
television habits of its members or adherents
would draw up a list of programs it
    a. described.
    b. proscribed.
    c. euphemized.
    d. postscripted.

_____ 9. The painter left his studio at noon to buy a new
    a. pica.
    b. scribbet.
    c. euphoria.
    d. scrim.

_____10. The king called in his chief scribe to prepare
a manumit and thereby
   a. be sure the crown would go to his son.
   b. set his wedding date.
   c. free all the slaves in the kingdom.
   d. order three new Cadillacs and a Bentley.

ANSWERS: 1—b; 2—c; 3—a; 4—c; 5—a; 6—b; 7—d; 8—b; 9—b; 10—c.

DUC, DUCT
DUK, DUKT

From the Latin *ducere* meaning "to lead," or *ductus* "leading"

WHENEVER someone or something is guided or directed in a course or action, we say they are "led." (If it is in the wrong direction, they are "misled.") Leading takes many forms, so the words from this root cover a variety of objects and situations.

The following word parts will be combined with the root in this unit to make new words. Use this list as a reference to find the meaning of words in this unit.

PREFIXES
con—with or jointly
ab—from or away
in—not
de—from or down
se—apart
tra(ns)—across

SUFFIXES
or—doer or agent
ile—capable of being or pertaining to

ROOTS AS AFFIXES
aqua—water
via—away

context
clues

DIRECTIONS: Pronounce each word in the left hand column and read aloud the sentences in the right hand column. On the basis of context clues in the sentences, fill in the blank space to make a correct definition.

151

aqueduct

AK–wuh–duhkt

- The Romans supplied water to their cities by building remarkable aqueducts over many miles of rough countryside from the source of supply.
- Aqueducts usually run downhill from the source of water because no pumps are used in these structures.

1. An aqueduct is _____

_____

viaduct

VEYE–uh–duhkt

- The railroad company had to build a long viaduct over a river in order to get the tracks from one mountainside to another.
- A viaduct over the existing two levels of traffic made the highway interchange more complex but the traffic flow improved.

2. Viaduct means _____

_____

conductor

kon–DUHK–tor

- The tour conductor had to make sure everybody in the group was on the bus before they left London.
- The conductor of any musical group has to learn the scores or arrangements in order to be really effective.

3. A conductor is _____

_____

duct

DUHKT

- The air conditioning duct has to be enlarged because it is not carrying enough cool air from the compressor unit to the room.
- Workmen installed a duct system to carry the water away from the location where it made puddles every time there was a heavy rain.

4. A duct is _____

_____

ductile

DUHK–tl

■ Gold is a ductile substance that is used to make a variety of objects and to decorate everything from personal jewelry to room ceilings.
■ The development of ductile plastics has resulted in whole new industries because the material can be formed into so many different shapes.

5. Ductile means _____

_____

abduct

ab–DUHKT

■ The pirate captain abducted the pretty girl from the boat on which she was traveling and made her his captive.
■ The abduction of the Lindbergh baby in the 1930's led to enactment of strict federal laws for this crime.

6. Abduct means _____

_____

induct

in–DUHKT

■ Mortimer had to perform many silly activities as part of his induction into the fraternity.
■ The government will continue to induct young men into the armed forces.

7. Induct means _____

_____

deduce

di–DOOS

■ Sherlock Holmes always managed to deduce the name of the criminal from the evidence he gathered.

■ Any student who gets six A papers may deduce he will get an A as the final grade.

8. Deduce means _____

_____

seduce

si–DOOS

■ It is easy to be seduced into thinking that work is easy when you do not pay enough attention to learning how to do it properly.
■ The vision of all the delicious-looking fancy cakes and pastries seduced Mildred into breaking her diet.

9. Seduce means _____

_____

traduce

truh–DOOS

■ Anonymous letters are often a method used to traduce someone's character even though that person is blameless.
■ "Do not traduce my good name," the hero warned the villain in the first act of the play.

10. Traduce means _____

_____

ANSWERS

1. An *aqueduct* is a structure for carrying large quantities of water.
2. *Viaduct* means a bridge.
3. A *conductor* is someone who leads.
4. A *duct* is a tube or channel that conveys something.
5. *Ductile* means capable of being fashioned into a new form.

6. _Abduct_ means to lead away forcibly; kidnap.
7. _Induct_ means to admit as a member.
8. _Deduct_ means to infer from or to draw conclusions.
9. _Seduce_ means to lead astray or to corrupt.
10. _Traduce_ means to slander, disgrace, malign or defame.

definitions

DIRECTIONS: In the space next to each number, write the letter that correctly defines the word at the left.

1. Viaduct means—a. a bridge b. one who leads c. behavior d. to capture   1._____
2. To conduct is—a. to capture b. to lead c. to infer d. to reduce   2._____
3. To capture is to—a. conduct b. deduce c. induct d. abduct   3._____
4. To deduce is to—a. capture b. lead away c. bridge d. infer   4._____
5. If it is easily fashioned into a new form it is—a. a duct b. ductile c. inductor d. an aqueduct   5._____
6. If something is without tubes or channels it is—a. ductile b. ductless c. deducing d. viaduct   6._____
7. If something is made smaller, its size is—a. deduced b. produced c. conduced d. reduced   7._____
8. To lead astray is to—a. deduce b. seduce c. abduct d. induct   8._____

9. A canal or passage for carrying a liquid is—a. an abductor
   b. an aqueduct   c. an inductor   d. a deducer   9._____

10. To draw conclusions is—a. to deduce   b. to conduct   c. to
    introduce   d. abduct   10._____

ANSWERS: 1—a; 2—b; 3—d; 4—d; 5—b; 6—b; 7—d; 8—b; 9—b; 10—a.

matching exercise

DIRECTIONS: Write the appropriate letter from the right hand
column in the space next to each number so that the numbered
words are defined.

_____ 1. aqueduct	**a.** to disgrace, defame
_____ 2. viaduct	**b.** to carry off forcibly or kidnap
_____ 3. conductor	**c.** to lead astray
_____ 4. ductile	**d.** a canal or passage for carrying liquid
_____ 5. duct	**e.** a bridge
_____ 6. abduct	**f.** something or someone who leads
_____ 7. induct	**g.** capable of being fashioned into a new form
_____ 8. deduce	**h.** without ducts
_____ 9. seduce	**i.** to lessen
_____10. traduce	**j.** a tube or channel that conveys something
	k. to infer, to draw conclusions
	l. to admit as a member

ANSWERS: 1—d; 2—e; 3—f; 4—g; 5—j; 6—b; 7—l; 8—k; 9—c; 10—a.

affixes at work

DIRECTIONS: Add your own words to the blanks at the bottom of the diagram.

<u>se</u>duce

secede
(withdraw from an organization)
_____

seclude
(remove or separate from)
_____

secret
(hidden)
_____

secure
(confident; without fear)
_____

select
(of special value; superior)
_____

_____

_____

Prefix: *se* means "apart from"

duct
_____

aquacade
(a water spectacle)
_____

aqualung
(underwater breathing apparatus)
_____

aquatic
(performed in or around water)
_____

aquaculture
(growing sea products for food)
_____

_____

_____

Prefix: *aqua* means "water"

FAK, FACT
FAK, FAKT

From the Latin *facere* meaning "to make" or "to do"

WORDS that tell about making things or kinds of actions, or promises, or copies—or compromises—share a common Latin root. That it appears in so many English words may be evidence of the emphasis our culture places upon accomplishing tasks.

The following word parts will be combined with the root in this unit to make new words. Use this list as a reference to find the meaning of words in this unit.

SUFFIXES

tion—action or state	**ure**—act or result
ous—marked by or given to	**al**—act or process or doing
ory—a place or thing	**ity**—state or quality or condition
ty—quality or state	**ate**—office or office-holder
or—doer or maker	**ile**—marked by or showing

ROOTS AS AFFIXES
totum—all
many—hand
art—art
simile—like

context

clues

DIRECTIONS: Pronounce each word in the left hand column and read aloud the sentences in the right hand column. On the basis of context clues in the sentences, fill in the blank space to make a correct definition.

faction

FAK–shun

■ One faction in the student government wanted to abolish the dress code, and they pushed hard to make their ideas known to everyone on campus.

159

■ Sampson belonged to a minority faction that believed the hairier a man was, the more powerful he was.

1. A faction is _____

_____

factious

FAK–shus

■ Ted and Alice finally decided they were too factious to continue living together because their arguments always woke the neighbors.
■ "I don't mean to be factious," John said, "but this is the tenth thing you've said in the last hour that I simply cannot agree with."

2. Factious means _____

_____

factitious

fak–TISH–us

■ Such a factitious story could only be shown eventually for the lie that it was.
■ Everything about her was factitious: her hair, her eyelashes, her seemingly smooth skin, her shining teeth, even her shape.

3. Factitious means _____

_____

factory

FAK–tuh–ree

■ Thousands of dolls came off the assembly line at the factory in time for Christmas.
■ If the factory does not have the capabilities to produce your invention, we will add the necessary machinery and manpower to make it.

4. A factory is _____

_____

factotum

fak–TOE–tum

■ The factotum in operas is always a humorous character because he already has many duties and is called upon to undertake many more.
■ Often the mother in a busy household begins to feel she is nothing more than a general factotum who receives no salary.

5. A factotum is _____

_____

faculty

FAK–ul–tee

■ You have a natural faculty for golf if you can hit the ball 100 yards at your first lesson.
■ It is necessary to call every faculty into play when you study hard to pass a test.

6. Faculty means _____

_____

manufacture

man–yuh–FAK–chur

■ Factories manufacture everything from matches to rockets.
■ The manufacture and sale of DDT was sharply curbed when it was discovered how harmful the substance was.

7. To manufacture means _____

_____

facetious

fuh–SEE–shus

■ Sometimes a facetious remark is misinterpreted and the speaker finds himself being glared at instead of being laughed with.
■ Mary was so embarrassed by the constant puns Jim made that she always warned him not to be so facetious in public.

8. Facetious means _____

_____

factor

FAK–tor

■ Businessmen often advertise in the paper that they will serve as factor for several companies while traveling to foreign countries.
■ If you do not have enough staff of your own, you could hire a factor to help handle the customers.

9. A factor is _____

_____

artificial

art–uh–FISH–ul

■ Some artificial flowers look as natural as real ones.
■ If the artificial flavoring is improved, you will not be able to tell the difference between it and the real thing.

10. Artificial means _____

_____

artifact

ART–uh–fakt

■ The archaeologists dug up some artifacts proving the people who lived at that spot had worked with metal tools.
■ There are many artifacts in every store.

11. An artifact is _____

_____

facility

fuh–SIL–uh–tee

■ If you show a facility for boxing, you should study the sport and perhaps you will advance in the Golden Gloves tournaments.
■ Any child who shows a facility for numbers ought to study advanced forms of mathematics.

12. Facility means _____

_____

facile

FAS–ul

■ Mr. Smith had such a facile mind that he jumped from one topic to another without ever seeming flustered.
■ Speaking may prove to be a more facile way of communicating your ideas than writing will.

13. Facile means _____

_____

facsimile

fak–SIM–uh–lee

■ The U.S. Copyright Law permits a certain number of facsimiles to be made from any book without charge or permission.
■ The copying machine can make a facsimile of anything put on the light-sensitive plate.

14. A facsimile is _____

_____

facilitate

fuh–SIL–uh–tate

- Use any method you can think of to facilitate learning words, including playing word games.
- If you really want to facilitate matters, you should stand at the door to collect fees when the audience enters.

15. Facilitate means _____

_____

ANSWERS

1. A *faction* is a group or clique within a large group.
2. *Factious* means opposing or given to dissension.
3. *Factitious* means artificial or contrived; made up.
4. A *factory* is a building in which things are made.
5. A *factotum* is a person hired to do a variety of work, as a chief servant in a household.
6. *Faculty* means a natural or acquired ability for a particular kind of action.
7. To *manufacture* means to make (by a human being).
8. *Facetious* means funny or frivolous and amusing.
9. A *factor* is an agent or person who does business for another.
10. *Artificial* means an object made by man as a substitute for something natural.
11. An *artifact* is an object made or modified by man.
12. *Facility* means a readiness or ease due to skill.
13. *Facile* means moving, acting, or working with ease.
14. A *facsimile* is an exact copy.
15. *Facilitate* means to make easier.

word comprehension

DIRECTIONS: Read the short paragraph. Then put a check next to each word in the list below that is described in the paragraph.

The manufacturing plant produced exact copies of old Indian relics. Although machines were used, the owner employed a handyman to do all the easy work.

———————— 1. faction

———————— 2. factious

———————— 3. factitious

———————— 4. factory

———————— 5. faculty

———————— 6. artifacts

———————— 7. facile

———————— 8. factor

———————— 9. facsimile

————————10. factotum

ANSWERS: 4, 6, 7, 9, 10.

scrambled

letters

DIRECTIONS: Make as many words as you can based on the root FACT from the following letters.

t r f c e l i a o i n u

(for instance the word *fact* can be made by selecting f, a, c, t, from the letters given).

1. _____

2. _____

3. _____

4. _____

5. _____

ANSWERS: 1—*faction*; 2—*factious*; 3—*factitious*; 4—*factor*; 5—*facile*.

crossword puzzle

ACROSS

4—a manmade object

DOWN

1—opposing; contentious
2—easy to do
3—artificial; sham, made up
5—an exact copy

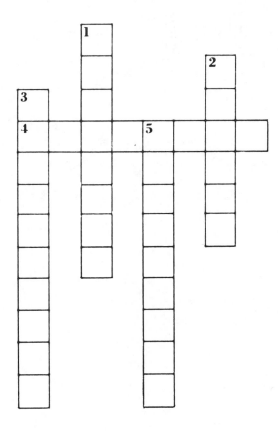

solution

HYDRO   MANU

HEYE-dro   *MAN-u*

MOT

MOTE

From the Greek *hydor* meaning "water"	From the Latin *manus* meaning "hand"	From the Latin *movere* meaning "to move"

MAN has learned to work in many ways—and to make many natural forces work *for* him. The power of the hand is limited; enhanced with the enormous force of water it can accomplish more than man alone. So it is, too, with forces that move—whether objects or ideas.

The following word parts will be combined with the root in this unit to make new words. Use this list as a reference to find the meaning of words in this unit.

PREFIXES
de—down or from
a—on or in or at
pro—before or in behalf of
re—back or again

SUFFIXES
ant—against or opposite
ic—pertaining to or like
ate—having or showing
al—of or belonging to
ensis—relating to
tion—action or state or condition
ive—tending to or having the nature of
or—doer or agent

ROOTS AS AFFIXES

elec—electric
cephal—head
foil—thin sheet or winglike structure
therap—to be a servant
plane—flat

script—write
mit—send
cure—care
fest—apparent to the senses
loco—from place to place

context
clues

DIRECTIONS: Pronounce each word in the left hand column and read aloud the sentences in the right hand column. On the basis of context clues in the sentences, fill in the blank space to make a correct definition.

hydrant

HEYE–drunt

■ In hot weather, police sometimes open the fire hydrants so children can splash in their water.
■ When the hydrant was opened, the field was flooded with enough water to help the crops grow.

1. A hydrant is _____

_____

hydraulic

heye–DRAW–lik

■ Since the lake nearby was such a ready supply of water, an hydraulic lift was installed to help move the building materials.
■ Wilson hooked up an hydraulic motor to the family hose.

2. Hydraulic means _____

_____

dehydrate

de–HEYE–drate

■ Foods that are dehydrated and packaged need only to have the water put back in them so they can be ready to eat.
■ Anyone spending a long time on the desert without sufficient water will find his body has become dehydrated.

3. Dehydrate means _____

_____

hydroelectric

hy–dro–i–LEK–trik

■ The new hydroelectric plant could not be built until the dam which would supply the water was completed.
■ Mr. Willoughby's job for the power company was to measure the intensity of flow in rivers to determine whether it was strong enough for use in hydroelectric plants.

4. Hydroelectric means _____

_____

hydrocephalus

heye–dro–SEF–uh–lus

- Most large heads are not due to an excess of water, for children normally have large heads in proportion to body size and are not hydrocephalic.
- Illness may cause body fluids to accumulate in the cranial cavity and thus result in hydrocephalus.

5. Hydrocephalus means _____

_____

hydrofoil

HEYE–druh–foil

- Boat builders are turning out larger hydrofoils than ever before to transport passengers who live on one side of a bay or lake and work on the other side.
- Riding in a hydrofoil feels somewhat like flying low over the water.

6. A hydrofoil is _____

_____

hydrotherapy

heye–dro–THER–uh–pee

- Hot circulating water is so useful a device for helping certain kinds of muscular ailments that home-size hydrotherapy units are now being manufactured.
- Physical therapy students at this school study the proper temperatures for water in different kinds of hydrotherapy.

7. Hydrotherapy is _____

_____

hydroplane

HEYE–druh–plane

- When the Smiths bought a house on Wyatt Lake, they also bought a hydroplane for quick transportation to the city.
- Just as a ski-equipped plane is useful to supply people living in remote northern areas in winter, a hydroplane is useful to supply people living along remote lakes.

8. A hydroplane is _____

_____

manual

MAN–yuh–wuhl

- Ditch-digging is manual labor.
- A manually operated washing machine is useful to people who live in places that have no electricity.

9. Manual means _____

_____

manuscript

MAN–yuh–skript

- Manuscript writing is a fine art and expensive to contract for, so most people today type or have printed most of their important documents.
- A publisher will no longer accept a manuscript in its most literal meaning; the book or article must now be typewritten to be submitted.

10. A manuscript is _____

_____

manumit

man–yuh–MIT

- The Emancipation Proclamation manumitted the slaves in the United States.
- Indentured servants in England needed someone to manumit them or they were condemned to indefinite servitude because they could never earn enough money to free themselves.

11. Manumit means _____

_____

amanuensis

uh–man–yuh–WEN–sus

- In ancient Rome, when wealthy men were illiterate, one who wanted to send letters would employ an amanuensis to write for him.
- An amanuensis can be found in the market place in case you need to have a letter written.

12. An amanuensis is _____

_____

manicure

MAN–uh–kyuhr

- Have a manicure before you wear your new rings because then your hands will be more attractive.
- A manicurist gets no business from people who bite their nails.

13. Manicure means _____

_____

manifest

MAN–uh–fest

- The difficulty of the work was readily manifest because even the best worker couldn't do the job.
- When I make my wants manifest, you will know what kind of furniture to show me.

14. Manifest means _____

_____

motion

MO–shun

- The rocking motion of the boat made Mary Ann seasick.
- Wasted motion when you type will make your arms and hands tired.

15. Motion means _____

_____

motivate

MO–tuh–vate

- The workers will turn out better work if they are motivated by the offer of prizes for accomplishment.
- The wife's continual nagging motivated the character in the play to murder her.

16. Motivate means _____

_____

motive

MO–tiv

- The gangster's motive for robbing the bank was to gain approval from other gang members rather than to get the money.
- The motive for doing good work is self-satisfaction.

17. Motive means _____

_____

motor

MO–tuhr

- The car runs when the motor is working right.
- Hubert built a motor so he could power the rocket he invented.

18. A motor is _____

_____

promote

pruh–MOTE

- You can promote your ideas about reorganizing the administration by speaking to students on the campus.
- The author made a tour of the country, appearing on radio and television programs, in order to promote the sale of his book.

19. To promote means _____

_____

locomotive

low–kuh–MO–tiv

- Hook another car onto the train and see if the locomotive can pull all of them.
- A diesel locomotive moves faster but releases no less pollution than a steam locomotive.

20. A locomotive is _____

_____

remote

ruh–MOTE

- The college president was too remote from the students and therefore did not realize how dissatisfied they were with his policies.
- Seeking peace and clean air, many young people have moved from cities to remote areas of the country.

21. Remote means _____

_____

ANSWERS

1. *A hydrant is a water outlet.*
2. *Hydraulic means a device that uses water power to move or operate it.*
3. *Dehydrate means to remove water or become waterless.*
4. *Hydroelectric means the generation or distribution of electricity from falling water or from another water source.*

5. _Hydrocephalus_ means an accumulation of fluid within the cranium that causes enlargement of the head.
6. A _hydrofoil_ is a boat that rides on wing-like "skis" that "lift" it out of water when it moves fast.
7. _Hydrotherapy_ is the treatment of disease by internal or external use of water.
8. A _hydroplane_ is an airplane with floats that can take off or land on water.
9. _Manual_ means what is done by hand.
10. A _manuscript_ is a book, document, or letter written by hand.
11. _Manumit_ means to release from slavery; to set free.
12. An _amanuensis_ is someone employed to write from dictation or to copy a manuscript.
13. _Manicure_ means a professional treatment of hands and fingernails.
14. _Manifest_ means readily perceived by the eye or easily understood.
15. _Motion_ means the act or process of moving or changing place or position.
16. _Motivate_ means to give impulse to do something.
17. _Motive_ means a reason or cause that prompts a person to act in a certain way.
18. A _motor_ is a small and powerful engine that imparts motion.
19. To _promote_ means to encourage progress.
20. A _locomotive_ is a self-propelled vehicle for pulling trains.
21. _Remote_ means far removed in space or time; distant.

matching exercise

DIRECTIONS: Write the appropriate letter from the right hand column in the space next to each number so that the numbered words are defined.

_____ 1. hydrant   **a.** done by hand

_____ 2. hydraulic   **b.** to release, to set free

_____ 3. dehydrate   **c.** easily understood

_____ 4. manual   **d.** a water outlet

_____ 5. manifest   **e.** far removed in space or time; distant

_____ 6. amanuensis   **f.** to move; draw on; give an impulse to

_____ 7. motivate   **g.** a reason; cause

_____ 8. remote   **h.** one employed to write from dictation, or to copy manuscripts

(_more_)

_____ 9. motive   **i.** the employment of water to move or operate devices

_____10 manumit   **j.** to become waterless; to remove water

                                               k. to lead by hand

ANSWERS: 1—d; 2—i; 3—j; 4—a; 5—c; 6—h; 7—f; 8—e; 9—g; 10—b.

true-false

DIRECTIONS: Read each sentence and decide whether it is true or false. If it is true, put a T in the space at the right. If it is false, write in an F.

1. A hydrant is a flower.   1._____
2. The word dehydrate indicates a lack of water.   2._____
3. Hydraulic implies the use of water to move or operate devices.   3._____
4. Motivate means to move, or to set in motion.   4._____
5. The cause or reason for something is its motive.   5._____
6. Promotion indicates that something is being done over again.   6._____
7. To free someone is to manumit him.   7._____
8. A man might possibly catch the disease amanuensis.   8._____
9. If a part is shaped like a hand it might be called a manumit.   9._____
10. A manicure indicates that electricity is being carried through a hand.   10._____

ANSWERS: 1—F; 2—T; 3—T; 4—T; 5—T; 6—F; 7—T; 8—F; 9—F; 10—F.

affixes at work

DIRECTIONS: Add your own words to the blanks at the bottom of the diagram.

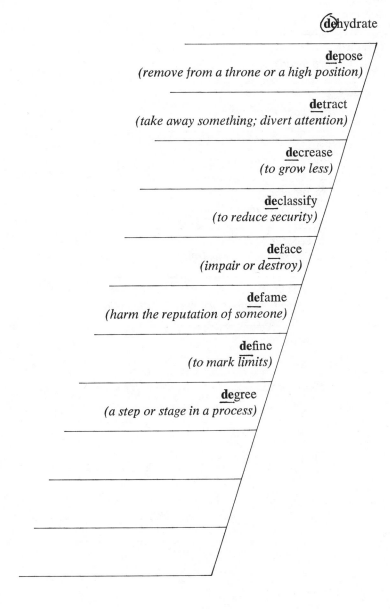

dehydrate

depose
(remove from a throne or a high position)

detract
(take away something; divert attention)

decrease
(to grow less)

declassify
(to reduce security)

deface
(impair or destroy)

defame
(harm the reputation of someone)

define
(to mark limits)

degree
(a step or stage in a process)

Prefix: *de* means "down" or "from"

(re)mote

review
(to look at again)

rebound
(to spring back)

rebirth
(to be born again)

recall
(to bring back to mind)

recede
(move back or away)

reconsider
(to consider again)

recover
(to get back or regain)

reflect
(to turn off or backward at an angle; to think)

Prefix: *re* means "again" or "back"

OLOGY
OL-o-je

From the Greek *logos* meaning "word" or "speech"

IF one studies special groups of words—that is, reads extensively—he will become knowledgeable in a particular branch of learning. He then becomes a specialist in that area.

"Ology" though a root, is often used as a suffix added to various roots in order to describe special fields of study and, when in its variable form of "ist," to describe persons who pursue that study as their work. For example, "biology" is the study of plants and animals; one who studies plants and animals is a "biologist."

The following list records only some of the many "ologies."

- Anthropology is the science of the culture and origin of man.
- Archaeology is the study of the history of mankind.
- Astrobiology is the study of life on other planets.
- Cetology is the study of whales.
- Hematology is the study of blood.
- Metrology is the study of weights and measures.
- Physiology is the science that studies how living plants and animals function under varied conditions.
- Theology is the study of religion.
- Zoology is the study of animals.

OTHER "–OLOGY" words abound to describe sciences and fields of studies. Among them are etymology (words); entomology (bugs); pathology (disease); neurology (nervous system); pharmacology (medicines); pharyngology (pharynx); ecology (the relation between plants and animals and their environment).

177

crossword puzzle

ACROSS

2—far removed; distant
4—to lead by hand
5—the act of movement

DOWN

1—to become waterless
3—done by hand; handwritten

solution

SCRIBE, SCRIPT
SKREYEB, SKRIPT

From the Latin *scribere* meaning "to write"

DESPITE the many forms of verbal and pictorial communication in use today, men still transmit most of their business by means of writing. Whether it is a computer printing hundreds of words a minute, or a high-speed press setting a newspaper photographically, or a schoolboy laboriously printing his first spelling words, writing is still a prime means of communication. It is especially useful because it is permanent and because, as Francis Bacon said, "Writing maketh an exact man."

The following word parts will be combined with the root in this unit to make new words. Use this list as a reference to find the meaning of words in this unit.

PREFIXES
er—doer or result of action
able—capable of being or able to
de—from or down
in—not
pre—before
pro—before or in behalf of or
   according to
sub—under or beneath
in—into
post—after
trans—across

SUFFIXES
et—small
ure—act of
tion—action or state or condition

ROOT AS AFFIX
manu—hand

context
clues

DIRECTIONS: Pronounce each word in the left hand column and read aloud the sentences in the right hand column. On the basis of context clues in the sentences, fill in the blank space to make a correct definition.

179

scribe (noun)

SKREYEB

- The scribe is an important person in communities where few people can write but who occasionally need to have letters written to other people.
- In ancient Egypt, every high-ranking noble employed a scribe to record his family history.

1. A scribe is _____

_____

scriber

SKREYE–buhr

- The jeweler ordered a new scriber because he wanted to be sure the lengthy engraving on the tray would be readable.
- Students of linoleum block printing know that a sharp scriber is a necessary tool for a clear and clean impression on the block.

2. A scriber is _____

_____

transcribable

trans–KREYE_buh–bl

- Any book that is printed is also transcribable by hand.
- The typewriter makes it possible to write letters faster than they are able to be transcribed.

3. Transcribable means _____

_____

describe

di–SKREYEB

- If you will describe your aches, Dr. Throckmorton guarantees to cure them.
- Rare indeed is a person who can describe a beautiful sunset in enough detail for an artist to paint it.

4. Describe means _____

_____

inscribe

in–SKREYEB

- Give a $50 donation and we will inscribe your name on our roll of benefactors.
- Some people make a hobby of collecting unusual sayings inscribed on tombstones.

5. Inscribe means _____

_____

scribbet

SKREYEB–et

- The artist used a scribbet to make a few "laugh lines" around the eyes of the portrait of Mrs. Jones.
- Use a scribbet to make the outline; then fill in the objects with paint in whatever color you wish.

6. A scribbet is _____

_____

scribble

SKRIB–uhl

- "Don't scribble on the ceiling with your new crayons," mother used to warn us before she left the house.
- Scribble on your test if you must, but only meaningful marks can count on the answer sheet that goes through the machine for grading!

7. Scribble means _____

_____

script

SKRIPT

- "Read this script," the director begged the actress, "before you turn down such a wonderful part."
- If you write in script instead of typing your report, be sure it is legible.

8. Script means _____

_____

manuscript

MAN–yuh–skript

- The book was submitted to the publisher as a manuscript and it was then sent to a printer for typesetting.
- The illustrated manuscripts penned by medieval monks are highly prized by museums today.

9. A manuscript is _____

_____

prescribe

pri–SKREYEB

- Not all doctors are willing to precribe methadone as a "replacement drug" for heroin addicts.

- A prescription of rest, fresh air, and good food never hurt anyone and has, in fact, helped many people.

10. Prescribe means _____

proscribe

pro–SKREYEB

- Totalitarian governments often have lists of proscribed books and anyone found reading or owning them is immediately arrested.
- Property of a proscribed person is often confiscated by the government which forces him into political exile.

11. Proscribed means _____

subscribe

sub–SKREYEB

- Hurry! Don't wait! Subscribe to *Fascinating Facts* for one year and get two free issues of *Sexy Sidelights*.
- Melissa didn't subscribe to everything Harold told her, but he certainly sounded convincing.

12. Subscribe means _____

Scripture

SKRIP–chuhr

- Every church service began with a reading from Scripture and then that passage was used as a basis for the sermon.
- Scripture is regarded by many as the true word of God to be taken literally.

13. Scripture is _____

inscription

in–SKRIP–shun

- An inscription on the coin enabled the archaeologist to prove it had been minted during one of Caesar's visits to Egypt.
- Be sure to put an inscription on the flyleaf of the book so your grandmother will remember you sent it as a birthday present.

14. Inscription means _____

postscript

POST–skript

- Mary had already signed the letter, so she added a postscript reminding Jennifer she would arrive on the 7:30 plane.
- There is a happy postscript to this unhappy tale, for they were married and lived happily ever after.

15. A postscript is _____

_____

ANSWERS

1. *A scribe is a person who writes.*
2. *A scriber is an engraving tool with a sharp point for writing or drawing designs.*
3. *Transcribable means capable of being re-written.*
4. *Describe means to tell how something looks or feels.*
5. *Inscribe means to write upon something.*
6. *A scribbet is a pencil used by a painter.*
7. *Scribble means to write without care or beauty.*
8. *Script means a cursive handwriting OR the words of a play or film.*
9. *A manuscript is a book, document or letter written by hand.*
10. *Prescribe means lay down a rule or course, as for a remedy to make someone well.*
11. *Proscribe means to denounce, condemn, or forbid.*
12. *Subscribe means to contribute or to receive and pay for something, such as a periodical. It may also mean to support or consent to something.*
13. *Scripture is a sacred or religious book or writing, especially the Bible.*
14. *Inscription means something engraved or written upon a surface.*
15. *A postscript is something written after the main body of a work.*

words in use

DIRECTIONS: Read the following paragraph. Then fill in each blank with the appropriate word from among the following choices.

prescribe	manuscript
scribbet	postscript
script	describe
scriber	proscribe

The _____ told an interesting story. It
              1

_____ a person who had been cursed for enter-
        2

ing an ancient Egyptian tomb. Doctors had _____
                          3

medicines for him to take and _____
                  4

activities that would be too strenuous, but to no avail for he eventually

died. It might be added as a _____ that in
                    5

many foreign lands this type of a situation would be a very credible story.

ANSWERS: 1—script; 2—described; 3—prescribed; 4—proscribed; 5—post-script.

true-false

DIRECTIONS: Read each sentence carefully and decide whether it is true or false. If it is true, put a T in the answer space at the right. If it is false, write in an F.

1. A scribe may be a writer or something to write with.   1._____
2. If you write without care or beauty you are a scribbet.   2._____
3. To prescribe is to tell someone what to do.   3._____
4. Writing at the beginning of a book is called a postscript.   4._____
5. Script may refer to many things: a cursive handwriting, a writing style or money printed by the government.   5._____
6. You are unorthodox if you are scriptural.   6._____
7. To proscribe is to tell someone what not to do.   7._____
8. A script used by actors may also be called a manuscript.   8._____
9. Scripture usually refers to hallowed religious writing.   9._____
10. Subscribe means a second–class writer.   10._____

ANSWERS: 1—F; 2—F; 3—T; 4—F; 5—F; 6—F; 7—T; 8—T; 9—T; 10—F.

crossword puzzle

ACROSS

3—a writer
4—to write down what not to do
5—to write down what to do

DOWN

1—to attribute to
2—very orthodox
6—a writing style

solution

POSTTEST

DIRECTIONS: In the space next to each number, write the letter that correctly completes the statement.

_____ 1. Dr. Watson was usually impressed with Sherlock Holmes' almost uncanny ability to
   a. deduce the culprit.
   b. seduce the winner.
   c. abduct the culprit.
   d. absorb the duction.

_____ 2. A manuscript today is usually typewritten, though there may still be some people who take the word literally and send publishers books that are
   a. written by hand.
   b. filled with scriptural quotations.
   c. delivered by special messenger.
   d. clothbound.

_____ 3. If you wanted somebody to wait on you constantly, you would hire
   a. a factory.
   b. a factor.
   c. a facsimile.
   d. a factotum.

_____ 4. In order to use dehydrated foods you must
   a. add water to them.
   b. keep them refrigerated until used.
   c. warm them in the oven at 350° for 10 minutes.
   d. open the can while it is at room temperature.

_____ 5. When Richard took to the woods with his canoe and camping gear I had no idea he would actually be so
   a. remote.
   b. remanded.
   c. manumitted.
   d. motive.

_____ 6. Theology lectures would most likely be given by
   a. dockworkers.
   b. ministers.
   c. puppeteers.
   d. theorems.

_____ 7. If you decided to study archaeology you would probably want to spend your summer
   a. digging.
   b. working in a hotel.
   c. clerking in a bank.
   d. fighting.

_____ 8. In ancient Egypt the scribe was an important member of noble households because he
   a. kept the wolf from the door.
   b. wrote down the family history.
   c. drew up plans for the family pyramid.
   d. recruited for private armies.

_____ 9. All the principals in the important anti-trust suit had to be supplied with information about hearings held before the trial; this was done by mailing each person a
   a. scripture.
   b. scribble.
   c. transcript.
   d. transformation.

_____10. You can often sell your products in other countries by hiring a reputable businessman to act as your
   a. facsimile.
   b. factor.
   c. benefactor.
   d. beneficience.

ANSWERS: 1—a; 2—a; 3—d; 4—a; 5—a; 6—b; 7—a; 8—b; 9—c; 10—b.

chapter 5

Words About Cultures

PRETEST

DIRECTIONS: In the space next to each number, write the letter that correctly completes the statement.

_____ 1. When a man is considered superannuated by a big company for which he has worked a long time, he is most likely to be
   a. given a job with more responsibility.
   b. retired.
   c. shifted into various departments in order to break in more young people.
   d. congratulated.

_____ 2. An example of the only picture in the following list which does not contain an anachronism is that of
   a. a jet plane flying over houses with TV antennas.
   b. a maiden in a long skirt and bustle watching television.
   c. a cigarette lighter being used in the 17th century.
   d. a man on the Crusades drinking a can of beer.

_____ 3. A chronicle is
   a. a location at which the movie was made.
   b. an historical record.
   c. an innovation based on the Bible.
   d. a series of paintings by Picasso.

_____ 4. When a load of turkeys is sent to a store on consignment, it means that
  a. the store pays the owner only for the turkeys sold.
  b. the turkeys are guaranteed to be tender and flavorful.
  c. they are transported by fast freight trucks.
  d. the turkey grower gives the store owner a discount price.

_____ 5. The main character in Moliere's play *The Misanthrope* shows in several ways that he
  a. worries about his future.
  b. wishes he could advance socially.
  c. dislikes other people.
  d. is obviously a fraud.

_____ 6. Before the beauty contest began, contestants were required to submit their measurements as recorded by the official
  a. anthropemetric device.
  b. misanthrope.
  c. philanthropic aide.
  d. anthropoid.

_____ 7. The punch line of a cartoon is usually in its
  a. line art.
  b. location.
  c. humorous intent.
  d. caption.

_____ 8. A generic drug is
  a. likely to be widely advertised by name to doctors.
  b. most helpful in serious cases of disease.
  c. used for surgical reasons.
  d. one that can appear under several trade names.

_____ 9. The starfish can survive the loss of a "leg" because it
  a. requires only the right genus to keep going.
  b. has the ability to regenerate.
  c. can be a progenitor.
  d. follows the law of primogeniture.

_____10. The Antivivisection League would be most likely to demonstrate in order to prevent the establishment of
a. a medical research center.
b. a barber college.
c. a Playboy Club.
d. etymological research.

_____11. If you sent someone your vita you would probably be
a. arrested.
b. applying for a job.
c. giving away something illegally.
d. ordering a new coat.

_____12. The announcement that the peace treaty just signed was unprecedented meant that
a. nothing like it has ever existed before.
b. it is likely to have no effect on the economy.
c. it was a copy of one previously prepared.
d. nothing would really persuade the armies to stop fighting.

_____13. Stop! That is private property and you cannot have
a. access!
b. an intercessor!
c. concession!
d. excess!

_____14. If you were to make a study of decadent civilizations, you would concentrate on those that were
a. revitalized.
b. brand new.
c. long dead.
d. dying.

_____15. News stories of women who kill their newly born children indicate they are guilty of
a. materialism.
b. uxoriousness.
c. infanticide.
d. fratricide.

_____16. One who commits matricide
        a. kills his king.
        b. repudiates his mother.
        c. agrees to accept patrimony.
        d. kills his mother.

ANSWERS: 1—b; 2—a; 3—b; 4—a; 5—c; 6—a; 7—d; 8—d; 9—b; 10—a; 11—b; 12—a; 13—a; 14—d; 15—c; 16—d.

ANNU
AN-you

From the Latin *annus* meaning "circuit of the sun" or "year"

MANY ancient customs and beliefs had to do with natural phenomena: the change of seasons, the passing of the sun across the sky, the nightly rise of the moon. Since the measuring of a year has always had so many implications in the economic, social, and religious lives of people, words based on that Latin root have to do with all three aspects of culture.

The following word parts will be combined with the root in this unit to make new words. Use this list as a reference to find the meaning of words in this unit.

PREFIXES
semi—half or partly
bi—two or double
tri—three or triple
super—above or beyond

SUFFIXES
al—of or belonging to
ity—state or quality
ist—one who does
ary—characterized by
tion—action or state or condition

ROOT AS AFFIX
ver(t)—turn

context
clues

DIRECTIONS: Pronounce each word in the left hand column and read aloud the sentences in the right hand column. On the basis of context clues in the sentences, fill in the blank space to make a correct definition.

annals

AN–uhlz

■ If you want to find authoritative information about the battle at Gettysburg, you may consult the annals of the American Historical Society.

193

■ Never before in the annals of our school have we had so many honor students.

1. Annals mean _____

_____

annual

AN–yuh–wuhl

■ The annual visit of the circus is always a big event in our town.
■ Doctors recommend an annual physical examination for everyone.

2. Annual means _____

_____

annuity

uh–NYOU–uh–tee

■ If you buy an annuity when you are at the peak of your earning power, you will be able to have an income additional to Social Security benefits.
■ An annuity is considered an investment because the money put in will come back to you later.

3. Annuity means _____

_____

annualist

AN–yuh–wuhl–ist

■ Saratoga is a summer resort popular with annualists.
■ The license bureau finds that many people who show up to buy hunting or fishing licenses the first day they are put on sale are sport annualists.

4. An annualist is _____

_____

annuary

AN–nyou–uh–ree

■ It is the custom for the senior class of a high school to have pictures in an annuary.
■ Organizations which maintain an annuary always have a record of past projects and meetings.

5. An annuary is _____

_____

annuation

AN–nyou–a–shun

■ The annuation report showed that to build a dam at the proposed site would greatly harm the ecology of that region.
■ Ecology students are most concerned with annuation studies because they show if animal life in an area begins to change.

6. Annuation means _____

_____

semi–annual

sem–ee–AN–yuh–wuhl

■ Some people are semi-annual churchgoers: they appear on Christmas and Easter.
■ Department stores find semi-annual sales are best held in the spring and fall.

7. Semi–annual means _____

_____

anniversary

an–uh–VER–suh–ree

■ Birthday anniversaries are generally not celebrated by people who prefer to have others forget how old they are getting.
■ Woe to the husband who forgets to give his wife a gift on their wedding anniversary!

8. Anniversary is _____

_____

biannual

beye–AN–yuh–wuhl

■ Most schools on the semester system require the student to go through biannual registration, one for the fall term, and one for the spring term.
■ Merton was surprised when, after asking every six months, Millicent finally accepted his biannual proposal of marriage.

9. Biannual means _____

_____

biennial

beye–EN–ee–uhl

■ The Venice Art Biennial always shocks people who forget how quickly the art world can change in just two years.

■ Our state requires biennial renewal of a driver's license, because getting licenses in alternate years relieves the annual crush.

10. Biennial means _____

_____

triennial

treye–EN–ee–uhl

■ Triennial elections were agreed upon because two years was not considered long enough for an official to learn to do his job well, yet four years was thought to be too long for one person to remain in office.
■ Because the junior high school accommodated grades 7 thru 9, the principal decided to recommend a triennial prom in order that every student have a chance to attend the event during his course of study.

11. Triennial means _____

_____

superannuated

sou–puhr–ANN–you–
way–ted

■ A superannuated horse is in danger of being killed and his carcass used for animal food.
■ Our society has not yet learned how to deal with the superannuated person who still has an active mind and is healthy enough to keep working.

12. Superannuated means _____

_____

ANSWERS

1. *Annals are a record of events kept yearly in chronological order.*
2. *Annual means appearing or happening yearly.*
3. *Annuity means an income payable at stated intervals.*
4. *An annualist is one who does something annually.*
5. *An annuary is a yearbook.*
6. *Annuation means observations about ecology made over a period of years.*
7. *Semi–annual means twice a year.*

8. *Anniversary* is a yearly recurrence of the date of a past event.
9. *Biannual* means twice a year.
10. *Biennial* means once every two years.
11. *Triennial* means once every three years.
12. *Superannuated* means retired because of age or infirmity.

true-false

DIRECTIONS: Read each sentence carefully and decide whether it is true or false. If it is true, put a T in the space at the right. If it is false, write in an F.

1. Annual indicates something is happening on a yearly basis.   1._____
2. If something occurs every two years it is said to be biannual.   2._____
3. If you are superannuated you are youthful and vigorous.   3._____
4. An annuary is a yearbook.   4._____
5. To annualize is to predict what is to come next year.   5._____
6. If an event occurs twice a year it is biennial.   6._____
7. An amount paid on a yearly basis is called an annuity.   7._____
8. A semi–annual magazine is published three times a year.   8._____
9. The word "annals" refers to a record of events, usually in a chronological order.   9._____
10. Annuation is a method of extracting fresh water from salt water.   10._____

ANSWERS: 1—T; 2—F; 3—F; 4—T; 5—F; 6—F; 7—T; 8—F; 9—T; 10—F.

matching exercise

DIRECTIONS: Write the appropriate letter from the right hand column in the space next to each number so that the numbered words are defined.

_____ 1. annual   **a.** occurring every three years

_____ 2. biannual   **b.** occurring every two years

(*more*)

——————— 3. superannuated   **c.** ecological observations made over a period of years

——————— 4. annuary   **d.** a record of events, usually in chronological order

——————— 5. annualize   **e.** appearing or happening yearly

——————— 6. biennial   **f.** twice a year

——————— 7. annuity   **g.** a yearbook

——————— 8. annuation   **h.** very old; retired because of age

——————— 9. annals   **i.** to compute for less than a year

———————10. triennial   **j.** income payable on a yearly basis

                                    k. twelve months a year

ANSWERS: 1—e; 2—f; 3—h; 4—g; 5—i; 6—b; 7—j; 8—c; 9—d; 10—a.

ANTHRO
AN-throw

From the Greek *anthropo* meaning "man"

A CULTURE is built by the people who live in it; their need for words about themselves and their beliefs dictate their vocabulary. In English, such words are likely to be built on the root "anthro."

The following word parts will be combined with the root in this unit to make new words. Use this list as a reference to find the meaning of words in this unit.

ROOTS AS AFFIXES
mis—hate
latry—worship of
metri—measure
phil—love
centri—center
gen(esis)—birth
geo—earth
graph—word or write
morph—shape
path—feel or suffer

SUFFIXES
ist—one who does or makes a practice of
ope—(same as *ist*)
oid—shaped like
ic—pertaining to

context
clues

DIRECTIONS: Pronounce each word in the left hand column and read aloud the sentences in the right hand column. On the basis of context clues in the sentences, fill in the blank space to make a correct definition.

anthropolatry

an–thruh–POL–uh–tree

■ Japanese worship of the emperor approached the dimension of anthropolatry.
■ Anthropolatry is considered a step beyond the worship of animals as gods.

1. Anthropolatry means _____

_____

misanthrope

MIS–uhn–thrope

■ Hermits very often undertake their unusual way of life because they are misanthropes.
■ A misanthrope would find little of cheer in all the achievements of men.

2. A misanthrope is _____

_____

philanthropist

fuh–LAN–thruh–pist

■ Contrary to a misanthrope, the philanthropist enjoys being with people because of his special interest in them.
■ A philanthropist who prefers to remain anonymous endowed the college and the local library as well as a new unit of the hospital.

3. A philanthropist is _____

_____

anthropometric

an–thruh–puh–MET–rik

■ Anthropometry shows that men being inducted into the armed forces now are taller and broader than their fathers were.
■ Clothing manufacturers rely on the reports of anthropometry in order to find the most standard size measurements.

4. Anthropometric means _____

_____

philanthropic

fil–an–THROP–ik

■ If you would like to join a philanthropic organization, the Community Chest office can recommend several that can use your services.
■ "I'm not running a philanthropic organization," Mr. Smith shouted when Herman asked if he could have a free pass to the movies.

5. Philanthropic means _____

_____

anthropocentric

an–thruh–puh–SEN–trik

■ Because humans often tend to regard the world as anthropocentric, we may be facing ecological disaster.
■ Scientists speculate on whether man will continue to be anthropocentric if life is discovered on other planets.

6. Anthropocentric means _____

_____

anthropogenesis

an–thruh–puh–JEN–
     uh–sus

- Anyone studying anthropogenesis cannot help but see how the physical features of man have changed since the Cromagnon period.
- Archaeologists are interested in anthropogenesis as a study to help understand their discoveries.

7. Anthropogenesis means _____

_____

anthropogeography

an–thruh–puh–jee–OG–
     ruh–fee

- Anthropogeography can account for the development of some people as nomads and some as farmers.
- If you would like to know more about why certain kinds of people prospered in cold climates and others in warm climates, you should take a course in anthropogeography.

8. Anthropogeography is _____

_____

anthropoid

AN–thruh–poid

- Monkeys, gorillas, orangutangs, and apes are anthropoids.
- Look at the anthropoid shape of that cloud; it looks just like a man!

9. Anthropoid means _____

_____

anthropomorphic

an–thruh–puh–MOR–fik

- The tree seemed to have a human shape and this anthropomorphic condition caused the natives to worship it as a king.
- Anthropomorphic religions choose man-shaped objects as idols.

10. Anthropomorphic means _____

_____

anthropopathy

an–thruh–POP–uh–thee

- The Greeks obviously had an anthropopathic religion because their gods had love affairs, wandering eyes, and carried grudges.

- Any religion that considers humans to be copies of their gods would be an example of anthropopathy.

11. Anthropopathy is _____

_____

ANSWERS

1. *Anthropolatry* means worship of a human as if he were a god.
2. A *misanthrope* is one who hates men.
3. A *philanthropist* is one who gives donations of work, property, or money to needy people; one who loves man.
4. *Anthropometric* means measuring the human body.
5. *Philanthropic* means giving support (in the form of money, work, or other aid) to needy people.
6. *Anthropocentric* means regarding man as the center of the universe.
7. *Anthropogenesis* means the development of the human race.
8. *Anthropogeography* is the branch of anthropology dealing with the geographical distribution of man and his relation to his environment.
9. *Anthropoid* means resembling man or in the shape of a man.
10. *Anthropomorphic* means ascribing a human form or attributes to a thing.
11. *Anthropopathy* means attributing human emotions to God.

words in use

DIRECTIONS: Read this passage. Then fill in each blank with the appropriate word from among the following choices.

anthropocentric   anthropoid
philanthropy   misanthropes
philanthropist   anthropolatry
anthropometric   anthropogenesis

The _____ gave everything he owned to

1

the poor human beings that he met. He spent so much time helping people

that many religious people actually were against him, for they felt he was

practicing _____ and was placing God

2

second. These religious individuals said that when one studied

_____ or the development of the human race

        3

it was easy to see that man was not the center of the universe, and that

anyone who practiced this _____ idea should

                              4

be condemned. The man who helped everyone answered by saying they were

_____, for they hated mankind.

        5

ANSWERS: 1—philanthropist; 2—anthropolatry; 3—anthropogenesis; 4—anthropocentric; 5—misanthropes.

fill in the blanks

DIRECTIONS: Fill in the blank in each sentence with the appropriate word from among the following choices.

anthropogenesis
anthropomorphic
anthropometric
anthropogeography
anthropoid

anthropopathy
philanthropist
misanthrope
anthropocentric
anthropolatry

1. The worship of man is called _____.

2. A _____ is one who hates mankind.

3. _____ refers to regarding man as the

    central fact of the universe.

4. A _____ is one who loves mankind.

5. The development of the human race is called _____.

                              (*more*)

6. _____ is that branch of anthropology

dealing with the distribution of mankind.

7. If it resembles man it is called _____.

8. _____ is ascribing human form or

attributes to something which is not human.

9. If you attribute human emotions to God it is said that you are

practicing _____.

10. _____ has to do with the measuring of

the human body.

ANSWERS: 1—anthropolatry; 2—misanthrope; 3—anthropocentric; 4—philan-thropist; 5—anthropogenesis; 6—anthropogeography; 7—anthropoid; 8—anthro-pomorphic; 9—anthropopathy; 10—anthropometric.

scrambled
words

DIRECTIONS: Unscramble the following words.
They are defined in parentheses.

1. dinothrapo: _____
   (it resembles man)

2. resisopanthogen: _____
   (the development of the human race)

3. prtotryanolah: _____
   (the worship of man)

4. treshaponim: _____
   (he hates man)

5. sitithroplanph: _____
   (he loves mankind)

ANSWERS: 1—anthropoid; 2—anthropogenesis; 3—anthropolatry; 4—misan-thrope; 5—philanthropist.

affixes at work

DIRECTIONS: Add your own words to the blanks at the bottom of the diagram.

(mis)anthrope

misogamist
(one who hates marriage)

misogynic
(hatred and distrust of women)

misology
(hatred of argument)

misoneism
(hatred of something new or of change)

Prefix: *mis* means "hatred"

misadventure
_____
(misfortune)
_____
misapprehend
(to misunderstand)
_____
mischance
(bad luck)
_____
miscount
(not count or calculate correctly)
_____
misgiving
(a feeling of doubt)
_____
misinterpret
(to understand wrongly)
_____
mismatch
(to mate unsuitably)
_____
misprint
(to print incorrectly)
_____

_____

_____

Prefix: *mis* means "badly"

CED CEED CESS
SEED SEED SES

From the Latin *cedere* meaning "to go" or "to yield"

PERHAPS it is the actions suggested by this root—all so basic to life—that have led to the formation of so many words from it. Certainly it would be hard to imagine any person without the possibility of "coming and going."

That our language has taken three forms from the same basic Latin verb probably shows how useful that word is to English-speaking peoples. The concepts of going or proceeding and of yielding or of giving appear so frequently that the words in this section comprise one of the longest lists in the book—and many other forms of the word were omitted in the interest of brevity.

The following word parts will be combined with the root in this unit to make new words. Use this list as a reference to find the meaning of words in this unit.

PREFIXES
ac—characteristic of or relating to
ante—before
con—together or with
de—from or down
ex—out of or away from
in—not
inter—between
pre—before
un—opposite or negative
pro—before or in behalf of
se—apart
re—back or again

SUFFIXES
ion—act or state or result
ence—act or condition
ent—doing or showing
ant—opposite or against
ure—condition of
ion—act or state

context
clues

DIRECTIONS: Pronounce each word in the left hand column and read aloud the sentences in the right hand column. On the basis of context clues in the sentences, fill in the blank space to make a correct definition.

207

access

AK–ses

■ If you want to gain access to the room, you need a key.
■ The president kept the door to his office open to show that all employees had access to him.

1. Access means _____

_____

accession

ak–SESH–uhn

■ The accession to the British throne has not always been as orderly and regular as it has been in this century.
■ Election as Vice President in the United States means automatic accession to the Presidency if the chief executive dies before his term of office is up.

2. Accession means _____

_____

accede

ak–SEED

■ Mary would not accede to George's wishes and give him the secret formula.
■ The boss was handed an ultimatum: accede to the demands of the strikers or risk having his plant burned down.

3. Accede means _____

_____

antecedent

ant–uh–SEED–uhnt

■ Everyone is not proud of all his antecedents; there are skeletons in almost every family closet.
■ If your antecedents came over on the *Mayflower,* you may join a special organization.

4. Antecedents are _____

_____

concede

kon–SEED

■ If you will concede that I am right, I will sign the paper you require as a record of the transaction.
■ Herman refused to concede that Martin won the election.

5. Concede means _____

_____

decadent

DEK–uh–dent

■ Some historians believe that Rome was already a decadent civilization at the time Julius Caesar ruled.
■ A person who loves luxury and surrounds himself with devices for pleasant and easy living is not necessarily decadent.

6. Decadent means _____

_____

excess

ek–SES

■ Eating an excess of food is just as unhealthy as eating an inadequate amount.
■ Most cultures emphasize that moderation in beliefs and activities is better than an excess of either.

7. Excess means _____

_____

incessant

in–SES–uhnt

■ The incessant crying of the baby finally woke all the neighbors.
■ Incessant demands for equal rights without any action on your part will not move me to grant such rights.

8. Incessant means _____

_____

intercede

in–ter–SEED

■ Marigold refused to intercede for Murgatroid because she knew he was only going to be punished for the wrongs he had already done to other people.
■ I will intercede for you in court if you will promise never to get into trouble again.

9. Intercede means _____

_____

precede

pri–SEED

■ Each scene in the play builds upon preced-
ing action and information.
■ A gentleman always allows a lady to precede
him into the car.

10. Precede means _____ /
_____

_____

precedent

PRES–uh–dent

■ Paying John's fine will establish a precedent
that all future traffic offenders will want to
follow.
■ Legal opinions are usually based on precedent
found in those cases that have previously been
tried.

11. Precedent means _____

_____

unprecedented

un–PRES–uh–den–ted

■ The crowd was unprecedented; never before
had so many people gathered at the funeral
of a tiddlywinks champion.
■ Professor Throttlebottom's willingness to
change the student's grade was an unprecedented action on his part.

12. Unprecedented means _____

_____

procedure

pruh–SEED–juhr

■ A surgical procedure must be perfectly organized in order to be most beneficial to the patient.
■ Outline the procedure to the senate; then ask
its members to follow the directions.

13. A procedure is _____

_____

process

PROS–uhs

■ The process of extracting fresh water from sea
water is familiar to scientists, but is generally
considered too expensive for commercial use.
■ Many manufacturing processes are being simplified and speeded up by the development of
machines which replace men.

14. A process is _____

_____

secede

si–SEED

■ The group that seceded from the White Knights and formed a new gang called themselves the Late Knights.
■ It is not easy for a state to secede from the Union.

15. Secede means _____

_____

secession

si–SESH–un

■ France threatened secession from NATO if demands for arms were not met.
■ The secession of the southern states led to the Civil War.

16. Secession means _____

_____

cede

SEED

■ "Cede the back 40 to your brother and I'll not marry you," announced the fortune-seeking man-about-town.
■ As part of the peace treaty concluding the Spanish-American War, Spain ceded control of the Philippines to the United States.

17. Cede means _____

_____

concession

kuhn–SESH–uhn

■ One of the concessions the conquered nation had to make was to allow its conquerers to build military bases on its land.
■ The college administration was forced to make concessions to the militants in order to prevent the president's office from being bombed.

18. Concession means _____

_____

recede

ri–SEED

■ When the flood waters recede there will be rich silt in which to plant your crops.
■ As a man's hairline begins to recede, he may decide to buy a hairpiece to cover the bald area.

19. Recede means _____

_____

NAME: _____

ANSWERS

1. <u>Access</u> means admittance or approach.
2. <u>Accession</u> means coming into possession of a right, dignity or office.
3. <u>Accede</u> means to give consent or agree.
4. <u>Antecedents</u> are forebearers.
5. <u>Concede</u> means to admit as true, just or proper.
6. <u>Decadent</u> means deteriorating or declining.
7. <u>Excess</u> means too much.
8. <u>Incessant</u> means continuing without interruption.
9. <u>Intercede</u> means to interpose in behalf of one in trouble.
10. <u>Precede</u> means to go before in place, order, rank, time, importance, etc.
11. <u>Precedent</u> means an established custom.
12. <u>Unprecedented</u> means unexpected.
13. A <u>procedure</u> is a method of performing a process.
14. A <u>process</u> is a systematic series of actions directed to some end.
15. <u>Secede</u> means to withdraw formally from an alliance or association.
16. <u>Secession</u> means the act of formally withdrawing from a group or association.
17. <u>Cede</u> means to grant or assign, as a territory.
18. <u>Concession</u> means to give up or yield.
19. <u>Recede</u> means to go back.

fill in the blanks

DIRECTIONS: Fill in the blank in each sentence with the appropriate word from among the following choices.

receded	antecedents
secede	decadent
intercede	concede
procedure	access
cede	accede

1. Anyone who has a special privilege of admittance to a place has

   _____ to that place.

2. To _____ is to give consent for something

   or to agree to something.

3. Those members of a family who lived before you are your

   _____ .

NAME: _____

4. To _____ an election is to admit defeat, or
   to surrender.

5. The tumbledown castle in the midst of grass-roofed huts and empty
   buildings with broken windows gave the town a _____
   look.

6. To _____ is to place one's self between
   two opposing forces.

7. The manner or method of registering for classes is the
   _____ that must be followed in order
   to enroll.

8. To _____ from a formal group organization
   is to withdraw from it.

9. To grant, assign, or transfer is to _____.

10. When flood waters have gone back to their original level, newsmen
    announce that they have _____.

*ANSWERS: 1—access; 2—accede; 3—antecedents; 4—concede; 5—decadent;
6—intercede; 7—procedure; 8—secede; 9—cede; 10—receded.*

words in use

DIRECTIONS: Read this passage. Then fill in each blank with the appropriate
word from among the following choices.

excess   decadent
conceded   procedures
intercede   precede
seceded   access
antecedents   incessant

NAME: _____

The immediate cause of the Civil War was that the southern states

_____ from the Union. This cut off
1

_____ between the northern and southern
2

states and one could only travel between the hostile lines by using

special _____. After many years of
3

_____ warfare the South finally
4

_____ victory to the North.
5

ANSWERS: 1—seceded; 2—access; 3—procedures; 4—incessant; 5—conceded.

scrambled
words

DIRECTIONS: Unscramble the following words. They are defined in parentheses.

1. edeces: _____
   (to withdraw formally from an alliance)

2. edecac: _____
   (to give consent or to agree)

3. tadecend: _____
   (departing, withdrawing or dying)

4. tederenic: _____
   (to come between two opposing forces)

5. rederopuc: _____
   (manner or method of action)

ANSWERS: 1—secede; 2—accede; 3—decadent; 4—intercede; 5—procedure.

CIDE
SEYE-d

From the Latin *caedere* meaning "to cut down" or "to kill"

SAD but true, this is a popular root for words in the English language; we spend a great deal of time killing living things. Who—or what—is killed is made known by the prefixes added to the root "cide," and hardly a day goes by that the news media do not use one of the many words that can be more readily understood when this root and its variations are familiar.

Terracide

The title of a book (by Ron Linton) telling how America is racing to destruction because it is killing its land. It comes from *terra,* the earth, and *caedere,* to kill.

The following word parts will be combined with the root in this unit to make new words. Use this list as a reference to find the meaning of words in this unit.

ROOTS AS AFFIXES
fratr—brother
gen—birth
homo—man
infant—infant or child
matr—mother
patr—father
reg—king or ruler
soror—sister
uxor—wife
av—bird
parr—parents
sui—oneself
insect—insect

context
clues

DIRECTIONS: Pronounce each word in the left hand column and read aloud the sentences in the right hand column. On the basis of context clues in the sentences, fill in the blank space to make a correct definition.

fratricide

FRA–truh–seyed

■ The first recorded example of fratricide is that of Cain killing Abel.
■ After her elder boy, Montmorency, committed fratricide, Mrs. Smith had only one son left.

1. Fratricide means _____

_____

genocide

JEN–o–seyed

■ Hitler sought to rid Germany of both Gypsies and Jews by genocide.
■ Historically, plagues and other instances of widespread disease have accomplished genocide in a way that men deliberately setting out to destroy a national group could not do.

2. Genocide is _____

_____

homicide

HO–muh–seyed

■ In legal terminology, a murderer is always accused of homicide.
■ One homicide which attracted international attention was the killing of Martin Luther King, Jr.

3. Homicide is _____

_____

infanticide

in–FAN–tuh–seyed

■ Because the child was born malformed, the father thought he was saving his child from a horrible life; he was, nevertheless, guilty of infanticide.
■ The ancient Spartan custom of killing undesirable babies was actually widespread infanticide.

4. Infanticide means _____

_____

matricide

MA–truh–seyed

■ Although some persons feel so bound to their mothers they wish they could be rid of them, few actually commit matricide.
■ Hamlet was horrified to find the poisoned drink meant for him was swallowed by Gertrude, thus making him guilty of matricide.

5. Matricide is _____

_____

patricide

PA–truh–seyed

■ The boy who set his home afire and killed his father because he resented him so intensely will be tried for patricide.
■ Only an orphan can be guilty of both matricide and patricide.

6. Patricide is _____

_____

regicide

REJ–uh–seyed

■ When Hamlet discovered that his uncle Claudius had killed the king, he realized Claudius was guilty of regicide.
■ Regicide is often a way of acquiring a throne for the aspirant by eliminating the present ruler.

7. Regicide means _____

_____

sororicide

suh–ROAR–uh–seyed

■ Brothers and sisters usually fight, but few brothers ever resort to sororicide.
■ The bereaved family mourned the sororicide which left them with only one of the identical twin girls, and she was in jail for the crime.

8. Sororicide means _____

_____

uxoricide

uk–SOR–uh–seyed

■ A man who made himself a widower would be guilty of uxoricide.
■ King Henry VIII committed uxoricide when he had Anne Boleyn beheaded.

9. Uxoricide is _____

_____

avicide

AV–uh–seyed

■ During the dove hunting season, many men are guilty of avicide.
■ Is it justifiable avicide that John James Audubon killed many birds in order to paint them?

10. Avicide means _____

_____

parricide

PAR–uh–seyed

■ In the movie thriller, Hiram took his parents out for a ride in his car and then committed parricide by jumping out just before he ran the car over a cliff, killing both his parents.
■ Lizzie Borden is probably the most famous parricide in the United States because of this rhyme about her: "Lizzie Borden took an axe/ And gave her mother forty whacks./When the job was neatly done,/She gave her father forty-one."

11. Parricide is _____

_____

suicide

SU–uh–seyed

■ An example of a ridiculous law is that the legal penalty for suicide should be death.
■ Some people believe only a coward would choose suicide as a way out of his personal problems.

12. Suicide means _____

_____

insecticide

in–SEK–tuh–seyed

■ Part of today's conservation problem is that insecticides have frequently killed beneficial insects as well as harmful ones.
■ The insecticide DDT was taken off the market because although it killed harmful insects it was also dangerous to man.

13. Insecticide is _____

_____

ANSWERS

1. *Fratricide* means killing one's brother.
2. *Genocide* is the deliberate and systematic killing of an entire national or racial group.
3. *Homicide* is murder or the deliberate killing of one person by another.
4. *Infanticide* means killing an infant.
5. *Matricide* is the act of killing a mother.
6. *Patricide* is the act of killing a father.
7. *Regicide* means killing a king or ruler.
8. *Sororicide* means the killing of a sister.
9. *Uxoricide* is the act of murdering one's wife.
10. *Avicide* means killing birds.
11. *Parricide* is the killing of a parent.
12. *Suicide* means the taking of one's own life.
13. *Insecticide* is a chemical combination that kills insects.

fill in the blanks

DIRECTIONS: Fill in the blank in each sentence with the appropriate word from among the following choices.

avicide	parricide
fratricide	patricide
homicide	sororicide
genocide	suicide
infanticide	regicide
insecticide	matricide
uxoricide	

1. The jury had found him guilty of assassinating the president and the

   penalty for _____ is death.

2. The Bible presents the first example of _____

   with the story of Cain and Abel.

3. Oedipus feared the prophecy of _____ so
   much that he left home in order not to kill the man he believed was
   his father.

4. King Henry VIII resorted to _____
   rather than to divorce.

5. The thought of _____ was constantly
   with Electra because of her intense hatred for her mother.

6. The driver of a car which accidentally kills someone is charged with

   _____.

7. If Hitler had lived after losing the war, he probably would have been
   tried and convicted of _____ for
   exterminating millions of Jews during World War II.

8. The Bible illustrates Solomon's wisdom by telling how he uses the
   threat of _____ to prove which of two
   women was the actual mother of a child.

9. In the story "What Ever Happened to Baby Jane?" a perfect example
   of _____ is that one sister tries to kill
   the other.

10. A taxidermist who specialized in birds would not be against

    _____.

ANSWERS: 1—regicide; 2—fratricide; 3—patricide; 4—uxoricide; 5—matricide; 6—homicide; 7—genocide; 8—infanticide; 9—sororicide; 10—avicide.

NAME: _____

true-false

DIRECTIONS: Read each sentence carefully and decide whether it is true or false. If it is true, put a T in the space at the right. If it is false, write in an F.

1. Fratricide means killing one's mother.   1._____
2. Genocide is the deliberate, systematic killing of an entire national or racial group.   2._____
3. Homicide is the extermination of insects.   3._____
4. The ancient custom of killing the first-born child was infanticide.   4._____
5. The assassination of President Kennedy is an example of regicide.   5._____
6. The boy who killed his mother was put on trial for matricide.   6._____
7. The killing of parrots is called parricide.   7._____
8. John was convicted of uxoricide because he killed his wife.   8._____
9. Sororicide would more likely take place in a sorority house than in a YMCA.   9._____
10. Insecticides frequently prevent crop damage caused by voracious insects.   10._____

ANSWERS: 1—F; 2—T; 3—F; 4—T; 5—T; 6—T; 7—F; 8—T; 9—T; 10—T.

THE SMITH FAMILY

By Mr. and Mrs. George Smith

CHRON
KRON

From the Greek *chronos* meaning "time"

IN THE Greek legend about the origin of the earth and the gods, Cronos (or Chronos), child of Earth and Heaven, was one of the chief nature deities. Cronos was imprisoned by his father but overpowered him, liberated his sisters and brother, and formed a new dynasty. Cronus, first an agricultural divinity, developed into one representing time. His children subsequently divided the universe among themselves with Zeus receiving dominion over the sky, Poseidon over the sea, and Hades over the underworld.

Cronos was the original representation of Father Time.

The following word parts will be combined with the root in this unit to make new words. Use this list as a reference to find the meaning of words in this unit.

PREFIXES
an—not
syn—together or along with
iso—equal

SUFFIXES
ic—pertaining to
al—of or belonging to
ism—act or state
ize—condition or act
icle—small
logy—study of or science

ROOTS AS AFFIXES
graph—word or write
meter—measure
scope—watch or sight

context
clues

DIRECTIONS: Pronounce each word in the left hand column and read aloud the sentences in the right hand column. On the basis of context clues in the sentences, fill in the blank space to make a correct definition.

chronic

KRON–ik

■ Chronic skin diseases are particularly hard to get rid of but are especially annoying because they are visible for such a long time.

223

■ The country seemed in a chronic state of civil war and no one could remember a peaceful period.

1. Chronic means _____

_____

chronicle

KRON–i–kuhl

■ Often the chronicles that soldiers keep on the battlefield are as accurate as any records kept officially by the army.
■ The official chronicles of the reign of King Henry V are not exactly like the plays Shakespeare wrote about that period.

2. A chronicle is _____

_____

chronography

kruh–NOG–ruh–fee

■ Keeping a diary is a familiar type of chronography.
■ Killjoy University decided to print a chronography in honor of its twelfth year of existence.

3. Chronography is _____

_____

chronological

kron–uhl–OJ–i–kuhl

■ Chronological paragraph development is especially suitable for any essay describing the changes occurring during a timed experiment.
■ Present your story chronologically so that the judge can follow exactly what happened and when each event occurred.

4. Chronological means _____

_____

anachronism

uh–NAK–ruh–niz–uhm

■ Sometimes an obvious anachronism is visible in a movie, such as a TV antenna on the roof of a house in what is supposed to be the background for a 19th century scene.
■ Sylvester spotted the anachronism in the photograph: the rifle in King Arthur's tent.

5. An anachronism is _____

_____

synchronize

SIN–kruh–neyez

■ "All right men, let's synchronize our watches," is a standard line in war movie scenes about a group which has to time its actions.
■ Some entertainers become very good at synchronizing their lip movements with the voice on a record.

6. Synchronize means _____

_____

isochronal

eye–SOK–ruhn–uhl

■ Since the vibrations of the machine are normally isochronal, any variation is immediate evidence of some malfunction.
■ The duration of a college semester or a college quarter is not isochronal.

7. Isochronal means _____

_____

chronology

kruh–NOL–uh–jee

■ World literature courses are often taught according to chronology, beginning with the *Iliad* and working forward to contemporary novels.
■ You can learn much about the chronology of an area by studying the layers uncovered by archaeological exploration.

8. Chronology is _____

_____

chronometer

kruh–NOM–uh–tuhr

■ Scientists working in observatories need chronometers rather than the simple clocks that are satisfactory for ordinary people like you and me.
■ Quick Henry, the chronometer! Time is passing by so quickly!

9. A chronometer is _____

_____

chronoscope

KRON–uh–skope

■ When even the chronometer is not accurate enough, you can use a chronoscope.

■ If you would use a chronoscope, perhaps you could measure the time it takes a bullet to get from here to there.

10. A chronoscope is _____

_____

ANSWERS

1. *Chronic means constant or continuing for a long time; recurring, especially concerning a disease.*
2. *A chronicle is an historical record according to time sequence.*
3. *Chronography is a record or description of past events.*
4. *Chronological means events arranged in the order of time.*
5. *An anachronism is a chronological error such as post or ante-dating of a thing or event.*
6. *Synchronize means to be simultaneous or to agree in time.*
7. *Isochronal means equal in length of time.*
8. *Chronology is the treating of events arranged according to their proper sequence.*
9. *A chronometer is an instrument for measuring time with extreme accuracy.*
10. *A chronoscope is an instrument for measuring minute intervals of time.*

fill in the blanks

DIRECTIONS: Fill in the blank in each sentence with the appropriate word from among the following choices.

chronoscope	synchronized
chronometer	chronography
isochronal	chronological
chronology	chronicle
chronic	anachronism

1. A _____ disease is one that has continued

for a long period of time.

2. An historical record is called a _____.

3. A _____ is a record or description of

   past events.

4. If an historical record of past events is written down in the same time

   order that the events occurred it is a _____

   account.

5. An _____ is an event that is erroneously

   placed or that occurs in a period in which it does not belong.

6. If two things or events occur simultaneously in time they are said

   to be _____.

7. _____ events occur at equal intervals of time.

8. The science treating events and arranging their dates in proper

   time sequence is called _____.

9. A _____ is an instrument for measuring

   time with extreme accuracy.

10. If we wish to measure very small intervals of time we would use a

   _____.

ANSWERS: 1—chronic; 2—chronicle; 3—chronography; 4—chronological; 5—anachronism; 6—synchronized; 7—isochronal; 8—chronology; 9—chronometer; 10—chronoscope.

true-false

DIRECTIONS: Read each sentence carefully and decide whether it is true or false. If it is true, put a T in the space at the right. If it is false, write in an F.

1. A chronic illness is one that continues for a long time. 1._____
2. Any record is a chronicle. 2._____

3. The science of dancing is called chronography. 3._____
4. Any record that is chronological contains an account of past
   events in the order of time in which they have occurred. 4._____
5. Anachronism refers to a national disorder. 5._____
6. If two events agree in time they are said to be synchronized. 6._____
7. Isochronal was a Greek philosopher. 7._____
8. Chronology is the science that deals with the making of
   watches. 8._____
9. A chronometer is an instrument for measuring time. 9._____
10. A chronoscope is a telescope with a timing device. 10._____

ANSWERS: 1—T; 2—F; 3—F; 4—F; 5—F; 6—T; 7—F; 8—F; 9—T; 10—F.

words in use

DIRECTIONS: Fill in the blank in each sentence with the appropriate word
from among the following choices.

chronoscope   synchronize
chronometer   chronography
isochronal   chronological
chronology   chronicle
chronic   anachronism

The patient had a _____ disease. The
                              1

doctors decided to administer drugs at specific time intervals, so a

_____ was used to make certain the patient
              2

was given his medication at exactly the times prescribed. In order to learn

more about the illness, one of the doctors kept a _____
                                                        3

of the patient's progress so other doctors could refer to it.

ANSWERS: 1—chronic; 2—chronoscope; 3—chronicle.

GEN
JEN

From the Latin *genus* meaning "kind" or "sort" and *genes* meaning "born" or "produced"

MANY words are needed to express cultural ideas involving the beginnings of people, things, or ideas. One convenient characteristic of the root "gen" is that it combines readily with other word parts to express this variety. Perhaps it is also significant that from this root come words ranging from "gene," a unit important in the conception of living things, all the way to "genocide" that describes their destruction.

The following word parts will be combined with the root in this unit to make new words. Use this list as a reference to find the meaning of words in this unit.

PREFIXES
con—with or together
pre—before or in behalf of
re—back or again
en—in or into

SUFFIXES
sis—abnormal condition
ure—act of
al—act or state
or—maker or doer
ate—office or officeholder
ion—the act of
ic—like or dealing with or caused by
er—maker or doer
logy—science or study of

ROOTS AS AFFIXES
prim—first
cide—kill or cut down

context
clues

DIRECTIONS: Pronounce each word in the left hand column and read aloud the sentences in the right hand column. On the basis of context clues in the sentences, fill in the blank space to make a correct definition.

229

gene

JEEN

■ The genes determine much about the physical appearance of a child.
■ Many ills of an individual are mistakenly blamed on genes when, in fact, they are the result of either environment or training rather than of heredity.

1. A gene is _____

_____

genealogy

je–ne–OL–uh–jee

■ The genealogy of the royal families was printed in many newspapers when the prince married the princess of another country.
■ The person you hire to find your family coat of arms will first have to make a study of your family's genealogy.

2. Genealogy is _____

_____

genesis

JEN–uh–suhs

■ The idea for the sit-in at the administration building had its genesis at an informal meeting of some students in the cafeteria.
■ The genesis of the private school was parental reluctance to send their children to a newly integrated school.

3. Genesis means _____

_____

primogeniture

preye–mo–JEN–uh–tuhr

■ The law of primogeniture means that there is often little money left for second and third sons to inherit from their parents.
■ When Clarence became king by virtue of primogeniture, his younger brother Richard was so enraged that he plotted to kill him to gain the throne.

4. Primogeniture means _____

_____

congenital

kuhn–JEN–uh–tl

■ Congenital drug addiction is possible for a new-born baby if both parents are addicted to drugs.
■ Congenital heart defects are now being corrected by early heart surgery.

5. Congenital means _____

_____

progenitor

pro–JEN–uh–ter

■ According to the Bible, Adam was the progenitor of human beings.
■ Henry Ford's first mass-produced automobiles were the progenitors of today's cars.

6. Progenitor means _____

_____

progeny

PROJ–uh–nee

■ The progeny of the champion dog were all registered with the American Kennel Club and were destined to become show dogs.
■ All the Barrymore progeny were well–known in show business.

7. Progeny means _____

_____

regenerate

ri–JEN–uh–rate

■ The busy executive said a quiet vacation in the mountains served to regenerate him for the coming year.
■ Some people find that religious experiences make them feel regenerated.

8. Regenerate means _____

_____

genteel

jen–TEEL

■ Never a harsh word passed the lips of Miranda because she was such a genteel lady.
■ No genteel person would ever let another be insulted or suffer any indignity.

9. Genteel means _____

_____

genius

JEEN–yuhs

■ Leo had a positive genius for making useful things out of old pieces of junk he found around the house.
■ Sometimes a genius is unrecognized in his time because his ideas are beyond the comprehension of his contemporaries.

10. Genius means _____

_____

genus

JEE–nuhs

■ In scientific terminology man belongs to the genus homo sapiens.
■ A single genus of plant or animal may become the lifetime study of many people searching for primary knowledge.

11. Genus means _____

_____

genetics

juh–NET–iks

■ Some scientists believe that through genetic selection man can eventually control the kind of people born.
■ High-yield crops are usually the result of experimentation with plant genetics.

12. Genetics is _____

_____

generate

JEN–uh–rate

■ If you generate enough ideas, some of them are bound to be good.
■ A good leader generates confidence in himself.

13. Generate means _____

_____

generation

jen–uh–RAY–shuhn

■ The generation of silent screen stars has almost passed away.
■ If there is a generation gap, it is up to both parents and children to close it.

14. Generation means _____

_____

genocide

JEN–uh–seyed

■ War is always a matter of genocide.
■ People killed in riots in this country are as much victims of genocide as people killed in groups by soldiers during every war.

15. Genocide means _____

_____

gender

JEN–der

■ If you learn French or Spanish, you must learn the gender of each noun in order to put either the masculine or feminine article with each.
■ One of the desires of our society is that each person be a strong representative of his gender.

16. Gender means _____

_____

generic

juh–NER–ik

■ Doctors sometimes order drugs by their generic rather than by their brand names.
■ "American" is a generic term while "Californian" is a more specific name for certain Americans.

17. Generic means _____

_____

engender

in–JEN–der

■ Riots engender fear in a city.
■ You can engender trust in someone you like by being honest with him.

18. Engender means _____

_____

ANSWERS

1. *A gene is a unit of heredity transmitted by the chromosome.*
2. *Genealogy is a record of the ancestry or family of a person.*
3. *Genesis means origin, creation, or beginning.*
4. *Primogeniture means the first-born child of the same parents who inherits property or title.*
5. *Congenital means existing at or from a person's birth, such as a physical disability.*
6. *Progenitor means forefather; a model for later developments.*

7. _Progeny_ means children or descendants.
8. _Regenerate_ means to produce anew or recreate.
9. _Genteel_ means well-born, refined or elegant.
10. _Genius_ means a person of exceptional natural intellect.
11. _Genus_ means a kind, sort or class.
12. _Genetics_ is a science pertaining to the hereditary characteristics.
13. _Generate_ means to bring into existence.
14. _Generation_ means an entire group of individuals born and living at about the same time.
15. _Genocide_ means the mass deliberate and systematic killing of a racial or political group.
16. _Gender_ means sex.
17. _Generic_ means that which is applicable to all members of a class or group.
18. _Engender_ means to create or produce.

matching exercise

DIRECTIONS: Write the appropriate letter from the right hand column in the space next to each number so that the numbered words are defined.

_____ 1. gene		**a.** first born child of same parents
_____ 2. genealogy		**b.** an origin, creation, or beginning
_____ 3. congenital		**c.** kind, sort, or class
_____ 4. progenitor		**d.** offspring, or descendant
_____ 5. genteel		**e.** recreate; produce anew
_____ 6. regenerate		**f.** killing of men
_____ 7. progeny		**g.** well-born; refined
_____ 8. genus		**h.** forefather; model for later development
_____ 9. genocide		**i.** a record based on accounts of the ancestry or family of a person
_____ 10. genesis		**j.** existing at or from one's birth
		k. unit of heredity transmitted by the chromosome

ANSWERS: 1—k; 2—i; 3—j; 4—h; 5—g; 6—e; 7—d; 8—c; 9—f; 10—b.

scrambled

words

DIRECTIONS: Unscramble the following words. They are defined in parentheses.

1. engred: _____
   (it means sex)

2. tinecolang: _____
   (existing at or from one's birth)

3. letegen: _____
   (refined; well-born)

4. sugne: _____
   (kind, sort, class)

5. sisenge: _____
   (an origin, creation, or beginning)

ANSWERS: 1—gender; 2—congenital; 3—genteel; 4—genus; 5—genesis.

words in use

DIRECTIONS: Fill in the blank in each sentence with the appropriate word from among the following choices.

gene	regenerate
genealogy	progeny
congenital	genus
progenitor	genocide
genteel	genesis

If a person is trying to figure out how his _____
                                                    1

will he necessarily must take into account that unit of heredity, the

_____. This would be particularly true of any

2

_____ concerned with family planning whose

3

prime consideration was the elimination of _____

4

defects.

ANSWERS: 1—progeny; 2—gene; 3—progenitor; 4—congenital.

PORT
PORT

From the Latin *portare* meaning "to carry"

ONE can carry an object, a thought, an emotion. One can bring things in or send them away or bear the weight of them. Words that come from the root "port" are indeed versatile.

Portfolios are in common use today; the portmanteau, a large, carry-all bag or suitcase is not often spoken of any longer. Lewis Carroll, the author of *Alice in Wonderland,* ascribed still another meaning to "portmanteau" when he used it for words that he invented by combining parts of other words such as "slithy," which he made up from "lithe" and "slimy."

The following word parts will be combined with the root in this unit to make new words. Use this list as a reference to find the meaning of words in this unit.

PREFIXES
de—down or from
im—into
re—back or again
sup—under or beneath
trans—across
ex—out or from

SUFFIXES
er—doer or dealer in
able—capable of
age—place
ment—result or means
tion—action or condition

ROOT AS AFFIX
folio—sheet or leaf

context

clues

DIRECTIONS: Pronounce each word in the left hand column and read aloud the sentences in the right hand column. On the basis of context clues in the sentences, fill in the blank space to make a correct definition.

porter

POR–tuhr

- If your suitcase is heavy, ask a porter to carry it for you when you get to the train.
- In Africa, porters have to be hired by safari managers because trucks cannot go everywhere

237

and because some equipment still has to be carried by people.

1. A porter is _____

_____

portable

PORT–uh–bl

- The portable hair dryer was a great invention for girls who like to swim but don't have time to sit in a beauty shop between the time they get out of the water and the time they go out on a date.
- What was advertised as a portable television set is actually much too heavy to carry around, so we keep it permanently on a stand in the living room.

2. Portable means _____

_____

portage

PORT–ij

- If the supplies are properly wrapped and stored, they are easy to handle when you have to portage your canoe from Lake Minnehaha to Ojibway River.
- The Boy Scout troop thought of earning money by setting up a portage service for tourists who could not manage their own equipment on the trek from one river to the other of the woodlands trip.

3. Portage means _____

_____

deportment

duh–PORT–ment

- Mary Lou's deportment was so bad she got an F on her report card because her constant jumping up and talking annoyed the rest of the class.
- Young ladies in finishing school used to learn deportment so they could always conduct themselves in the proper manner under any conditions.

4. Deportment means _____

_____

deport

duh–PORT

- The government tried to deport the proven Mafia kingpin as an undesirable alien.
- People who enter the country illegally can expect to be deported if they are caught.

    5. Deport means _____

_____

import

im–PORT

- Tobacco does not grow in England, so all cigarette tobacco has to be imported.
- Sylvester made a fortune importing Panama hats and selling them in Kansas.

    6. Import means _____

_____

report

ruh–PORT

- An accurate report of the accident was difficult to obtain because each witness had a different view of what happened.
- The general's aide was entrusted with the job of writing the report of the troop's withdrawal from the campus.

    7. A report is _____

_____

supporter

suh–PORT–uhr

- Supporters of the presidential candidate worked long hours to assure his election.
- If you are a supporter of guaranteed income for poor families, you should write your congressman telling him to vote for legislation that will assure that money is allotted.

    8. A supporter is one who _____

_____

transportation

trans–puhr–TAY–shuhn

- The Secretary of Transportation administers all roads, waterways, and airways because all of them are used for carrying people and supplies.
- Cheap transportation of their finished product has led many manufacturers to locate their plants on the canal that connects with the gulf.

    9. Transportation means _____

_____

portfolio

port–FO–lee–o

■ Mr. Hodgkins put the papers in his portfolio and walked out of the meeting, showing his displeasure with the merger plans.
■ The teacher told his students that when they turned in papers at the end of the term, each student had to provide himself with a separate portfolio.

10. A portfolio is _____

_____

exporter

ek–SPORT–er

■ Mr. Jones was an exporter specializing in electrical appliances that could not be made in Venezuela.
■ Cuba was formerly an exporter of huge amounts of sugar to the United States.

11. An exporter is one who _____

_____

ANSWERS

1. *A* <u>*porter*</u> *is someone who carries baggage for passengers or does errands for pay.*
2. <u>*Portable*</u> *means able to be carried.*
3. <u>*Portage*</u> *means to carry boats and supplies overland from one navigable body of water to another.*
4. <u>*Deportment*</u> *means behavior or the manner of conducting oneself.*
5. <u>*Deport*</u> *means to banish or send away from a country.*
6. <u>*Import*</u> *means to bring goods into one country or place from another.*
7. *A* <u>*report*</u> *is a record of proceedings.*
8. *A* <u>*supporter*</u> *is one who upholds someone or something, or that which bears up.*
9. <u>*Transportation*</u> *means the act or business of moving passengers and goods.*
10. *A* <u>*portfolio*</u> *is a flat or small case for carrying papers.*
11. *An* <u>*exporter*</u> *is one who sends things abroad.*

true-false

DIRECTIONS: Read each sentence carefully and decide whether it is true or false. If it is true, put a T in the space at the right. If it is false, write in an F.

1. Portage refers to the occupation of carrying baggage for passengers at a train station.   1._____

2. If a package can be carried it is said to be portable. 2._____
3. A word that tells how boys and girls behave themselves at parties is deportment. 3._____
4. If one of our citizens were an excellent scientist, the government would probably deport him. 4._____
5. A person who sends surfboards to Africa is an importer. 5._____
6. A report is a record of proceedings. 6._____
7. Transportation is the act or business of moving goods and passengers. 7._____
8. A flat case for carrying papers is a portfolio. 8._____
9. An exporter is in the business of bringing marijuana into the country. 9._____
10. One who upholds the Constitution of the United States is a supporter of the Constitution. 10._____

ANSWERS: 1—F; 2—T; 3—T; 4—F; 5—F; 6—T; 7—T; 8—T; 9—F; 10—T.

fill in the blanks

DIRECTIONS: Fill in the blank in each sentence with the appropriate word from among the following choices.

porter   portable
portage   deportment
deport   import
report   transportation
supporter   portfolio
exporter

1. One whose occupation is to carry baggage for passengers is called a

   _____.

2. An _____ is one who sends ties and shirts

   to other countries.

3. A flat case for carrying papers is called a _____.

4. The Simpson Company, whose business is moving passengers and

goods, appealed to the _____ secretary

to permit a rate increase.

5. If a statue is _____ it can be carried.

6. To _____ is to banish a person.

7. _____ is another word used to describe

people's manners and general behavior.

8. When boats and supplies are carried overland from one navigable body

of water to another it is called _____.

ANSWERS: 1—porter; 2—exporter; 3—portfolio; 4—transportation; 5—porta-ble; 6—deport; 7—deportment; 8—portage.

words in use

DIRECTIONS: Fill in the blank in each sentence with the appropriate word from among the following choices.

portfolio   portage
deportment   portable
import   transportation
deport   porter

The _____ carried the passenger's

1

_____, but the other piece of baggage was not

2

considered _____ for it weighed twelve–hundred

3

pounds.

ANSWERS: 1—porter; 2—portfolio; 3—portable.

affixes at work

DIRECTIONS: Add your own words to the blanks at the bottom of the diagram.

deport**ment**

investment
(the act of investing)

atonement
(the act of atoning for or asking forgiveness)

government
(the act of governing)

replacement
(the act of replacing)

abridgement
(the act of making smaller)

judgment
(the act of judging)

enjoyment
(the act of enjoying)

Suffix: *ment* means "the act or process of"

(ex)port

example
(person or thing that serves as a pattern)

exasperate
(incite or inflame to anger)

excavate
(to form a hole or cavity)

exceed
(greater than or superior to)

excise
(to remove by cutting)

exclude
(to shut out)

Prefix: *ex* means "out of or from; free from or without"

SIGN
SEYE-n

From the Latin *signum* or *signatus* meaning "mark," "sign" or "token"

THE FIRST storekeeper who put a symbol outside his shop announcing who he was and what he sold began modern advertising—and was the forerunner of gigantic and elaborate electric neon displays.

All signs, however, are not material objects. A lifted eyebrow or a smile are signs, too. The English words coming from this Latin root, then, have developed both objective and subjective concepts.

The following word parts will be combined with the root in this unit to make new words. Use this list as a reference to find the meaning of words in this unit.

PREFIXES
in—into
de—down or from
en—in or into
as—to or toward
re—back or again
con—with or together

SUFFIXES
al—of or belonging to
tory—suitable
ure—condition or act of
et—little
ant—that which
fy—make
ize—act or manner
ate—product of
tion—action or condition
ia—pertaining to
ment—condition

context
clues

DIRECTIONS: Pronounce each word in the left hand column and read aloud the sentences in the right hand column. On the basis of context clues in the sentences, fill in the blank space to make a correct definition.

245

signal

SIG–nuhl

- The colors of traffic lights are so well known they constitute a signal anywhere in the world.
- A hood up on a car by the side of the road is a signal of distress on the highway.

1. A signal is _____

_____

signatory

SIG–nuh–tor–ee

- The signatory countries to the NATO treaty agree to military obligations should any of them become involved in a war.
- If you are a signatory for a friend's loan from the bank, you become liable for his car payments if he cannot meet them.

2. A signatory is _____

_____

signature

SIG–nuh–chuhr

- John Hancock was the first man to put his signature to the Constitution of the United States.
- Your signature is all that is needed for a loan from this company.

3. A signature is _____

_____

signet

SIG–nit

- The signet on the official's ring was pressed into soft wax that sealed the letter so that the recipient knew before opening the letter who had sent it.
- Herkimer's father gave him a signet ring with the family crest as a birthday present.

4. A signet is _____

_____

insignificant

in–sig–NIF–uh–kuhnt

- Mervin was not only small, but he also looked insignificant.
- Her contribution to the class was so small as to be insignificant.

5. Insignificant means _____

_____

signify

SIG–nuh–feye

- Everybody who agrees, signify by saying "aye."
- The flag, a white martini glass on a blue background, signifies that drinks are being served on board the yacht.

6. Signify means _____

_____

signalize

SIG–nuh–leyes

- Madama Montague's diamonds signalized her husband's wealth.
- The extra large trailer with leather furniture, soft rugs, bar, tape and stereo equipment, and other trappings signalized the dressing room of the movie star known for his love of luxury.

7. Signalize means _____

_____

design

di–ZEYEN

- If you want to design buildings, you have to study drafting and take architectural courses.
- The design of football uniforms has changed as the game developed as well as when new fabrics and materials were developed.

8. Design means _____

_____

designate

DEZ–ig–nate

- The road will be designated a dead end as soon as the sign comes from the county road department workshop.
- Horace designated Homer to be his alternate in case he was not able to attend the club meeting on the night of the important vote.

9. To designate is to _____

_____

insignia

in–SIG–nee–uh

- A man's military unit is evident by the insignia he wears on his uniform.
- Boy Scouts wear insignia showing what rank they have attained and which badges they have earned.

10. An insignia is _____

_____

ensign

EN–sin

- The pirate ensign flying from the main mast struck fear in the heart of every merchant sailor who spied it at sea.
- The dove is an ensign of peace.

11. An ensign is _____

_____

assignation

as–ig–NAY–shuhn

- Myrtle sneaked out of the house because if her father ever discovered she was on her way to an assignation with Harold he would have prevented her from leaving.
- The assignation arranged, both Simpson and Marlene went about their usual routines until it was time for them to meet.

12. An assignation is _____

_____

resign

ri–ZEYEN

- The mayor was forced to resign when graft was discovered in his administration.
- Student power forced the dean to resign.

13. Resign means _____

_____

assign

uh–SEYEN

- If you are not willing to be assigned to classes, you will have to choose them quickly so that registration can proceed.
- The private was assigned guard duty while the sergeant went off to the NCO club.

14. Assign means _____

_____

assignment

uh–SEYEN–ment

- The assignment is to find out how many beans are in the glass beaker.
- Miss McDivot gave the assignment for the next day just before the bell rang.

15. Assignment means _____

_____

consign

kuhn–SEYEN

■ This company will consign the goods to you only upon receipt of a satisfactory financial statement.
■ The ship was consigned to another nation as payment of a national debt.

16. Consign means _____

_____

ANSWERS

1. A *signal* is a sign or agreed upon means of communication that is used to convey information.
2. A *signatory* is one bound by the terms of a signed document.
3. A *signature* is the written, stamped, or inscribed name of a person.
4. A *signet* is a seal, especially one used to seal private letters or to mark official use.
5. *Insignificant* means unimportant; trifling matters or details.
6. *Signify* means to make known or to communicate.
7. *Signalize* means to make conspicuous; to point out with care.
8. *Design* means to make, draw, or prepare.
9. To *designate* is to indicate or make recognizable by some mark, sign or name.
10. An *insignia* is a badge, emblem or other mark of office or distinction.
11. An *ensign* is a flag or banner or emblem.
12. An *assignation* is an appointment for a meeting, especially a rendezvous or tryst.
13. *Resign* means to give up or to surrender.
14. *Assign* means to allot, appoint, or mark out, as a position.
15. *Assignment* means anything fixed or specified.
16. *Consign* means to give or hand over formally.

fill in the blanks

DIRECTIONS: Fill in the blank in each sentence with the appropriate word from among the following choices.

insignificant   signature
signify   ensign
assignation   consign
designate   resign
signal   insignia
signatory   signet

1. A _____ means a sign or means of agreed

   upon communication.

2. If you want to borrow money, you need another person to be a

   _____ for the loan.

3. An _____ is a flag or a banner.

4. A _____ is a person's name which he

   puts at the end of a letter.

5. _____ means unimportant.

6. To make known by words or signs is to _____.

7. To indicate or make recognizable by some mark is to

   _____.

8. _____ refers to badges and emblems, usually

   indicating an office.

9. To give up or surrender is to _____.

10. If you _____ something you give it, or

    hand it over formally.

ANSWERS: 1—signal; 2—signatory; 3—ensign; 4—signature; 5—insignificant; 6—signify; 7—designate; 8—insignia; 9—resign; 10—consign.

matching exercise

DIRECTIONS: Write the appropriate letter from the right hand column in the space next to each number so that the numbered words are defined.

_____ 1. signal	**a.** to give or hand over formally
_____ 2. signatory	**b.** a badge or emblem used as a mark of office
_____ 3. signature	**c.** give up, surrender
_____ 4. signet	**d.** to indicate or make recognizable by a mark
_____ 5. insignificant	**e.** a sign or means of communication
_____ 6. signify	**f.** bound by the terms of a signed document
_____ 7. designate	**g.** a seal
_____ 8. insignia	**h.** a written name of a person
_____ 9. resign	**i.** to make known by words or signs
_____10. consign	**j.** unimportant
	k. to appoint

ANSWERS: 1—e; 2—f; 3—h; 4—g; 5—j; 6—i; 7—d; 8—b; 9—c; 10—a.

scrambled

words

DIRECTIONS: Unscramble the following words. They are defined in parentheses.

1. fisingy: _____
    (to make known by words or signs)

2. ginest: _____
    (a seal)

3. ganils: _____
    (a sign or means of communication)

4. genris: _____
    (to give up)

5. gainsini: _____
    (a badge or emblem)

ANSWERS: 1—signify; 2—signet; 3—signal; 4—resign; 5—insignia.

"Extinction is when you don't learn to live in man's environment."

VITA

VIVA

VEYE-tuh

VEE-vuh

From the Latin *vita* meaning "life"   From the Latin *vivus* meaning "alive" or "living"

Both words are also related to the Latin *vivere* meaning "to live"

A CULTURE is a way of life. It is therefore only fitting that words formed from this root be applicable to many aspects of life—everything from science to descriptions of how people look and live.

> *La dolce vita* means "the good life" and usually refers to excessive self-indulgence. It was exemplified in a movie of the same name.

The following word parts will be combined with the root in this unit to make new words. Use this list as a reference to find the meaning of words in this unit.

ROOTS AS AFFIXES
parous—to give birth to
sec(t)—to cut
scope—watch or sight
amin(e)—ammonia

SUFFIXES
id—marked by
ous—given to or full of action
arium—place relating to
ity—state or quality or condition
al—act or process or doer
tion—action or condition
a—pertaining to
ic—dealing with or like

PREFIX
anti—against or hostile towards

context

clues

DIRECTIONS: Pronounce each word in the left hand column and read aloud the sentences in the right hand column. On the basis of context clues in the sentences, fill in the blank space to make a correct definition.

253

vivid

VIV–id

- Mary Ann has such a vivid personality she is the natural leader among her friends.
- If you have a vivid imagination you will be a good reader, because you can visualize what the author describes.

1. Vivid means _____

_____

vivacious

vi–VAY–shuhs

- Henry's vivacious manner always gave a lift to everyone he met.
- The most vivacious teacher was in the physical education department, thus making a good case for emphasis on sports to keep a person healthy and on-the-go.

2. Vivacious means _____

_____

vivarium

veye–VAIR–ee–uhm

- The managers of the vivarium got salt water for the shark to live in and were able to develop a humid climate for the orchids to grow in, but they had difficulty regulating a climate cold enough for the polar bear.
- Every greenhouse is actually a vivarium.

3. A vivarium is _____

_____

viviparous

veye–VIP–uhr–uhs

- Humans are viviparous animals and babies immediately enter a strange environment when they are born.
- Among the animals that are not viviparous are chickens and alligators.

4. Viviparous means _____

_____

antivivisection

an–ti–viv–uh–SEK–shun

- Antivivisection laws in many states have inhibited medical study and surgical advances while not actually preventing cruelty to animals as supposed.
- Antivivisectionists should also be opposed to using humans in surgical experimentation.

5. Antivivisection means _____

_____

vital

VEYE–tuhl

- The heart performs what is probably the most vital function because the circulation of fresh blood is necessary to life.
- The census bureau concerned with vital statistics sends annual reports of births and deaths to the federal government.

6. Vital means _____

_____

vitality

veye–TAL–i–tee

- Mrs. Smith had such great vitality that she ran a mile daily, even though she was 85 years old last month.
- If you keep your body healthy and your mind active, you should also have great vitality.

7. Vitality means _____

_____

vitamin

VEYE–tuh–min

- Vitamins are prescribed for daily consumption by both children and adults who wish to stay healthy.
- Vitamins are important in an age where packaged or dehydrated foods are not often nutritious.

8. A vitamin is _____

_____

vitascope

VEYE–tuh–skope

- Sixty years ago you might ask your date to look at a vitascope with you and marvel at the way pictures moved.
- After you take the movies and have them developed, set up the vitascope so we can all see pictures of your trip.

9. A vitascope is _____

_____

vita

VEYE–tuh

■ The personnel manager asked Hubert to send in his vita so that information about him would be on file.
■ When you write a letter of application, it is customary to include a vita so that the prospective employer will know what other jobs you have held, your age, education, etc.

10. A vita is _____

_____

vivification

viv–uh–fi–KAY–shuhn

■ The mad scientist attempted vivification of his wax creations by transplanting human organs into them.
■ Vivification made the wooden Pinocchio into a real boy.

11. Vivification means _____

_____

ANSWERS

1. _Vivid_ means full of life, or presenting the appearance of life.
2. _Vivacious_ means lively or animated; sprightly.
3. A _vivarium_ is a laboratory where animals and plants are kept alive under conditions simulating their natural environment.
4. _Viviparous_ means bringing forth living young rather than eggs.
5. _Antivivisection_ means opposed to cutting into or dissecting a living animal or human.
6. _Vital_ means necessary for life.
7. _Vitality_ means exuberant physical strength or mental vigor.
8. A _vitamin_ is an organic substance essential to normal metabolism and health. (_Word was coined by C. Funk_)
9. A _vitascope_ is a kind of motion picture projector.
10. A _vita_ is a brief biographical resume of one's career. (_Another term for curriculum vitae._)
11. _Vivification_ means to give life to or animate; to enliven.

true-false

DIRECTIONS: Read each sentence carefully and decide whether it is true or false. If it is true, put a T in the space at the right. If it is false, write in an F.

1. Vivacious means lively, full of life or high spirited.   1._____
2. If a color is light or pale we say it is vivid.   2._____ .
3. A chicken, which lays eggs for reproduction, is an example
   of a viviparous animal.   3._____
4. If you are against cutting up animals for experimentation you
   are an antivivisectionist.   4._____
5. Water is vital for human life.   5._____
6. If one has exuberant physical or mental vigor we say he has
   vitality.   6._____
7. The word part *vita* in the vitamin refers to a life–giving force.   7._____
8. Another name for a moving picture projector is a vitascope.   8._____
9. A vivarium is a steam bath.   9._____
10. When we use vita as a word rather than a root it is something
    in written form.   10._____

ANSWERS: 1—T; 2—F; 3—F; 4—T; 5—T; 6—T; 7—T; 8—T; 9—F; 10—T.

matching exercise

DIRECTIONS: Write the appropriate letter from the right hand column in the space next to each number so that the numbered words are defined.

_____ 1. vivacious
_____ 2. vivid
_____ 3. viviparous
_____ 4. antivivisection

_____ 5. vitality

a. revival, restoration of life
b. a life history; autobiography
c. necessary to life
d. exuberant physical strength or mental vigor
e. laboratory where plants and animals are kept under conditions simulating their natural environment

(*more*)

--------- 6. vitamin

--------- 7. vital

--------- 8. vivarium

--------- 9. vita

---------10. vivification

f. to bear young live

g. presenting the appearance of life

h. lively; animated

i. a philosophy that is against experimental cutting or dissecting of living organisms

j. a group of organic food substances necessary to normal health

ANSWERS: 1—h; 2—g; 3—f; 4—i; 5—d; 6—j; 7—c; 8—e; 9—b; 10—a.

fill in the blanks

DIRECTIONS: Fill in the blank in each sentence with the appropriate word from among the following choices.

vita

vitascope

vitality

vivacious

vivarium

vital

vitamins

vivification

viviparous

vivid

antivivisectionist

1. _____ means lively or animated.

2. If something is full of life or presents the appearance of life we say it is

    _____.

3. _____ animals give birth to live young.

4. An _____ is against the cutting of animals

    for experimental purposes.

5. If something is necessary to life it is said to be _____.

6. _____ means that someone has exuberant physical strength or mental vigor.

7. _____ are a group of organic substances essential to normal health.

8. Another name for a motion picture projector is a _____.

9. A _____ is a laboratory where animals and plants are kept alive under conditions simulating their natural environment.

10. _____ is a word that describes a resume or short autobiography of an individual.

ANSWERS: 1—vivacious; 2—vivid; 3—viviparous; 4—antivivisectionist; 5—vital; 6—vitality; 7—vitamins; 8—vitascope; 9—vivarium; 10—vita.

POSTTEST

DIRECTIONS: In the space next to each number, write the letter that correctly completes the statement.

_____ 1. Insurance companies often advise young people to plan for their retirement by
    a. purchasing an annuity.
    b. observing their anniversary date with meaningful gifts.
    c. purchasing an annualist.
    d. making triennial visits to a doctor for checkups.

_____ 2. Which of the following shows the proper chronology
    a. The Revolutionary War, the Civil War, the Spanish-American War.
    b. The French and Indian War, the Korean War, the Civil War.
    c. The Vietnam War, the Russian Revolution, the Spanish Civil War.
    d. The War of 1812, the Crusades, the French Revolution.

_____ 3. The lieutenant in war movies always tells his men to synchronize their watches so that
    a. they can each arrive at the right spot at the right time.
    b. he can show off his wristwatch.
    c. he can utter the famous line in a new way.
    d. they can each be the subject of a closeup shot.

_____ 4. A signet is
    a. a small swan.
    b. a tiny signal flag.
    c. a small seal.
    d. a miniaturized transistor.

_____ 5. People who refuse to consider any elements in the universe except man may be called
    a. eccentric.
    b. right.

    c. anthropocentric.
    d. antithetic.

_____ 6. If you leave your money to a philanthropic organization, you can be sure it will be used to
    a. further the smuggling of drugs.
    b. give annual gratuities to all people named "Phil."
    c. help incite riots.
    d. help people in need.

_____ 7. During the French Revolution, the guillotine was used for
    a. capitalistic enterprises.
    b. hungry workers.
    c. militant peasants.
    d. decapitating aristocrats.

_____ 8. Vivacious people are usually
    a. unhappy.
    b. melancholy.
    c. pleasant.
    d. dejected.

_____ 9. If you drink to excess you will most likely end up
    a. full.
    b. drunk.
    c. slimmer.
    d. healthier.

_____10. Sylvester's wife yelled at him to stop the _____ hammering.
    a. incessant
    b. decadent
    c. procedural
    d. decession

_____11. According to military rank, the person who would precede a major in a parade is a
    a. lieutenant colonel.
    b. private.
    c. lieutenant.
    d. sergeant.

———12. When the enemy capitulates, we will draw up a
    a. division of labor.
    b. peace treaty.
    c. table of organization.
    d. map.

———13. You would consult a genealogist if you were
    a. searching for lost gold.
    b. anxious to cure a painful boil.
    c. studying genes and chromosomes.
    d. looking for a family crest.

———14. The grade on a report card that tells parents how their children behave in class is
    a. for deportment.
    b. for export only.
    c. portage.
    d. portable.

———15. A widower might be guilty of
    a. uxoricide.
    b. transportation.
    c. avicide.
    d. transmigration.

ANSWERS: 1—a; 2—a; 3—a; 4—c; 5—c; 6—d; 7—d; 8—c; 9—b; 10—a; 11—a; 12—b; 13—d; 14—a; 15—a.

chapter 6

Words About Science

PRETEST

DIRECTIONS: In the space next to each number, write the letter that correctly completes the statement.

_____ 1. When Mr. Winsome was presented an aster he
   a. had it developed.
   b. put it in water.
   c. looked through it.
   d. took off in it.

_____ 2. When a doctor wants to know if a growth is cancerous he orders a
   a. biogenesis.
   b. biopsy.
   c. antibiotic.
   d. symbiosis.

_____ 3. Winthrop had a persistent itch so he consulted
   a. a dermatologist.
   b. a carnelian.
   c. incarceration.
   d. a dermatopsy.

_____ 4. Agraphia deals with the
   a. inability to write.
   b. inability to listen.
   c. lie detector.
   d. mirror writing.

_____ 5. The science of handwriting is called
        a. chirography.
        b. laryngographia.
        c. macrographia.
        d. graphology.

_____ 6. The insotonic scale
        a. was hard to remove from the fish.
        b. sounded strange to Jane.
        c. always indicated exact weight.
        d. assures equal pay for equal work.

_____ 7. Given the four choices below, Lucite is a substance best suited for
        a. seasoning.
        b. clothing.
        c. windshields.
        d. planting.

_____ 8. A pyromaniac feels he must have
        a. skates.
        b. money.
        c. matches.
        d. paint.

_____ 9. Verbal pyrotechnics can best be described as
        a. sparkling rhetoric.
        b. correct enunciation.
        c. shyness.
        d. soundly constructed.

_____10. If a nerve or nerves are inflamed, the condition
is called
        a. neurotomy.
        b. neuroblast.
        c. neuritis.
        d. neurotoid.

_____11. A shape similar to that of a nerve is called
        a. neurotomy.
        b. neuritis.
        c. neurotic.
        d. neurotoid.

_____12. A person who is psychic is supposed to pos-
sess a
        a. mental illness.
        b. psychodrama.

        c. supernormal faculty.
        d. high threshold.

_____13. Something that is psychogenic originates
        a. in the genes.
        b. in the mind.
        c. in the ocean.
        d. in the body.

_____14. Resonance is a desirable quality in
        a. where people live.
        b. a singer.
        c. a plumber.
        d. what people eat.

_____15. John felt antipathy toward Humbert, so his
best course of action was to
        a. embrace him.
        b. avoid him.
        c. find a mutual friend.
        d. disclose the secret.

_____16. If you suspect pathodontia, you should
        a. make an appointment with a dentist.
        b. call the people immediately.
        c. step on it.
        d. report it to an administrator at school.

_____17. Science fiction and horror movies often make
use of the principle of
        a. telergy.
        b. telecourse.
        c. telethermometers.
        d. teleology.

_____18. People who say the same thing simultaneously
sometimes claim they communicate by
        a. telegony.
        b. teletype.
        c. telepathy.
        d. telemetry.

ANSWERS: 1—b; 2—b; 3—a; 4—a; 5—b; 6—b; 7—c; 8—c; 9—a; 10—c; 11—d; 12—c; 13—b; 14—b; 15—b; 16—a; 17—a; 18—c.

"Say something in computerese."

AST   ASTR
AST   *AS-truh*

From the Greek *aster* meaning "star"

RUSSIA has its cosmonauts who travel through the cosmos; the United States has its astronauts who journey among the stars. Man has long felt an affinity for the stars. They are believed to influence his life; he uses them for navigation; he writes poems about them; he marvels at them. Never mind the scientific data that tells such unromantic things about them as their unbelievably high temperatures or distances so great they must be measured in light years. Stars continue to fascinate man and to be included, in varied forms, in his vocabulary.

The following word parts will be combined with the root in this unit to make new words. Use this list as a reference to find the meaning of words in this unit.

ROOTS AS AFFIXES
meter—measure
labe—to take
naut—sailor
nomy—system of laws

SUFFIXES
oid—shaped like
isk—small
ic—dealing with or like
logy—science or study of

PREFIX
dis—separation from or reversal

context
clues

DIRECTIONS: Pronounce each word in the left hand column and read aloud the sentences in the right hand column. On the basis of context clues in the sentences, fill in the blank space to make a correct definition.

disaster

diz–AS–tuhr

■ A typhoon was the latest natural disaster to hit Japan and it caused extensive flooding of low lands.

267

■ Seven critics called the play a disaster, and it closed after a week.

1. A disaster is _____

_____

astronometer

as–truh–NOM–i–tuhr

■ According to the measurements made by the most finely tuned astronometer, the newest star discovered by man is several light years away.
■ Since the astronometer was refined it can give more accurate readings to show that the universe is much larger than we thought it was.

2. An astronometer is _____

_____

asteroid

AS–tuh–roid

■ There are dozens of asteroids among the planets revolving around the sun.
■ Some asteroids are so small they have only recently been discovered because previously they seemed like stars.

3. Asteroids are _____

_____

asterisk

AS–tuh–risk

■ The asterisk is a symbol developed by printers to call attention to something important.
■ The asterisk on a typewriter keyboard is easy to spot because it has more points than any other special mark.

4. An asterisk is _____

_____

aster

AS–tuhr

■ Asters are desirable for gardens because they bloom late and thus make the garden look pretty for a longer time.
■ When asters add their colorful bloom to the fields, you know autumn has arrived.

5. An aster is _____

_____

NAME: _____

astrolabe

AS–truh–lab

■ Columbus had an astrolabe with him to aid navigation, but frequent cloudy nights hid the stars and hindered its use.
■ The astrolabe is an indispensable instrument for celestial navigation.

6. As astrolable is _____

astronaut

AS–truh–not

■ If astronauts ever travel to stars, rather than to planets, they will literally live up to their name.
■ The United States has aquanauts, who pioneer in under-water exploration, as well as astronauts, who pioneer space travel.

7. An astronaut is _____

astronautics

as–truh–NOT–iks

■ Frobisher joined a firm specializing in astronautics because he was deeply interested in space exploration.
■ One of the newest offshoots of physics and engineering in space-age science is astronautics.

8. Astronautics is _____

astronomy

uh–STRON–uh–mee

■ Students fascinated by planets and stars will often spend extra time at the telescopes in the astronomy laboratory.
■ The science of astronomy began with pre-historic star gazers, perhaps out with their dates.

9. Astronomy is _____

astrology

uh–STROL–uh–jee

■ An astrologist will cast your horoscope for the coming year when you tell him your birth date so he can check the stars at the time of your birth.

■ If you follow the rules of astrology, your life will be directed by the stars.

10. Astrology is _____

_____

ANSWERS

1. A _disaster_ is a calamitous event or one causing great damage.
2. An _astronometer_ is a device for measuring the distance of stars.
3. _Asteroids_ are star-like, tiny heavenly bodies.
4. An _asterisk_ is a starlike mark used in printing.
5. An _aster_ is a plant with a star-shaped flower.
6. An _astrolabe_ is an instrument used in navigation that calculates the altitude of stars.
7. An _astronaut_ is one who travels through space.
8. _Astronautics_ is the science of construction of space vehicles.
9. _Astronomy_ is the study of heavenly bodies.
10. _Astrology_ is a method of predicting the future by means of the stars and heavenly bodies.

matching exercise

DIRECTIONS: Write the appropriate letter from the right hand column in the space next to each number so that the numbered words are defined.

_____ 1. disaster

_____ 2. astronometer

_____ 3. asteroid

_____ 4. asterisk
_____ 5. astrolabe
_____ 6. astronaut
_____ 7. astronomy

_____ 8. astrology

a. the pseudo–science of prediction by means of the stars
b. one who navigates or travels through space
c. an instrument used in navigation by calculating star altitude
d. the study of heavenly bodies
e. star like; a very small heavenly body
f. a starlike mark used in printing
g. a device for measuring the distance of the stars
h. misfortune
i. the science of construction of space vehicles

ANSWERS: 1—h; 2—g; 3—e; 4—f; 5—c; 6—b; 7—d; 8—a.

true-false

DIRECTIONS: Read each sentence carefully and decide whether it is true or false. If it is true, put a T in the space at the right. If it is false, write in an F.

1. Asterisk is a disease. 1._____
2. Disaster means misfortune. 2._____
3. An astronaut is one who navigates or travels through space. 3._____
4. The pseudo–science of prediction by means of the stars is called astronomy. 4._____
5. The astrolabe is an instrument to detect submarines. 5._____
6. A plant with a star shaped flower is the aster. 6._____
7. Asteroid is a mineral found near volcanoes. 7._____
8. Astrology refers to the study of plants with star shaped flowers. 8._____
9. A star shaped mark used in printing is the asterisk. 9._____
10. The astronometer is a device for measuring the distance of stars. 10._____

ANSWERS: 1—F; 2—T; 3—T; 4—F; 5—F; 6—T; 7—F; 8—F; 9—T; 10—T.

fill in the blanks

DIRECTIONS: Fill in the blank in each sentence with the appropriate word from among the following choices.

astronomy   astronaut
astronautics   astronometer
asteroid   disaster
asterisk   astrolabe
aster   astrology

1. The pseudo–science of prediction by means of the stars is called

   _____.

2. _____ means misfortune.

3. A device for measuring the distance of the stars is a _____.

4. An _____ is a very small heavenly body.

5. An _____ is used by a printer to refer to something at the bottom of the page.

6. The _____ is a plant with a star shaped flower.

7. The _____ is an instrument used in navigation to calculate star altitude.

8. One who navigates or travels through space is an _____.

9. _____ is the study of heavenly bodies.

10. The _____ industry would be anxious to hire space-minded engineers.

ANSWERS: 1—astrology; 2—disaster; 3—astronometer; 4—asteroid; 5—asterisk; 6—aster; 7—astrolabe; 8—astronaut; 9—astronomy; 10—astronautics.

BIO
BEYE-o

From the Greek *bios* meaning "life"

It is difficult to talk about life itself, especially in its scientific aspects, without using several words based on the root *bio*. It appears in common words such as "biography" and "antibiotic." And it is a part of great numbers of specialized words. Some of the latter are in the following list.

The following word parts will be combined with the root in this unit to make new words. Use this list as a reference to find the meaning of words in this unit.

PREFIXES
auto—self
anti—against or hostile
sym—same or like
ex—out or from

SUFFIXES
sis—condition of
ic—dealing with or like
cence—act or state or condition

ROOTS AS AFFIXES
logy—study or science of
graph—word or write
cide—kill or cut down
sphere—ball or globe
chemistry—study of chemical reactions
opsy—appearance
lumin—light
taxis—arrangement
gen—birth
dyn—power

context
clues

DIRECTIONS: Pronounce each word in the left hand column and read aloud the sentences in the right hand column. On the basis of context clues in the sentences, fill in the blank space to make a correct definition.

biology

beye–OL–uh–jee

- Merton's life-long fascination with plants and animals led him to major in biology at college.
- Many think that the secret of the beginning of life may be discovered in the biology laboratory.

1. Biology is _____

_____

biography

beye–OG–ruh–fee

- When you read Morrison's biography of Columbus, you will marvel at the navigational ability of the man who discovered America.
- The biography of Marie Curie, discoverer of radium, by her daughter, Eve, contains many personal family memories and anecdotes.

2. A biography is _____

_____

autobiography

aw–tuh–beye–OG–ruh–fee

- How can you write your autobiography when your life is just beginning?
- In his autobiography, George Grubetz is unflattering to everyone but himself.

3. An autobiography is _____

_____

biochemistry

beye–o–KEM–uh–stree

- One chapter in the biochemistry book is about the chemical processes of reproduction.
- Biochemistry is required of medical students because it combines two subjects of use to the future doctor.

4. Biochemistry is _____

_____

biopsy

BEYE–op–see

- The surgeon did a biopsy on the patient to determine whether the tumor was diseased.
- Before treatment is decided upon, tissue-thin sections of the biopsy will be studied under the microscope.

5. A biopsy is _____

_____

biocide

BEYE–uh–seyed

- This biocide in a spray can kill most garden pests.
- Be sure to read the label carefully before using a biocide to destroy termites.

6. A biocide is _____

_____

biosphere

BEYE–uh–sfear

- Future space probes may find forms of life outside the biosphere.
- Virus could conceivably live in the deepest oceans and at the outer limits of the biosphere.

7. Biosphere means _____

_____

antibiotics

ant–eye–beye–OT–iks

- Antibiotics work by killing the bacteria that contain diseases.
- Antibiotics are grown like plants in laboratories.

8. Antibiotic means _____

_____

bioluminescence

beye–o–loo–muh–
  NES–nts

- The firefly is one of the insects which uses bioluminescence both as a defense and as a way of attracting mates.
- A faint glow sometimes seen at night on the ocean is the bioluminescence of plankton.

9. Bioluminescence means _____

_____

symbiosis

sim–beye–O–suhs

- The small fish attracts food to the Man-of-War and then eats unused bits; thus, the two animals exist in a state of symbiosis.
- The tapeworm is a pure parasite which harms its host, so symbiosis is not the case here.

10. Symbiosis means _____

_____

biotaxis

BEYE–o–taks–uhs

- Anthropologists study biotaxis so they can determine which classification a tribe they are studying belongs to.
- A study of biotaxis is likely to leave you classifying everybody you meet.

11. Biotaxis means _____

_____

biogen

BEYE–o–juhn

- If you can see a biogen under the microscope, you have seen one of the most basic units of life.
- A cell lives because of its biogen.

12. A biogen is _____

_____

bioexology

beye–o–x–OL–o–jee

- Anybody who studies biology also studies something about bioexology so he can determine how plants and animals coexist.
- Animals require plants for both food and oxygen, so bioexology is important because it determines how these two different groups of living things can get along together.

13. Bioexology means _____

_____

biodynamics

BEYE–o–deye–NAM–iks

- Early philosophers believed that biodynamics was the key to human life because the special force represented was measurable.
- Biodynamics was believed to move every aspect of a person's life.

14. Biodynamics is _____

_____

ANSWERS

1. *Biology is the study of plants and animals.*
2. *A biography is the life history of a particular person.*
3. *An autobiography is one's own life story written by himself.*

4. *Biochemistry* is the study of the chemical process of living things.
5. A *biopsy* is the removal of living tissue for examination.
6. A *biocide* is a chemical that kills pests.
7. *Biosphere* is a layer of earth and atmosphere which contains living things.
8. *Antibiotic* is a substance produced by living tissue which kills bacteria.
9. *Bioluminescence* means the production of light by living organisms.
10. *Symbiosis* means two organisms living together for mutual benefit.
11. *Biotaxis* means the classification of living organisms.
12. A *biogen* is a basic unit that makes up a cell.
13. *Bioexology* means the interrelation of plants and animals.
14. *Biodynamics* is the doctrine of the vital force.

words in use

DIRECTIONS: Read the following passage. Then fill in each blank with the appropriate word from among the following choices.

biogenic   bioexology
symbiotic   biocide
biosphere   biogen
autobiography   biotaxy
antibiotic   biopsy

The scientist implied in his _____ that for
                                        1

authentic _____ it is sometimes necessary to
                        2

take a _____ to determine that two organisms
                    3

living together are existing in a truly _____
                                                        4

state. He was a specialist in _____, that science
                                              5

which deals with the interrelationship existing between plants and animals.

ANSWERS: 1—autobiography; 2—biotaxy; 3—biopsy; 4—symbiotic; 5—bio-exology.

NAME: _____

fill in the blanks

DIRECTIONS: Fill in the blank in each sentence with the appropriate word from among the following choices.

bioexology   bioplasm
autobiography   biopsy
biogen   biometry
biogenic   biodynamics
symbiosis   biotaxis

1. The remora and the shark, two species of fish that live together in a

   mutually beneficial way, are said to live in _____.

2. _____ is the science of calculating the

   human life span.

3. Living matter is called _____.

4. The doctrine of vital life force is called _____.

5. _____ is the classification of human

   organisms.

6. If something is produced from living organisms it is said to be

   _____.

7. After Frank Fiddle wrote the history of his life, he sent the

   _____ to a publisher.

8. _____ is the removal of living tissue for

   examination.

9. _____ deals with the interrelationship

between plants and animals.

10. The basic unit that makes up a living cell is a _____.

*ANSWERS: 1—symbiosis; 2—biometry; 3—bioplasm; 4—biodynamics; 5—bio-
taxis; 6—biogenic; 7—autobiography; 8—biopsy; 9—bioexology; 10—biogen.*

true-false

DIRECTIONS: Read each sentence and decide whether it is true or false. If it
is true, put a T in the space at the right. If it is false, write in an F.

1. The written life history of an individual is his biodynamics.   1._____
2. The removal of living tissue for examination is called biogen.   2._____
3. Symbiosis is two different organisms living together in a
   beneficial relationship.   3._____
4. Biocide is another name for a pesticide.   4._____
5. A biopsy is the basic unit of a cell.   5._____
6. The science of calculating the human life span is called biometry.   6._____
7. A bioscope is another name for a motion picture projector.   7._____
8. The science which studies the distribution of plants and animals over the earth is biogeography.   8._____
9. Biogenesis deals with the development of life from pre-exist-
   ing life.   9._____
10. Someone who writes his own life history is called biogenic.   10._____

ANSWERS: 1—F; 2—F; 3—T; 4—T; 5—F; 6—T; 7—T; 8—T; 9—T; 10—F.

affixes at work

DIRECTIONS: Add your own words to the blanks at the bottom of the diagram.

biometry

telemetry
(the science of measuring distant objects)

micrometry
(measurement with a micrometer)

geometry
(branch of mathematics that deals with measurement of points, lines, angles, surfaces, etc.)

psychometry
(psychological technique of mental measurement)

hypsometry
(the measurement of heights)

hygrometry
(science of measuring humidity)

pyrometry
(science that measures extremely high temperatures)

Suffix: *metry* means "the art or science of measuring"

The suffix *meter* means "that which measures or a measurer"; therefore

hygrometer is an instrument used to measure moisture in the air.

hypsometer is an instrument used to measure the heights of trees.

speedometer is an instrument that measures miles per hour traveled.

cyclometer is a device to record revolutions of a wheel.

photometer is used to measure light intensity.

cardiometer is an instrument to measure heart action.

altimeter measures altitude.

Words People Use

CARN
KARN

DERM
DUHRM

From the Latin *carn* meaning "flesh"	From the Greek *derma* meaning "skin" or "covering"

SKIN and flesh are actually the same; the covering for the skeleton and other basic parts of animals. In order to live and therefore to grow and maintain their bodies, animals must take in nourishment. Therefore, these two roots, "carn" and "derm" are the basis of many words concerned with the formation and appearance of the flesh. Many also describe more abstract meanings or implications than those associated with the human body.

The following word parts will be combined with the root in this unit to make new words. Use this list as a reference to find the meaning of words in this unit.

PREFIXES
re—back or again
in—in
hypo—under or beneath

ROOTS AS AFFIXES
vor—to eat or devour
epi—outside or near to
pach—thick

SUFFIXES
age—belonging to or place
al—of or belonging to
ate—product or rank
ous—marked by or full of
itis—inflammation of
tion—the act of
is—one who or person
logy—study or science of

context
clues

DIRECTIONS: Pronounce each word in the left hand column and read aloud the sentences in the right hand column. On the basis of context clues in the sentences, fill in the blank space to make a correct definition.

carnage

KAR–nij

■ The earthquake caused such carnage it was hard to find a single survivor when the tremors finally stopped.

283

■ War always results in senseless carnage, whether on the battlefield among soldiers or in the countryside among civilians.

1. Carnage means _____

_____

carnal

KARN–uhl

■ Burlesque houses and X-rated movies cater to man's carnal desires.
■ One school of thought in ancient Greece believed that only when the carnal appetites were satisfied could intellectual needs be met.

2. Carnal means _____

_____

carnival

KAR–nuh–vuhl

■ A carnival was originally a last fling before the restrictions of Lent.
■ The Mardi Gras is an example of carnival in its purest form and therefore the New Orleans sequence in the film *Easy Rider* was an example of the true carnival spirit.

3. Carnival means _____

_____

carnivore

KAR–nuh–vor

■ The fearful-looking brontosaurus, unlike the carnivores among dinosaurs, ate only swamp plants.
■ Vultures, jackels, and other hungry carnivores surrounded the zebra's carcass for a feast.

4. A carnivore is _____

_____

carnivorous

kar–NIV–uh–ruhs

■ Although the hyena is the most despised of the carnivorous animals, it performs the necessary service of waste collector among animals, for when it is finished, not much of the kill remains.

■ People, dogs, and other carnivorous animals have teeth especially suited to tearing and chewing meat.

5. Carnivorous means _____

_____

reincarnation

re–in–kar–NAY–shuhn

■ The Hindu belief in reincarnation does not see death as final but rather as only a transitory phase before the beginning of a new life in another form.
■ Mitchell was certain that through reincarnation he would reappear as a fish in his next life.

6. Reincarnation means _____

_____

incarnate

in–KAR–nuht

■ The devil incarnate appeared, though he wore regular business clothes and his tail and pointed ears were not visible.
■ "An incarnate being can't just disappear into thin air," the detective exclaimed!

7. Incarnate means _____

_____

dermatitis

der–muh–TEYET–uhs

■ Poison ivy rash and diaper rash are both forms of dermatitis.
■ A lotion may soothe the itching of dermatitis on your rough, red hands.

8. Dermatitis is _____

_____

dermatologist

der–muh–TOL–uh–jest

■ A serious skin infection requires the attention of a trained dermatologist.
■ A plastic surgeon may work with the dermatologist to treat skin disfigurement.

9. A dermatologist is _____

_____

epidermis

ep–uh–DUHR–muhs

- The outer layer of cells becomes the epidermis and thus protects you from extremes of weather.
- Cynthia's epidermis became wrinkled and leathery from constant sun tanning, but she would not consent to the kind of skin-restoring operations that would remove this layer and expose another while the cells replenished themselves.

10. The epidermis is _____

_____

pachyderm

PAK–i–duhrm

- Both hippos and rhinos have the same type of skin as elephants, and are also pachyderms.
- Pachyderms make excellent movers of supplies on long trips through dense jungle country because they are large, have tough skins, and can carry enormous loads.

11. Pachyderm means _____

_____

hypodermic

heye–puh–DUHR–mik

- A hypodermic syringe may be used to inject medication.
- The hypodermic needle must be kept exceedingly clean because it pierces the skin and can easily transmit disease.

12. Hypodermic means _____

_____

ANSWERS

1. *Carnage means great destruction of life.*
2. *Carnal means bodily pleasures or marked by sexuality.*
3. *Carnival means a festival.*
4. *A carnivore is a flesh-eating animal.*
5. *Carnivorous means an animal that eats the flesh of other animals.*
6. *Reincarnation means coming back to life, or the flesh, again.*
7. *Incarnate means in the flesh.*

8. _Dermatitis_ is an inflammation of the skin.
9. A _dermatologist_ is a doctor who specializes in skin diseases.
10. The _epidermis_ is the outer layer of skin.
11. A _pachyderm_ is a thick-skinned animal.
12. _Hypodermic_ means an injection under the skin.

fill in the blanks

DIRECTIONS: Fill in the blank in each sentence with the appropriate word from among the following choices.

dermatologist   reincarnation
epidermis   incarnate
dermatitis   carnelian
carnivore   carnage

1. The Greeks were responsible for the great _____

    that took place when they sacked Troy.

2. If a person is extremely evil he is sometimes referred to as the devil

    _____.

3. The skin condition called "acne" is a form of _____.

4. A lion is a _____.

5. Being reborn or coming into the flesh again is called

    _____.

6. The outer layer of the skin is called the _____.

7. A _____ is a skin specialist.

ANSWERS: 1—carnage; 2—incarnate; 3—dermatitis; 4—carnivore; 5—reincarnation; 6—epidermis; 7—dermatologist.

matching exercise

DIRECTIONS: Write the appropriate letter from the right hand column in the space next to each number so that the numbered words are defined.

_____ 1. carnage   **a.** skin like

_____ 2. incarnate   **b.** coming back into the flesh again

_____ 3. dermatitis   **c.** skin specialist

_____ 4. reincarnation   **d.** the top layer of skin

_____ 5. epidermis   **e.** great destruction of life

_____ 6. dermatologist   **f.** in the flesh

_____ 7. carnivore   **g.** a flesh-eating animal

     h. inflammation of the skin

ANSWERS: *1—e; 2—f; 3—h; 4—b; 5—d; 6—c; 7—g.*

words in use

DIRECTIONS: Read the following paragraph. Then fill in each blank with the appropriate word from among the following choices.

dermatitis   carnage
carnival   epidermis
incarnidine   reincarnation
dermatologist   carnivorous
carnivore   incarnate

The _____ informed us that certain

   1

_____ animals are apt to get

   2

_____. This would occur on the outer layer

   3

of their skin or the _____ and would appear

   4

red.

ANSWERS: 1—dermatologist; 2—carnivorous; 3—dermatitis; 4—epidermis.

true-false

DIRECTIONS: Read each sentence and decide whether it is true or false. If it is true, put a T in the space at the right; if it is false, write an F.

1. Carnage is a cake decoration.   1._____
2. Bodily pleasures are called carnal pleasures.   2._____
3. Incarnate means in the flesh.   3._____
4. Dermoid means skinlike.   4._____
5. Inflammation of the skin is called dermatitis.   5._____
6. A dermatologist is a foot specialist.   6._____
7. A meat eating animal is called a carnivore.   7._____

8. The word carnival refers to a festive holiday season that occurs just before Lent.　　8._____
9. Plastic surgery of the skin is called dermatology.　　9._____
10. Reincarnation is a method of treating skin disorders.　　10._____

ANSWERS:　1—F; 2—T; 3—T; 4—T; 5—T; 6—F; 7—T; 8—T; 9—F; 10—F.

"What do you know! A sexagenarian turns out to be a guy in his sixties."

GRAPH GRAPHIA
GRAF *GRAF-ee-uh*

From the Latin *graphicum* meaning a "stylus" or "writing implement"; also from the Greek *graphein*

THE root *graph* takes several forms in English. At times it can stand alone, as in the word "graph" which means a pictorial example of verbal information. It is most frequently used, however, as a word part—as in the familiar word "autograph"—where it means "write."

Psychographology
A study dealing with the revelations of
abnormal behavior through analysis of
handwriting.

The following word parts will be combined with the root in this unit to make new words. Use this list as a reference to find the meaning of words in this unit.

PREFIXES
a—without or not
poly—many
macro—large or thick

SUFFIXES
logy—science or study of
er—one who does or result of action
ic—belonging to or like or pertaining to

ROOTS AS AFFIXES

streph—turn
derm—skin
opthol—eye
erg—work
echo—repeat or imitate
chiro—hand
cart—map

crypt—hidden
demo—the people
seismo—earthquake or vibration
biblio—book
ocean—ocean
ortho—straight or upright

291

context

clues

DIRECTIONS: Pronounce each word in the left hand column and read aloud the sentences in the right hand column. On the basis of context clues in the sentences, fill in the blank space to make a correct definition.

agraphia

uh–GRAF–ee–uh

■ Even though a person once knew how to write, agraphia would make it impossible for him to do so.
■ Agraphia forced Frank to place long distance calls rather than to write business letters.

1. Agraphia is _____

_____

polygraph

POL–ee–graf

■ The suspect requested that the police let him submit to questioning with a polygraph in order to prove his innocence.
■ "Use the polygraph," the employment director said, "and be sure we hire truthful employees."

2. A polygraph is _____

_____

strephographia

STREF–o–GRAF–ee–uh

■ One of the reasons Michaelangelo's notebooks took so long to decipher is that he used strephographic writing in them.
■ Jim realized that his friend Tim's "secret writing" was only strephographia because when he saw the writing in a mirror he could decipher it immediately.

3. Strephographia is _____

_____

graphology

GRAF–ol–o–jee

■ A sign outside the graphologist's office was embellished with a large hand.
■ If it weren't for the pseudo-science of graphology, Milton would never have practiced to change his handwriting.

4. Graphology is _____

_____

dermographia

DERM–o–GRAF–ee–uh

■ The skin responds to the slightest stimulus if an individual has dermographia.
■ "Speaking of dermographia," dead-panned John, "if you have the skin you don't need writing paper."

5. Dermographia is _____

_____

macrographia

MAK–roe–GRAF–ee–uh

■ People with macrographia find it difficult to write on small pieces of paper.
■ The student's macrographia made it necessary for him to take a great many blue-books to every essay exam.

6. Macrographia is _____

_____

optholmograph

op–THAL–moe–GRAF

■ An opthalmograph will show that many poor readers actually keep looking back over what they have already read instead of moving their eyes ahead to the next passage.
■ Opthalmographic instruments provide useful printed records to show how people look at letters and words.

7. An opthalmograph is _____

_____

ergograph

ER–go–GRAF

■ Space scientists are interested in ergographic measurements as a guide to studying how much work an astronaut is capable of doing in space.
■ The readings on an ergograph would show that sedentary people show more strain after swimming than do athletic people.

8. An ergograph is _____

_____

echographia

EK–o–GRAF–ee–uh

■ Paul knew perfectly well who Henry VIII's wives were, but echographia prevented him from writing the answer on the test.

■ Cynthia failed the course even though she knew the answers for the final test because she had echographia and could not write the responses.

9. Echographia is _____

_____

chirography

KEYE–rog–ra–fee

■ Lawyers often employ chirographic specialists in preparing forgery cases.
■ People who have studied chirography scoff at machines such as those in airports or other public places which purport to analyze handwriting.

10. Chirography is _____

_____

cartographer

kar–TOG–ruh–fer

■ The expedition to the newly-discovered land included a cartographer who was charged with making an accurate map of the territory.
■ When the new atlas was published, cartographers eagerly examined it for accuracy.

11. A cartographer is _____

_____

cryptography

krip–TOG–ruh–fee

■ The enemy communications code was broken by a spectacular feat of cryptography.
■ Specialists in cryptography still cannot unravel the meaning of the Mayan glyph writing.

12. Cryptography is _____

_____

demographic

de–muh–GRAF–ik

■ Demographic studies show that the population center of the state is gradually changing as industry relocates.
■ The university employed an expert in demographic studies when it began its department of urban sociology.

13. Demographic is _____

_____

seismograph

SEYEZ–muh–graf

- An earthquake in Los Angeles registered on the seismograph in New York.
- The seismograph provided a clue to the location of underground disturbances later identified as a movement in the San Andreas fault.

14. A seismograph is _____

_____

bibliography

bib–lee–OG–ruh–fee

- Every research paper should include a bibliography to enable anyone to find the reference books used.
- Submit a bibliography and the teacher will help you decide which books will be most useful.

15. A bibliography is _____

_____

oceanography

o–shuh–NOG–ruh–fee

- The ship was specially outfitted to conduct oceanographic experiments during its long voyage.
- Jacques Cousteau sent back specimens of shrimp for study at the Institute of Oceanography.

16. Oceanography means _____

_____

orthography

or–THOG–ruh–fee

- Study your orthography so you can spell correctly.
- The orthography of Spanish is easy because words are spelled as they are pronounced.

17. Orthography is _____

_____

ANSWERS

1. *Agraphia is an inability to write.*
2. *A polygraph is a lie detector.*
3. *Strephographia is mirror writing.*
4. *Graphology is the study of handwriting.*
5. *Dermographia is skin writing.*

6. *Macrographia* is unusually large writing.
7. An *opthalmograph* is an instrument that measures eye movements.
8. An *ergograph* is an instrument that measures muscle fatigue.
9. *Echographia* is an inability to write answers to questions.
10. *Chirography* is the science of handwriting.
11. A *cartographer* is a map maker.
12. *Cryptography* is the practice of secret or code writing.
13. *Demographic* means the science of vital and social statistics of populations.
14. A *seismograph* is an instrument which records earthquakes and tremors.
15. A *bibliography* is a list of readings on a particular subject.
16. *Oceanography* is the study of the seas and oceans.
17. *Orthography* is correct spelling.

fill in the blanks

DIRECTIONS: Fill in the blank in each sentence with the appropriate word from among the following choices.

polygraph   cryptography
agraphia   ergograph
graphology   opthalmograph
bibliography   oceanography
macrographia   strephographia

1. Several physical responses are recorded on a _____

   to determine if a person is telling the truth.

2. Someone with _____ could not take any

   job requiring him to write.

3. The _____ can be used to measure animal

   as well as human work.

4. _____ is a popular but inexact method

   of finding out about a person's personality.

5. The _____ works by directing a beam of

   light at the cornea of a person's eye.

6. Books about _____ and spy activities usually

    appeal to young boys.

7. If you want to know a great deal about a subject, compile a

    _____ and then read all the items listed on it.

8. Rachel Carson's book *Edge of the Sea* is a good introduction to

    _____.

9. Not all students who write big have _____;

    some are merely trying to fill up the pages to impress the teacher.

10. Children sometimes play spy games in which one form of cryptography

    is _____.

ANSWERS: 1—polygraph; 2—agraphia; 3—ergograph; 4—graphology; 5—opthalmograph; 6—cryptography; 7—bibliography; 8—oceanography; 9—macrographia; 10—strephographia.

words in use

DIRECTIONS: Read the following paragraph. Then list the technical name for each part of the description of Mr. Simmons in the blanks below.

Mr. Simmons was a most unusual man. Among other things, he thought he could tell all about a person's personality just by looking at his handwriting. Another odd thing was the way he wrote; you had to hold the paper up to a mirror in order to read the words. And his writing was so large he needed a whole sheet of paper—horizontally—just to write his name. We asked him to sign our notebooks so people would believe we had actually met him.

1. _____
2. _____
3. _____

ANSWERS: 1—graphology; 2—strephographia; 3—macrographia.

matching exercise

DIRECTIONS: Write the appropriate letter from the right hand column in the space next to each number so that the numbered words are defined.

———— 1. strephographia   **a.** a lie detector

———— 2. macrographia   **b.** a pseudo-science

———— 3. agraphia   **c.** the science of handwriting

———— 4. cryptography   **d.** the study of man

———— 5. cardiograph   **e.** a light signal

———— 6. monograph   **f.** mirror writing

———— 7. chirography   **g.** repetitive writing of a question

———— 8. opthalmograph   **h.** measures muscle fatigue

———— 9. polygraph   **i.** large handwriting

————10. graphology   **j.** writing on one subject

     k. instrument to record heartbeat

     l. inability to write

     m. secret writing

     n. instrument to measure eye movement

ANSWERS: *1—f; 2—i; 3—l; 4—m; 5—k; 6—j; 7—c; 8—n; 9—a; 10—b.*

affixes at work

DIRECTIONS: Add your own words to the blanks at the bottom of the diagram.

(**poly**)graph

polyandry
(practice of having more than one husband at a time)

polybasic
(having more than one hydrogen atom)

polychotomous
(divided into many parts)

polychromatic
(multicolored)

polydactyl
(having more than the normal number of digits)

polyglot
(speaking or writing several languages)

Prefix: *poly* means "many"

(a)graphia

atypical
(not normal; unusual)

anarchy
(absence of government)

anarthria
(inability to articulate words as result of brain damage)

amentia
(a condition of lack of development of mental capacity)

apraxia
(loss of physical coordination)

asexual
(lacking sex or functional sex organs)

Prefix: *a* means "without or not"

ISO

MORPH

EYES-o

MORF

From the Greek *isos* meaning "equal"	From the Greek *morphe* meaning "form"

THE MOST useful descriptions of objects—or even of people—are likely to be those which tell about shape. Two useful word roots from the Greek help speakers of English to make many words that tell about how things surrounding us look. Equality, *isos,* a kind of form, is important enough to merit a whole special group of words expressing that relationship and separate from other forms.

The following word parts will be combined with the root in this unit to make new words. Use this list as a reference to find the meaning of words in this unit.

PREFIXES
meta—among, with or after
a—not
dis—away from or negative

SUFFIXES
ous—marked by or given to
sis—condition of, esp. abnormal
ic—pertaining to or like or belonging to
logy—science or study of

ROOTS AS AFFIXES

bar—bar
sceles—legs
tope—place
pod—foot
cracy—government or rule

tonic—tension
anthro—man
genesis—beginning
metric—measure

context

clues

DIRECTIONS: Pronounce each word in the left hand column and read aloud the sentences in the right hand column. On the basis of context clues in the sentences, fill in the blank space to make a correct definition.

301

isobar

EYE–suh–bar

- The areas on the weather map along this wavy isobar will have a strong band of showers.
- The points joined by the isobar have the same barometric pressure.

1. An isobar is _____

_____

isosceles

eye–SOS–uh–lez

- The roof of the A-frame looks like a snow-bound isosceles triangle.
- An isosceles triangle is elongated because only two sides are equal.

2. Isosceles means _____

_____

isotope

EYE–suh–tope

- A most useful form of uranium is the isotope U235.
- A variation in the number of electrons creates an isotope of a chemical element.

3. An isotope is _____

_____

isopods

EYE–suh–podz

- Those black, bug-like creatures with the many legs are marine isopods.
- Closer examination of the isopod will show that its numerous feet are equal.

4. An isopod is _____

_____

isotonic

eye–suh–TON–ik

- The musical tones of the isotonic scale are strange to the listener accustomed to the usual scale progressions.
- Hubert measured the osmotic (diffusion of fluids through a porous membrane) pressure of the two chemical solutions and discovered they were isotonic.

5. Isotonic means _____

_____

isocracy

eye–SOK–ruh–see

■ If everybody in the club wanted to be the boss, it would turn into an isocracy instead of a democracy.
■ No family should be run as an isocracy because children do not deserve powers equal to those of their parents.

6. Isocracy _____

_____

metamorphosis

met–uh–MOR–fuh–suhs

■ An example of metamorphosis is the caterpillar becoming a moth.
■ A fascinating story by Franz Kafka describes the metamorphosis of a man into a giant cockroach.

7. Metamorphosis means _____

_____

morphogenesis

mor–fuh–JEN–uh–suhs

■ "In this class," the embryology professor announced, "you will study the morphogenesis of the organs of the chick through various stages of development."
■ It is fascinating to follow the morphogenesis of the heart from a tiny mass of cells to a complex mechanism.

8. Morphogenesis means _____

_____

amorphous

uh–MOR–fuhs

■ John said he was a poet, but his works were so amorphous that everyone found them meaningless.
■ In Judy's skilled hands the amorphous ball of clay became a beautiful piece of sculpture.

9. Amorphous is _____

_____

anthropomorphic

an–thruh–puh–MOR–fik

■ The anthropomorphic Greek gods were capable of such human emotions as jealousy, fear, and sexual love.

■ Many primitive tribes gave anthropomorphic attributes to rocks or trees, and then prayed to influence them.

10. Anthropomorphic means _____

_____

dismorphic

dis–MORF–ik

■ Scientists have indicated that dismorphic children often result when one or both parents has taken large amounts of LSD prior to conception.
■ The ancient Chinese custom of binding the feet of girl babies produced a dismorphic foot.

11. Dismorphic means _____

_____

morphology

mor–FOL–uh–jee

■ If you want to know all about the duck-billed platypus, you would have to study its morphology so that you would understand the reasons for its special shape and habits.
■ The impression found in the sandstone was identified as an early form of fern on the basis of its morphology.

12. Morphology is _____

_____

isometric

eye–suh–MET–rik

■ Isometric exercises are based on the principle that equal forces pitted against each other result in good muscle tone.
■ Isometric matching is important if you want to plan an experiment that will require a control group of children physically matched to the experimental group.

13. Isometric means _____

_____

NAME:

ANSWERS

1. An *isobar* is a line joining the points of equal barometric pressure.
2. *Isosceles* means a triangle with only two equal sides.
3. An *isotope* is a form of some chemical element.
4. An *isopod* is anything that has equal length feet.
5. *Isotonic* means of equal tension.
6. *Isocracy* means everyone having the same power to rule.
7. *Metamorphosis* means a change of form.
8. *Morphogenesis* means the development or transformation of the organs of the body.
9. *Amorphous* means having no defined shape.
10. *Anthropomorphic* means resembling human form.
11. *Dismorphic* means something out of its regular or usual shape.
12. *Morphology* is the study of the form and structure of plants and animals.
13. *Isometric* means having equal measurements.

true-false

DIRECTIONS: Read each sentence carefully and decide whether it is true or false. If it is true, put a T in the space at the right. If it is false, write in an F.

1. Amorphism refers to an object or organism having many shapes. 1._____
2. An animal with only one foot is called an isopod. 2._____
3. Anything that is dismorphic is out of shape. 3._____
4. An isosceles triangle has only two sides which are alike. 4._____
5. If two objects have the same shape we may refer to them as isomorphic. 5._____
6. Forces, conditions, or mechanisms that have or can produce equal force are said to be isodynamic. 6._____
7. Isotonic is a drug used for the common cold. 7._____
8. Anthropomorphic implies animal shapes. 8._____
9. The development of the organs within the body is called morphogenesis. 9._____
10. The word isodont indicates that an organism has feet that are all the same size. 10._____

ANSWERS: 1—F; 2—F; 3—T; 4—T; 5—T; 6—T; 7—F; 8—F; 9—T; 10—F.

fill in the blanks

DIRECTIONS: Fill in the blank in each sentence with the appropriate word from among the following choices.

isosceles   isotope
metamorphosis   isotonic
amorphism   anthropomorphic
isopod   morphology
dismorphic   isodynamic

1. The science that studies the form of bodily organs is called

    _____.

2. Anything that is out of its regular shape we may call _____.

3. If an organism is _____ then it resembles

    human form.

4. If a triangle has two equal sides it is called an _____

    triangle.

5. The word _____ implies equal tension.

6. If an organism has many feet all equal in length, then the organism

    is termed an _____.

7. The shapeless form of water may be described by the word

    _____.

ANSWERS: 1—morphology; 2—dismorphic; 3—anthropomorphic; 4—isosceles;
5—isotonic; 6—isopod; 7—amorphism.

crossword puzzle

ACROSS
2—the science that studies
    the forms of organs
3—a triangle with two equal sides
4—out of shape

DOWN
1—resembling human form
5—having equal parts

solution

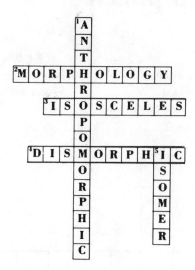

LUC, LUM   PYR
LUK, LUM   *PEYER*

From the Latin *lucere* meaning "to light" or "to shine"

From the Greek *pyr* meaning "fire"

LIGHT and fire are closely related. For instance, light is given off by fire. Historically, both light and fire have also been closely related in religious and symbolic significance. Lighting the funeral pyre, for instance, is an ancient custom observed even today among many cultures. Many words using the same root, "pyre," tell about the special uses of fire.

The following word parts will be combined with the root in this unit to make new words. Use this list as a reference to find the meaning of words in this unit.

ROOTS AS AFFIXES
technic—art or craft
meter—measure
olatry—worship

PREFIXES
il—in or into
trans—across
e—out, out of, or from

SUFFIXES
id—one marked by or showing
ite—formed or showing or treated with
ary—belonging to or place for
ous—full of
ate—product of or showing
iac—of or relating to
oid—shaped like or in the form of

context

clues

DIRECTIONS: Pronounce each word in the left hand column and read aloud the sentences in the right hand column. On the basis of context clues in the sentences, fill in the blank space to make a correct definition.

lucid

LOU–suhd

■ Morris' lucid explanation of the mathematics problem made it seem perfectly clear to the two girls he was tutoring.

■ Only lucid thought helped Sidney begin to understand why he always talked in class when the teacher tried to explain new material.

1. Lucid means _____

_____

Lucite

LOU–seyet

■ If see-through Lucite handbags ever come back into style, I will be ready because I have several put away in my closet.
■ Boat windshields of Lucite make sightseeing clear and keep splashed water off the customers.

2. Lucite is a tradename for _____

_____

luminary

LOU–muh–ner–ee

■ The ballroom seemed aglow with the social luminaries that came to the dance in order to support the Cancer Research Fund.
■ That nighttime luminary, the moon, has lost some of its romance now that astronauts have walked on it.

3. Luminary means _____

_____

luminous

LOU–muh–nuhs

■ "Don't leave me, John," begged Irene, looking up at him through eyes luminous with tears.
■ The Washington monument, luminous in the moonlight, was a breathtaking sight.

4. Luminous means _____

_____

illuminate

il–OU–muh–nate

■ Three floodlights will illuminate the entire stage.
■ Professor Sinbad illuminated a complex problem in his calculus class today.

5. Illuminate means _____

_____

translucent

trans–LOU–suhnt

■ Be sure you put translucent rather than transparent glass in the bathroom window that faces the kitchen window of the people next door.
■ The discovery of translucent material made it practical to put windows in houses of people who previously preferred to have privacy rather than light.

6. Translucent means _____

_____

elucidate

uh–LOU–suh–date

■ The politician likes to elucidate his statements by beginning, "Let me make this perfectly clear . . ."
■ The scientist who cannot elucidate his material for a layman doesn't communicate with people.

7. Elucidate means _____

_____

pyromaniac

peye–ro–MAY–nee–ak

■ The twelve fires during the last two weeks were deliberately set by a pyromaniac.
■ Just because Milton likes to watch flames in the fireplace doesn't mean he is a pyromaniac.

8. A pyromaniac is _____

_____

Pyrex

PEYE–reks

■ If you are going to pour boiling water into a glass, you had better be sure the glass is Pyrex.
■ A Pyrex baking dish may be used instead of a metal pan, but adjust the oven time for glass.

9. Pyrex is a trademark of _____

_____

pyrotechnics

peye–ruh–TEK–niks

■ The Fourth of July in the United States is usually celebrated by startling and beautiful pyrotechnical displays.
■ The Chinese long ago discovered the art of pyrotechnics; this was a direct outgrowth of their discovery of gunpowder.

10. Pyrotechnics means _____

_____

pyrometer

peye–ROM–i–tuhr

- The wax boiled at such a high temperature that a pyrometer had to be used to measure it.
- The average household thermometer goes little beyond the boiling temperature of water; other substances require a pyrometer for measuring.

11. A pyrometer is _____

_____

pyrolatry

peye–ROL–uh–tree

- The islanders built a huge fire at the site of their temple because theirs was a pyrolatreous religion.
- Pyrolatry was so ingrained in the civilization that the people would not accept the substitute of either religious idols or of ideas.

12. Pyrolatry is _____

_____

ANSWERS

1. *Lucid* means shining, transparent or clear.
2. *Lucite* is a trademark name for a class of plastic used chiefly as a substitute for glass.
3. *Luminary* means of or characterized by light, as a heavenly body or a person of intellectual or moral eminence who is an inspiration (light) to others.
4. *Luminous* means radiating or emitting light.
5. *Illuminate* means to light up.
6. *Translucent* means allowing light to pass through.
7. *Elucidate* means to clarify or bring to light.
8. A *pyromaniac* is someone who is obsessed with fire.
9. *Pyrex* is a trademark of a glassware that will not break when heated.
10. *Pyrotechnics* means of or having to do with fireworks.
11. A *pyrometer* is an instrument for measuring high temperatures.
12. *Pyrolatry* is the worship of fire.

fill in the blanks

DIRECTIONS: Fill in the blank in each sentence with the appropriate word from among the following choices.

pyrometer	pyrolatry
pyromaniac	translucent
luminous	luminary
Pyrex	

1. _____ is a glassware in which it is safe

    to cook.

2. The worshippers of fire on the desert island practiced _____.

3. Buy a new _____ if you need to

    measure high temperatures in the kiln.

4. Many windows are made of frosted glass because it is

    _____ but keeps out prying eyes.

ANSWERS: 1—Pyrex; 2—pyrolatry; 3—pyrometer; 4—translucent.

matching exercise

DIRECTIONS: Write the appropriate letter from the right hand column in the space next to each number so that the numbered words are defined.

_____ 1. Pyrex

_____ 2. pyrolatry

_____ 3. pyrometer

_____ 4. translucent

a. to reflect light

b. the worship of fire

c. a poison that causes fever

d. a glassware that will not break when heated

e. light can shine through

f. an instrument for measuring high temperatures

ANSWERS: 1—d; 2—b; 3—g; 4—e.

words in use

DIRECTIONS: Read the following passage. Then fill in each blank with the appropriate word from among the following choices.

pyromancy	pyromania
illuminated	lurid
elucidate	pyrolatry
luminary	pyrotechnics

As the evening passed, the _____
1

_____ the sky. Through the brightness of the
2

night there were some who practiced _____
3

for they actually worshipped fire.

ANSWERS: 1—pyrotechnics; 2—illuminated; 3—pyrolatry.

314   Words People Use

NEUR(O)
NOOR-o

From the Greek *neur-* meaning "nerve" or "sinew"; a combining form which means "nerve," "nerves," or "the nervous system"

WHEN a nerve is referred to in any of the sciences, the root *neuro* is almost certain to appear. Occasionally *nerv* from the Latin "nervus," will be seen and it refers to the tendons or sinews. But whenever a combining form is used, *neuro* can be expected. In fact, "neurology," the study of the nerves of the body is described in this manner (*neuro* = nerve, *ology* = the study of).

The following word parts will be combined with the root in this unit to make new words. Use this list as a reference to find the meaning of words in this unit.

ROOTS AS AFFIXES
longo—tongue
pathy—suffering or disease
psych—mind
lalo—speech or speech organs
asthen—weakness
blast—formative or embryonic
bio—life

SUFFIXES
oid—in the shape of
algia—pain
itis—inflammation
tomy—to cut
osis—condition of, esp. abnormal
ist—person who
logy—science or study of
gen—to be born or something that produces

context
clues

DIRECTIONS: Pronounce each word in the left hand column and read aloud the sentences in the right hand column. On the basis of context clues in the sentences, fill in the blank space to make a correct definition.

315

longoneurosis

LON–guh–new–ROW–sis

- The patient's longoneurosis made it difficult for him to pronounce words.
- As a result of nerve injuries involving the speech mechanism, Mr. Johnson suffered from longoneurosis.

1. Longoneurosis is _____

_____

neurotoid

NOOR–uh–toyd

- Calcium deposits had modified the shape of John's nerve fibers until they were no longer neurotoid.
- The artificial nerves in Mary's hand were neurotoid.

2. Neurotoid is _____

_____

neuralgia

new–RAL–juh

- Simple remedies such as aspirin that promise relief from pain of nerve fibers described as neuralgia are often effective.
- An arm afflicted by neuralgia can be just as painful as that caused by muscle strains, for the nerves are very sensitive.

3. Neuralgia is _____

_____

neuritis

new–REYE–tis

- Neuritis may occur anywhere in the body where there are nerves susceptible to inflammation.
- The pain caused by neuritis is often relieved by the application of warm compresses to the inflamed area.

4. Neuritis is _____

_____

neurotomy

new–ROT–uh–mee

- A neurotomy is a radical surgical procedure indicated in cases where the nerve being severed can bring relief from a physical ill.
- Marmaduke recovered quickly from the neurotomy, though he no longer had any sensation in his little finger.

5. Neurotomy is _____

_____

neurosis

new–ROW–sis

■ Of the several theories about the causes of a neurosis, all agree that it is some kind of stress which results in an inability to function.
■ Since a neurosis seldom has an organic cause, there is a theory that it is learned behavior.

6. Neurosis is _____

_____

neuropathy

new–ROP–uh–thee

■ A diagnosis of neuropathy is so inclusive that it does not state the particular disease of the nervous system the patient has.
■ Neuritis is a form of neuropathy.

7. Neuropathy is _____

_____

psychoneurosis

SEYE–ko–new–ROW–sis

■ Although there is some evidence that psychoneurosis tends to run in a family, science has not yet conclusively shown that it is hereditary.
■ Mary's urge to wash her hands constantly was diagnosed as a psychoneurosis because the illness had no physiological basis.

8. Psychoneurosis is _____

_____

neurotic

new–ROT–ik

■ Sylvester's neurotic behavior was evidenced by his constant looking over his shoulder and his constant twitching of the left eye.
■ Gertrude was not really sick, but she complained constantly because she had become a neurotic.

9. Neurotic is _____

_____

laloneurosis

LUH–lo–nuh–row–sis

■ The patient's frequent lip and tongue spasms made speech so difficult that therapy was recommended for his laloneurosis.

■ It would be next to impossible for someone with laloneurosis to become a radio announcer.

10. Laloneurosis is _____

_____

neurasthenia

nyur–uhs–THEE–nee–uh

■ Gladys had such a severe case of neurasthenia that she had to stop work in order to spend her time in bed resting.
■ Neurasthenia cannot be helped simply by taking vitamin pills and tonics to pep you up.

11. Neurasthenia is _____

_____

neuroblast

NYUR–uh–blast

■ The neuroblast showed clearly under the microscope even though it had not yet developed to the stage that it could be called an actual nerve cell.
■ Because of the growth pattern of the neuroblast, there were new nerve cells forming.

12. A neuroblast is _____

_____

neurology

nyur–ROL–uh–jee

■ When Herman decided to specialize in neurology, he had no idea that he would have to undertake a research project about how people react under the pressures of wartime combat.
■ The strain was too much for Wilbur and he finally had to consult a neurologist to find out the source of his constant stiff neck and tight stomach.

13. Neurology is _____

_____

neurogenic

nyu–ruh–GEN–ik

■ Virgil's constant habit of raising his right hand and then lowering it turned out to be neurogenic and thus was not just a habit.
■ Millicent had a neurogenic difficulty that made her smile when she became nervous.

14. Neurogenic means _____

_____

neurobiologist

nyur–uh–beye–OL–uh–
    juhst

■ A competent neurobiologist can trace a disease of the nervous system through its entire pattern of growth.
■ A neurobiologist must know something about how bones, muscles and tissues grow or else he cannot trace the development of the nerves.

15. A neurobiologist is _____

_____

ANSWERS

1. _Longoneurosis_ is a speech disorder caused by a mental disorder.
2. _Neurotoid_ is something shaped like a nerve.
3. _Neuralgia_ is a pain in a nerve.
4. _Neuritis_ is an inflammation of a nerve.
5. _Neurotomy_ is the surgical cutting of a nerve.
6. _Neurosis_ is a mental disorder.
7. _Neuropathy_ is any disease of the nervous system.
8. _Psychoneurosis_ is any mental disorder.
9. _Neurotic_ is having a neurosis.
10. _Laloneurosis_ is a functional spasm in the lips and tongue.
11. _Neurasthenia_ is a weakness of the nervous system.
12. A _neuroblast_ is a sprout or embryonic stage of a nerve cell.
13. _Neurology_ is the study of the nervous system.
14. _Neurogenic_ is what originates in the nervous system.
15. A _neurobiologist_ is one who studies the pattern of growth of nerves.

words in use

DIRECTIONS: Read the following paragraphs. Then check the phrases below which describe words in the paragraph.

A psychologist should be familiar with the field of neurology, for many neurotic patients are given neurological examinations. The results of these examinations help to determine whether an illness is neurogenic or psychogenic (i.e., whether a patient has neurasthenia or neuritis).

_____ 1. Someone who examines eyes.
_____ 2. A specialist in mental illness.
_____ 3. An individual with a neurosis.
_____ 4. The embryonic nerve cell.
_____ 5. The study of the nervous system.
_____ 6. Having its origin in the nerves.
_____ 7. Surgical cutting of a nerve.
_____ 8. A condition of heightened fatigue and of aches and pains.
_____ 9. Inflammation of a nerve or nerves.
_____10. A speech impediment.

John felt that he would like to specialize in the study of the nervous system so he wanted to attend medical school. He was interested not only in diseases which have their origin in the nervous system, but also in those speech disorders which have their origin in the mind. He was thinking of combining these with a specialty of surgically severing nerves for the purpose of eliminating pain in a nerve or nerves.

_____ 1. neurography.
_____ 2. neurology
_____ 3. neurobiotaxis.
_____ 4. neurotoid.
_____ 5. neurogenic.
_____ 6. laloneurosis.
_____ 7. neurasthenia.
_____ 8. neurotomy.
_____ 9. neuroblast.
_____10. neuralgia.

ANSWERS—Paragraph I: 2; 3; 6; 8; 9.
ANSWERS—Paragraph II: 2; 5; 6; 8; 10.

matching exercise

DIRECTIONS: Write the appropriate letter from the right hand column in the space next to each number so that the numbered words are defined.

_____ 1. neurotomy   **a.** a speech impediment

_____ 2. neuropathy   **b.** a condition of heightened fatigue

_____ 3. neuroblast   **c.** reflex arcs

_____ 4. neuro   **d.** any disease of the nervous system

(*more*)

_____ 5. neurosis   **e.** inflammation of a nerve or nerves

_____ 6. neurasthenia   **f.** surgical cutting of a nerve

_____ 7. neurogenic   **g.** a combining form meaning nerve

_____ 8. neurography   **h.** the embryonic nerve cell

_____ 9. neurology   **i.** a synonym for psychoneurosis

_____10. neurotoid   **j.** having its origin in the nerves

      k. a system of brain patterns

      l. the study of the nervous system

      m. like or formed like a nerve

ANSWERS: 1—f; 2—d; 3—h; 4—g; 5—i; 6—b; 7—j; 8—k; 9—l; 10—m.

fill in the blanks

DIRECTIONS: Fill in the blank in each sentence with the appropriate word from among the following choices.

psychoneuroid	neurotoid
neuritis	neuralgia
neurobiologist	laloneurosis
neurotomy	neurosis
neurasthenia	neuroblast
neurology	neurogenic
neurobiologist	neuropathy

1. "I couldn't possibly play tennis today," Herbert said, "because my

   _____ has flared up again and made my

   arm sore."

2. Although the patient seemed to have recovered from the auto accident,

   injured nerves left him with _____ which

   made it difficult for him to speak.

3. Sometimes the surgical procedure called _____

   is indicated to relieve pain resulting from nerve injuries.

4. A shorter form of the word psychoneurosis, and one often used

   synonymously with it, is _____.

5. Hazel's husband was annoyed because she always felt "all in" and

   complained of assorted aches and pains, but her physician said she had

   _____.

6. The nerve cell is a _____ in its earliest

   growing stage.

7. _____ or the study of the nervous system is

   necessary to complete understanding of how the human organism

   reacts under various kinds of stress.

8. A twitch affecting facial muscles such as those in the eye or cheek

   often is diagnosed as _____.

9. Someone studying nerve growth could be called a _____.

ANSWERS: 1—neuritis or neuralgia; 2—laloneurosis; 3—neurotomy; 4—neurosis; 5—neurasthenia; 6—neuroblast; 7—neurology; 8—neurogenic; 9—neurobiologist.

322   **Words People Use**

PATH
PATH

From the Greek *pathos* meaning "suffering," "disease" or "feeling"

THE FACT that this single root word has many meanings is indicative of the variety of ideas it is used to describe. The medical profession makes wide use of "path" root words to explain everything from the cause of disease to different philosophies of treating disease and suffering. As common a word as "sympathy" comes from this root, and there are other words that allow us to communicate different shades of meaning to tell specifically how we feel toward others.

The following word parts will be combined with the root in this unit to make new words. Use this list as a reference to find the meaning of words in this unit.

PREFIXES
a—not (a negative form of root)
em—in
sym—same or like
anti—against or hostile

SUFFIXES
ic—caused by or like
y—result or quality
ist—one who or person
sis—condition of (esp. abnormal)
gen—beginning or producing
logy—study or science of

ROOTS AS AFFIXES
dont—teeth
homeo—like or the same as
allo—variation or departure from normal

context
clues

DIRECTIONS: Pronounce each word in the left hand column and read aloud the sentences in the right hand column. On the basis of context clues in the sentences, fill in the blank space to make a correct definition.

apathetic

ap–uh–THET–ik

■ Marvin remained strangely apathetic to his surroundings even when there was great excitement in the room.

323

■ Even the most apathetic person will find something to laugh about in this film!

1. Apathetic means _____

_____

pathetic

puh–THE–tik

■ The wet, bedraggled protestors picking up their soggy signs after capitulating to the stronger group were a pathetic sight.
■ Tom made a weak, pathetic attempt to climb the rope and then gave up.

2. Pathetic means _____

_____

empathy

EM–puh–thee

■ The reader feels such empathy for the Sanchez family that he feels part of their life in Mexico.
■ Real empathy permits you to understand another person's feelings.

3. Empathy means _____

_____

sympathy

SIM–puh–thee

■ I am in complete sympathy with your beliefs and will be glad to assist you in any way possible.
■ Mrs. Wilson's great sympathy for unwanted animals made her house a refuge for stray cats and abandoned dogs.

4. Sympathy means _____

_____

antipathy

an–TIP–uh–thee

■ Bob and Carol discovered they had such natural antipathy toward each other that they were soon divorced.
■ Broderick's antipathy to violence made him a poor soldier.

5. Antipathy means _____

_____

pathos

PAY–thos

- The movie was so filled with pathos that most of the women in the audience could be heard sniffling and some were openly crying.
- Great sums were collected for the victims of the flood because Mr. Johnson could evoke such pathos in his speeches that everyone was moved to contribute.

6. Pathos means _____

_____

pathology

puh–THOL–uh–jee

- The class in pathology will include the study of several rare tropical diseases.
- Winthrop learned all he could about the pathology of the nervous system, hoping to find a cure for the disease.

7. Pathology is _____

_____

pathologist

puh–THOL–uh–juhst

- Since a diagnosis could not be reached, a pathologist was called to examine the supposedly diseased tissue sample.
- A pathologist is trained to recognize abnormal cellular changes.

8. A pathologist is _____

_____

pathodontia

path–uh–DON–chuh

- Dentists take courses in pathodontia so they can recognize the symptoms of disease before it has progressed too far.
- It didn't take a pathodontist to discover that the tooth was causing an infection throughout Henry's mouth.

9. Pathodontia means _____

_____

pathogenesis

path–uh–JEN–uh–suhs

- The pathogenesis of the Asian Flu strain recently isolated indicates it is easily transmitted and develops quickly once "caught" by an individual.

■ During the pathogenesis of his rare disease, Sylvester was hospitalized so doctors could observe him frequently.

10. Pathogenesis means _____

_____

homeopathic

ho–me–uh–PATH–ik

■ Dr. Simpson believed in homeopathic medicine, so he refused to write prescriptions that eliminated symptoms entirely.
■ Marvin decided on a homeopathically–oriented doctor, believing that he could therefore save money on drug store costs.

11. Homeopathy means _____

_____

allopathy

uh–LOP–uh–thee

■ The medicine was designed to have an allopathic effect and produce counter symptoms to Harold's cold.
■ If you have a burn, an allopathic method of treating it is to soothe the area.

12. Allopathy means _____

_____

ANSWERS

1. *Apathetic means without feeling.*
2. *Pathetic means arousing pity.*
3. *Empathy means participating in another's feelings.*
4. *Sympathy means to be in agreement about feelings with another person.*
5. *Antipathy means an aversion or basic repugnance.*
6. *Pathos means a feeling of pity or compassion.*
7. *Pathology is the study of the causes and nature of disease.*
8. *A pathologist is one who is skilled in studying the causes and nature of disease.*
9. *Pathodontia concerns the diseases of the teeth.*
10. *Pathogenesis means the development of a disease.*
11. *Homeopathy means the method of treating disease by giving small doses of drugs that would produce symptoms similar to those of the disease in a healthy person.*
12. *Allopathy is a method of treating disease by the use of drugs to eliminate symptoms.*

true-false

DIRECTIONS: Read each sentence carefully and decide whether it is true or false. If it is true, put a T in the space at the right. If it is false, write in an F.

1. An apathetic person is one who lacks feeling. 1._____
2. A situation that is pathetic is one that arouses pity. 2._____
3. Pathodontia refers to the classification of elephants. 3._____
4. Pathology is the study of the causes and nature of disease. 4._____
5. If you have antipathy for someone you like him very much. 5._____
6. Some doctors practice allopathic medicine. 6._____
7. Pathos is an emotion of sympathy. 7._____
8. The development of a disease is termed pathogenesis. 8._____
9. The word homeopathic refers to a mental disease. 9._____
10. Empathy is a French word used to indicate a happy ending in a story. 10._____

ANSWERS: 1—T; 2—T; 3—F; 4—T; 5—F; 6—T; 7—T; 8—T; 9—F; 10—F.

matching exercise

DIRECTIONS: Write the appropriate letter from the right hand column in the space next to each number so that the numbered words are defined.

_____ 1. apathetic
_____ 2. pathetic
_____ 3. empathy
_____ 4. pathogenesis
_____ 5. pathos
_____ 6. antipathy
_____ 7. allopathic
_____ 8. pathologist
_____ 9. pathology
_____10. pathodontia

a. disease of the teeth
b. a person skilled in pathology
c. an emotion of sympathy
d. a method of treating diseases
e. the study of the causes and nature of disease
f. participating in another's feelings
g. arousing pity
h. dislike; feelings against something
i. the lack of feeling
j. a mental disease

ANSWERS: 1—j; 2—g; 3—f; 4—j; 5—c; 6—h; 7—d; 8—b; 9—e; 10—a.

crossword puzzle

ACROSS
2—an emotion of sympathy
4—participating in another's
   feeling

DOWN
1—the development of a disease
2—arousing pity
3—the study of the nature and
   causes of disease

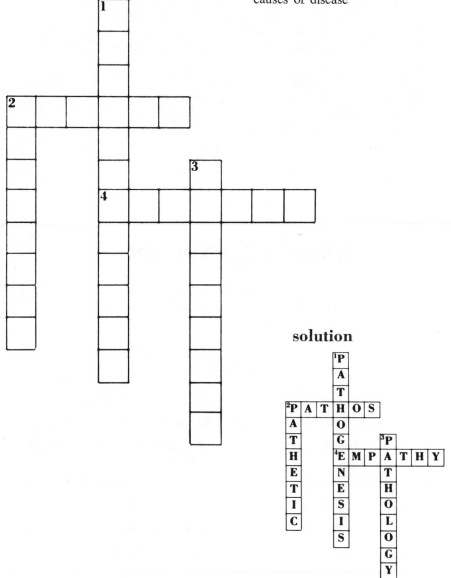

solution

			¹P						
			A						
			T						
²P	A	T	H	O	S				
A			O						
T			G			³P			
H			⁴E	M	P	A	T	H	Y
E			N			T			
T			E			H			
I			S			O			
C			I			L			
			S			O			
						G			
						Y			

PSYCHE
SEYE-ke

From the Greek *psycho* meaning "mind" or "soul"

THE WORD part *psyche* is basic to the word psychology itself. Literally, "psychology" means "the study of the mind." But since a study of the mind has so many ramifications, the word part *psyche* is employed in two different ways, so that it becomes a part of many descriptive words in the field.

As a prefix, *psyche* may be combined with another root, as in *psycho-neurotic* (since the part "neurotic" is also a root word), or *psychology* (-logy means "the study of").

The word *psyche* by itself has become a part of everyday language in a variety of forms, especially in slang such as "psycho" and "psych out."

> In Greek mythology, Psyche was a beautiful girl beloved by Eros (Cupid).

The following word parts will be combined with the root in this unit to make new words. Use this list as a reference to find the meaning of words in this unit.

ROOTS AS AFFIXES
soma—body
physics—physics or natural science
drama—drama or action on stage
graph—write or word
therapy—service of attendant
analysis—a releasing (study)

SUFFIXES
ic—caused by or dealing with
sis—condition of, esp. abnormal
ist—one who or person
gen—born or something that produces

context
clues

DIRECTIONS: Pronounce each word in the left hand column and read aloud the sentences in the right hand column. On the basis of context clues in the sentences, fill in the blank space to make a correct definition.

329

psychosomatic

SEYE–ko–so–MAT–ik

■ When Marybelle's husband Sidney exhibited the same signs of morning-sickness she did during the early months of pregnancy, her obstetrician assured her Sidney's illness was psychosomatic.
■ It is possible to have a psychosomatic toothache and yet experience great physical pain.

1. Psychosomatic illness is _____

_____

psychophysics

SEYE–ko–FIS–iks

■ A specialist in psychophysics might be employed by car safety experts interested in the quick braking capabilities of their product.
■ A psychophysicist would be interested in measuring the time it takes a sprinter to leave the starting bloc after he hears the starter's gun.

2. Psychophysics means _____

_____

psychodrama

SEYE–ko–DRAM–uh

■ The opportunity to participate in psychodrama and act out one's feelings is often a great help in understanding those feelings.
■ The therapeutic value of psychodrama is that it permits people to act out before a trained person the situations he might not have courage to perform under ordinary circumstances.

3. Psychodrama is _____

_____

psychograph

SEYE–ko–GRAF

■ Monroe's psychograph showed his personality traits made him well-suited for a job which involved meeting the public.
■ Many employers now ask for psychographs of prospective employees in order to make personality assessments before hiring people.

4. A psychograph is _____

_____

psychogenic

SEYE–ko–JEN–ik

■ A mania is psychogenic because behavior stems from a mental condition.
■ Sylvester's rash was psychogenic rather than the result of poison ivy.

5. Something psychogenic has _____

_____

psychiatrist

seye–KEYE–uh–trist

■ Psychiatrists can administer drugs in the treatment of patients because they are first physicians before specializing in mental disorders.
■ The fact that California is said to have more medical schools and mental institutions than any other state in the country indicates there are probably more psychiatrists there than in other states.

6. A psychiatrist is _____

_____

psychotherapy

SEYE–ko–THER–uh–
    pey

■ Sometimes psychotherapy takes the form of group discussions of individual problems among patients.
■ Free association is a form of psychotherapy.

7. Psychotherapy is _____

_____

psychic

SEYE–kik

■ ESP (Extra–Sensory Perception) is a psychic phenomenon.
■ Mental telepathy is a form of psychic power.

8. A psychic person _____

_____

psychosis

seye–KO–sis

■ Anyone suffering from a psychosis probably has a mental disorder which makes the pursuit of a normal life impossible.
■ The single word "psychosis" can be used to describe a wide variety of abnormal mental conditions.

9. A psychosis is _____

_____

psychoanalysis

SEYE–ko–uh–NAL–uh–
  sis

■ Psychoanalysis is usually a lengthy treatment for it requires that a patient explore his own subconscious.

■ Although psychoanalysis is a recent development, many writers of previous centuries have explored the minds of their characters with psychoanalytical methods.

10. Psychoanalysis is _____

_____

ANSWERS

1. *Psychosomatic illness is caused by the mind affecting the body.*
2. *Psychophysics is the study of the effect physical processes have on mental processes.*
3. *Psychodrama is acting out one's problems.*
4. *A psychograph is a chart outlining one's personality traits.*
5. *Something psychogenic has its origin in the mind.*
6. *A psychiatrist is a specialist in the treatment of mental disorders.*
7. *Psychotherapy is concerned with the diagnosis and treatment of mental disorders.*
8. *A psychic person possesses supernormal mental powers.*
9. *A psychosis is a severe mental disorder.*
10. *Psychoanalysis is a method of treating mental disorders.*

word comprehension

DIRECTIONS: Read the paragraph. Then put a check next to each sentence below that describes something in the paragraph.

The psychic went to the psychologist for psychometrics. Examination revealed a psychosomatic condition that might respond to psychotherapy.

_____ a. A medical doctor is involved.
_____ b. Problems were acted out.
_____ c. Mental tests were taken.
_____ d. Someone called an "ology" expert.

(*more*)

_____ e. The person involved had supernormal powers.
_____ f. There was a physical condition with mental causes.
_____ g. A study was made of the patient's writing.
_____ h. Treatment for mental illness was recommended.
_____ i. The person consulted was a specialist in the study of life forms.

ANSWERS: c; e; f; h.

words in use

DIRECTIONS: The italicized words in the following paragraphs can be stated more briefly by using single words. Match the number of each underlined group of words with a synonym from the column which follows the paragraph. Write the letter indicating the synonym next to the appropriate number.

John had an interesting ability. *Just by concentrating he could make*
                                                        1

things move. His brother Frank tried the same thing but paradoxically he

found his left leg suddenly paralyzed. He went immediately to a doctor who

told him the *paralysis was caused by his mind.* The doctor game him some
                          2

mental tests, then recommended a *specialized treatment which involved act-*
      3   4
ing.

_____ a. psychosomatic
_____ b. psychophysics
_____ c. psychodrama
_____ d. psychic
_____ e. psychotherapy
_____ f. psychograph
_____ g. psychogenic
_____ h. psychoauditory
_____ i. psychometrics
_____ j. psychosocial

ANSWERS: 1—d; 2—a or g; 3—i; 4—c.

true-false

DIRECTIONS: Read each sentence carefully and decide whether it is true or false. If it is true put a T in the space at the right. If it is false, write in an F.

1. Psychodynamic refers to a form of therapy where the patient acts out his problem.   1._____
2. If he practices psychiatry he is a medical doctor.   2._____
3. Psychosomatic illnesses are psychogenic.   3._____
4. Psyche is a root which means mind.   4._____
5. Psychomotor refers to mind and machine.   5._____
6. If a person has psychometry he has a mental illness.   6._____
7. A person with psychic powers might be able to tell what you were thinking.   7._____
8. Something which originates in the mind is said to be psychogenic.   8._____
9. Psychodrama is a form of psychotherapy.   9._____
10. A bell is likely to elicit a psychoauditory response.   10._____

ANSWERS: 1—F; 2—T; 3—T; 4—T; 5—F; 6—F; 7—T; 8—T; 9—T; 10—T.

SON PHON AUD
SON FON AWD

From the Latin *sonare* meaning "to speak" or "sound"	From the Greek *phone* meaning "sound" or "voice"	From the Latin *audire* meaning "to hear"

SONIC booms, telephones, phonograph records, audio amplifiers—all these are among the noise-makers of our society, the sounds that we are now told pollute the air so much we may eventually become a nation of people with damaged hearing. While most of us would dread being deaf, not much is being done to prevent the kind of "deafness" that results from the constant assault upon the eardrums. So radios and TV sets continue to play while people study, and there remains some mystical relationship between the quality of music and the size of the amplifiers over which it is played.

The following word parts will be combined with the root in this unit to make new words. Use this list as a reference to find the meaning of words in this unit.

ROOTS AS AFFIXES
meter—measurement
graph—word or write
micro—small
uni—one
ultra—beyond or to an extreme

PREFIXES
tele—distant or from afar
eu—good or well
caca—bad or evil
super—above or beyond or in addition to
sym—same or like
re—back or again
dis—away from or negation

SUFFIXES
ible—able, fit or likely
ence—act, state or condition
or—doer, action or state
tion—state, quality or condition
arium—place for
ic—caused by or dealing with
ant—doing or showing
ous—full of
ance—act, state or condition

335

context clues

DIRECTIONS: Pronounce each word in the left hand column and read aloud the sentences in the right hand column. On the basis of context clues in the sentences, fill in the blank space to make a correct definition.

audible

AWD–uh–buhl

- Selma's normally loud voice was barely audible when she had a cold.
- Careful design of the lecture hall will insure that every speaker will be audible even in the last row.

1. Audible means _____

_____

audience

AW–dee–ents

- The large audience came to hear the college president speak but stayed to stage a sit-in at the administration building.
- Mertin's wife was his best audience; she always laughed at his old stories even though others readily said they had heard the stories before.

2. An audience is _____

_____

audio

AW–dee–o

- The picture quality was perfect but the audio portion of the film was so bad nobody could understand what any character was saying.
- Audio teaching aids include recordings and live lectures.

3. Audio means _____

_____

audiometer

aw–dee–OM–uh–tuhr

- The specialist used a portable audiometer to come into the classroom and test each child's hearing.
- Before the audiometer was developed, it was hard to tell the exact amount of hearing loss a person suffered.

4. An audiometer is _____

_____

auditor

AW–duh–tuhr

- Instead of taking the lecture course for credit, Jim registered as an auditor just so he could sit in on the class.
- An auditor will attend every meeting of the legislature and report to the League of Women Voters on the progress of the bills they favor.

5. An auditor is _____

_____

audition

aw–DISH–uhn

- The chorus girls had to audition before they were selected to sing on the television program.
- Myrtle was a little nervous the day she had to audition for the part in the drama club production, but she impressed the teacher enough to win out over four others.

6. An audition is _____

_____

auditorium

aw–duh–TOH–ree–uhm

- Two hundred students gathered in the auditorium to hear the lecture.
- This auditorium was designed by experts so that any size crowd could hear the performance perfectly and even "stage whispers" would be audible anywhere.

7. An auditorium is _____

_____

phonetic

fuh–NET–ik

- English is difficult because words are not always spelled phonetically and thus there is no connection between the way a word looks and the way it sounds.
- The phonetic history of a language shows many changes in pronunciation over the years.

8. Phonetic means _____

_____

phonograph

FO–nuh–graf

■ The early phonograph used cylinders instead of disks to reproduce sounds.
■ The invention of phonograph records made it possible to store a library of great symphonies in a small space.

9. A phonograph is _____

_____

telephone

TEL–uh–fown

■ The telephone uses a small electromagnet to transmit electrical impulses set up by the voice.
■ Telephone operation differs from radio transmission because it makes use of electricity.

10. A telephone is _____

_____

microphone

MEYE–kruh–fown

■ Sound waves are magnified by the microphone.
■ A microphone is essential to make the speaker heard in the large auditorium.

11. A microphone is _____

_____

euphonic

you–FON–ik

■ The politician always beautifies his militant opinions with euphonic terms so his listeners don't really get the full impact of what he is saying.
■ Euphonic phrases are often used to disguise unpopular ideas.

12. Euphonic means _____

_____

cacophony

kuh–KOF–uh–nee

■ The jungle air at dawn was a cacophony of shrill bird calls and weird animal noises.
■ The junior high school band made a valiant effort to play together, but the result was more cacophonous than euphonious.

13. Cacophony means _____

_____

symphony

SIM–fuh–nee

■ You cannot produce a symphony if you will not play together.
■ It is amazing that such a variety of instruments can produce such harmony, such a symphony of sounds.

14. Symphony means _____

_____

resonant

REZ–uh–nuhnt

■ The waves of sound from his resonant voice reverberated through the room.
■ The resonant quality of fine, strong instruments adds a mellow tone to any orchestra.

15. Resonant means _____

_____

sonorous

SON–uhr–uhs

■ The sonorous notes of the choir resounded through the entire cathedral.
■ The white-haired senator addressed the congress in such rumbling, sonorous tones that the members all marveled at the richness of his voice.

16. Sonorous means _____

_____

unison

YOU–nuh–suhn

■ The twins were so much alike, they even answered questions in unison.
■ When the teacher entered, the entire class stood up and said in unison, "Good morning, teacher."

17. Unison means _____

_____

supersonic

sou–puhr–SON–ik

■ Supersonic aircraft must be specially designed so they will not break apart when they exceed the speed of sound.
■ It takes a moment for the sound of a supersonic plane to catch up with the sighting of the aircraft.

18. Supersonic means _____

_____

ultrasonic

uhl–truh–SON–ik

■ Sound waves of extreme intensity can do strange things, and these ultrasonic waves are now being used to wash the dirt off dishes.
■ Certain ultrasonic frequencies are being used to selectively destroy cells in surgery much as a high, piercing sound can shatter glass.

19. Ultrasonic means _____

_____

sonar

SO–nar

■ Modern commercial fishing vessels are equipped with sonar to help them find deep layers of shrimp by listening for variations in sounds beneath the sea.
■ The bat uses a kind of sonar when he emits high squeals that bounce back to him and warn him of obstacles.

20. Sonar is _____

_____

dissonance

DIS–uh–nuhns

■ The entire audience, unless it is singing in unison, will produce a cacophony of dissonance.
■ Martin's rock band, its music based on dissonance, shocked people who were used to careful harmony.

21. Dissonance means _____

_____

sonata

suh–NOT–uh

■ The sonata for violin and piano was performed beautifully.
■ The sonata form is basic to the symphony and to the concerto.

22. Sonata means _____

_____

ANSWERS

1. *Audible* means what can be heard.
2. An *audience* is a group of people assembled to hear something.
3. *Audio* means related to sound.
4. An *audiometer* is an instrument for measuring hearing.
5. An *auditor* is one who listens.
6. An *audition* is an examination by listening.
7. An *auditorium* is a room or hall where groups of people gather to listen.
8. *Phonetic* means the sounds of speech.
9. A *phonograph* is a record player, a device from which recorded sound is heard.
10. A *telephone* is a device over which sound is transmitted.
11. A *microphone* is an instrument that transforms sound into electric current or voltage which serves to magnify the sound of the human voice.
12. *Euphonic* means pleasant sounding.
13. *Cacophony* means unpleasant sounding.
14. *Symphony* means sounding together, as a group of musicians.
15. *Resonant* means continuing to sound or echoing.
16. *Sonorous* means giving out a deep, resonant sound.
17. *Unison* means sounding together, as one.
18. *Supersonic* means greater than or past the speed of sound (in a certain medium).
19. *Ultrasonic* means a sound so high it is beyond the normal range of hearing.
20. *Sonar* is a device that uses sound waves to detect underwater objects.
21. *Dissonance* means lack of harmony.
22. *Sonata* means a musical composition for one or two instruments and in a prescribed form of three or four contrasting movements.

matching exercise

DIRECTIONS: Write the appropriate letter from the right hand column in the space next to each number so that the numbered words are defined.

———— 1. resonant   **a.** harmony

———— 2. sonorous   **b.** a piece of music

———— 3. unison   **c.** able to be heard

———— 4. consonance   **d.** an examination by listening

———— 5. audible   **e.** an instrument for measuring hearing

———— 6. audiometer   **f.** obsessed with sound

(*more*)

_____ 7. audition

_____ 8. sonata

g. continuing to sound; echoing

h. giving out sound

i. a record player

j. together

ANSWERS: 1—g; 2—h; 3—j; 4—a; 5—c; 6—e; 7—d; 8—b.

true-false

DIRECTIONS: Read each sentence carefully and decide whether it is true or false. If it is true, put a T in the space at the right. If it is false, write in an F.

1. If it can be heard it is in unison.   1._____
2. Sonorous means the same as cacophony.   2._____
3. Phonasthenia is the science of sound.   3._____
4. An echoing sound is a resonant sound.   4._____
5. Sound is measured with an audiometer.   5._____
6. Audible means something is done by two or more individuals at the same time.   6._____
7. Dissonance refers to spelling.   7._____
8. A phonetic is an instrument for measuring sound.   8._____
9. Euphonic is a sound made with your mouth.   9._____
10. A sonata is a hall for group listening.   10._____

ANSWERS: 1—F; 2—F; 3—F; 4—T; 5—F; 6—F; 7—F; 8—F; 9—F; 10—F.

fill in the blanks

DIRECTIONS: Fill in the blank in each sentence with the appropriate word from among the following choices.

auditorium	euphonious
audiology	cacophony
audible	phonics
audient	phonasthenia
audiometer	phonate
resonant	unison
sonorous	consonance
dissonance	

1. A machine called an _____ measures hearing.

2. If it is continuous and echoing a sound is said to be _____.

3. If it can be heard it is _____.

4. The science of hearing is called _____.

5. The _____ was filled with students.

6. _____ is the science of sound.

7. _____ and harmony have the same meaning.

8. The two students, working in _____,

    finished the project together.

ANSWERS: 1—audiometer; 2—resonant; 3—audible; 4—audiology; 5—auditorium; 6—phonics; 7—consonance; 8—unison.

scrambled
words

DIRECTIONS: Unscramble the following words. Each is defined in parentheses.

1. sorouson _____
    (it means giving out sound)

2. inonus _____
    (to do things together)

3. atanos _____
                                    (a musical piece)

4. ibulade _____
                                    (it can be heard)

5. demuriteao _____
                                    (it measures hearing)

ANSWERS: *1—sonorous; 2—unison; 3—sonata; 4—audible; 5—audiometer.*

TELE

TEL-uh

From the Greek *tele* meaning "distant"

TELE has special meaning beyond simply "distant"; it usually refers to the transmission or sending of something over a distance as in the words *television* (sending something visible, i.e., a picture, over a distance) or *telephone* (a device used for the transmission of sound over great distances).

By using *tele* as a prefix to any word describing an instrument, it is possible to describe that instrument operating or transmitting information over a distance such as:

> teletypewriter (often shortened to teletype)
> telectroscope
> telebarometer
> telegraphoscope
> telethermometer

The following word parts will be combined with the root in this unit to make new words. Use this list as a reference to find the meaning of words in this unit.

ROOTS AS AFFIXES

cast—to throw
gnosis—knowledge or to know
gram—written down
gony—produced or generated
graph—word or writing
kinesis—movement
meter—measurement

prompter—to bring forth
path—feeling
photo—light
thesia—feeling
erg—work
scope—seeing too much

SUFFIXES
ic—caused by or dealing with
y—result, action or quality
gen—to be born, or something that produces
osis—condition

345

context
clues

DIRECTIONS: Pronounce each word in the left hand column and read aloud the sentences in the right hand column. On the basis of context clues in the sentences, fill in the blank space to make a correct definition.

telecast

TEL–uh–kast

■ Millions of people around the world watched the telecast of the first men walking on the moon.
■ Early telecasts had only unclear black–and–white pictures, but they were an exciting innovation for people who had only known radio communication.

1. Telecast means _____

_____

telegenic

tel–uh–JEN–ik

■ In order to be a television star, one must be telegenic as well as personable or articulate.
■ The most telegenic person may not be particularly attractive in person.

2. Telegenic means _____

_____

telegnosis

tuh–leg–NO–suhs

■ Mind readers and fortune–tellers are practitioners of telegnosis.
■ Many people who claim professional powers of telegnosis are actually either frauds or astute observers of people and human nature.

3. Telegnosis means _____

_____

telegony

tuh–LEG–uh–nee

■ Mr. Smith has brown eyes, so when Mrs. Smith gave birth to a child with blue eyes she could hardly blame the occurrence on telegony, even though her previous husband had blue eyes.
■ Telegony does not operate on race horses any more than on other animals; a winning horse is more often sired by a race horse than by a draft horse, even though the dam is a race horse.

4. Telegony means _____

_____

telegram

TEL–uh–gram

■ The arrival of a telegram was once such an unusual event in ordinary households that people were sure it carried bad news.
■ Telegrams are often used to confirm prices quoted in telephone conversations.

5. A telegram is _____

_____

telegraph

TEL–uh–graf

■ The telegraph became a practical means of communication only after it became possible to produce electricity cheaply and in quantity.
■ The poles and wires of the telegraph companies became the symbol of fast westward expansion in the U.S.

6. Telegraph means _____

_____

telekinesis

tel–i–kuh–NEE–suhs

■ Sometimes spiritualists demonstrate what they claim are their psychic powers by demonstrating through telekinesis how they can move a table or chair.
■ When Samantha, the "witch" on the television program, straightens up a messy room without touching anything in it, she is demonstrating telekinesis.

7. Telekinesis means _____

_____

telemeter

te–LEM–uh–tuhr

■ Telemetric devices enable men in ground control stations to gather data from unmanned space devices.
■ Visual sightings in astronomy are reinforced and confirmed by telemeters.

8. Telemeter means _____

_____

Teleprompter

TEL–uh–prom(p)–tuhr

■ The Teleprompter is a device that is seldom seen on camera, yet it makes it possible for TV performers to be letter-perfect in their dialogue.
■ Many political speakers find it difficult or impossible to remember long speeches, so they rely on the Teleprompter.

9. Teleprompter is _____

_____

telepathy

tuh–LEP–uh–thee

■ It is repetitious to use the word mental in the phrase "mental telepathy."
■ People who claim they can communicate by telepathy often are only those who have like experience or knowledge which they call upon simultaneously.

10. Telepathy means _____

_____

telephoto

tel–uh–FO–toe

■ The photographer was able to show how the runner broke his stride on the opposite side of the stadium because his camera was equipped with a telephoto lens.
■ The development of the telephoto lens made possible spying and reconnaissance missions from high-flying airplanes.

11. Telephoto means _____

_____

telescope

TEL–uh–skope

■ Until recently, man's closest look at the moon has been through a telescope.
■ The rifle used to kill President Kennedy was equipped with a telescopic sight.

12. Telescope means _____

_____

telesthesia

tel–uhs–THEE–zee–uh

■ Mitzi claimed that her telesthesia proved Clara was trying to reach her even though everyone knew Clara was in New York.

■ Telesthesia is probably at work in authentic cases of ESP.

13. Telesthesia means _____

_____

telergy

TEL–uhr–jee

■ It is more difficult to authenticate cases of telergy than of telesthesia because while the latter involves sensations, the former involves the mind.
■ Michael insisted that through telergy Mr. Mammond had implanted the idea of murder which he subsequently carried out.

14. Telergy means _____

_____

ANSWERS

1. *Telecast* means to broadcast by television.
2. *Telegenic* means having physical qualities that televise well.
3. *Telegnosis* means supernatural or occult knowledge; clairvoyance.
4. *Telegony* means heredity or the transmission of traits to children.
5. A *telegram* is a written message transmitted over a distance.
6. A *telegraph* is an apparatus to send messages over a distance by means of an electric device.
7. *Telekinesis* means the physical movement of objects from one place to another without contact or apparent physical means.
8. *Telemeter* is an instrument for determining the distance of another object.
9. *Teleprompter* is a device with a magnified script in front of a speaker so he can read his lines.
10. *Telepathy* means mentally transmitting ideas or feelings between persons at some distance from each other.
11. *Telephoto* means a lens that produces a large image of a distant object.
12. *Telescope* is an optical instrument for making distant objects appear closer.
13. *Telesthesia* means the sensation or perception received at a distance without normal use of the recognized sense organs.
14. *Telergy* means the supposed influence of one brain over another at a distance.

words in use

DIRECTIONS: Fill in each blank with the proper word from among the following choices.

telegnosis   telemeter
telethermometer   telegenic
telecast   telepathy
telegram   telegony

The news _____ pictured the
                    1

_____ showing the distance of the UFO to
                2

the astronomer. Thinking that it might contain intelligent beings he

concentrated with all his strength trying to use _____
                                                            3

to make contact with them. When he was unsucussful he sent a

_____ to Washington, D.C. asking for
                4

directions in handling the situation. He was told to use the

_____ to get a reading of the heat of the object.
            5

ANSWERS: 1—telecast; 2—telemeter; 3—telepathy; 4—telegram; 5—telethermometer.

true-false

DIRECTIONS: Read each sentence carefully and decide whether it is true or false. If it is true, put a T in the answer space at the right. If it is false, write in an F.

1. A telethermometer is used to measure air pressure.   1._____
2. Telegony is actually an hereditary term.   2._____
3. Clairvoyance is a synonym for telegnosis.   3._____
4. A telephoto is one that bears a written message.   4._____
5. If you can move objects just by thinking about them you can
   demonstrate telekinesis.   5._____
6. Telegenic means hereditary.   6._____
7. A telemeter is used to measure atmospheric pressure.   7._____
8. A teleprompter may be used to give cues to people speaking
   on TV.   8._____
9. Telepathy is the mental transmission of feelings between per-
   sons who are a distance from one another.   9._____
10. The lack of physical sensation in the hands and feet is prop-
    erly termed telesthesia.   10._____

ANSWERS: 1—F; 2—T; 3—T; 4—F; 5—T; 6—F; 7—F; 8—T; 9—T; 10—F.

matching exercise

DIRECTIONS: Write the appropriate letter from the right hand column in the space next to each number so that the numbered words are defined.

_____ 1. telemeter
_____ 2. telephoto
_____ 3. telekinesis

_____ 4. telegenic

_____ 5. telegony

_____ 6. telethermometer

_____ 7. telepathy

_____ 8. telebarometer

_____ 9. Teleprompter
_____10. telergy

a. hereditary
b. suitable for television broadcast
c. the influence one brain has over another at a great distance
d. a device with magnified script in front of a speaker on TV
e. an instrument for determining the distance of an object
f. a mental transmission of feelings between persons at a distance from each other
g. an instrument that records temperature at a distance
h. a lens used to produce a large image of a distant object
i. the psychic movement of objects from one place to another without physical contact
j. used to measure atmospheric pressure
k. a long TV program
l. relating to telium

ANSWERS: 1—e; 2—h; 3—i; 4—b; 5—a; 6—g; 7—f; 8—j; 9—d; 10—c.

POSTTEST

DIRECTIONS: In the space next to each number, write the letter that correctly completes the statement.

_____ 1. If you look through the telescope on a clear night you might see
        a. an asteroid.
        b. an asterisk.
        c. an aster.
        d. an astrologer.

_____ 2. Carlos Baker wrote Ernest Hemingway's
        a. autobiography.
        b. biography.
        c. fiction.
        d. non-fiction.

_____ 3. The ergograph is an apparatus for studying
        a. brain damage.
        b. muscle fatigue.
        c. temporal sequences.
        d. mirror writing.

_____ 4. An instrument often used in the study of reading is a
        a. polygraph.
        b. myograph.
        c. kymograph.
        d. opthalmograph.

_____ 5. An important clue to weather is indicated on the map by
        a. isosceles.
        b. isotopes.
        c. isobars.
        d. isometrics.

_____ 6. If you wanted to illuminate a street you would
        a. paint a new strip down the middle.
        b. set the date for the neighborhood sale.
        c. install parking meters.
        d. install lights.

_____ 7. A pyromaniac is most likely to be delighted by
      a. fire engines.
      b. sweets.
      c. the appearance of pretty girls.
      d. new clothing styles.

_____ 8. A neurosis is a
      a. neuroblast.
      b. physiological disorder.
      c. neurotomy.
      d. mental disorder.

_____ 9. A person who had experienced a neurotomy would have had
      a. a neurosis.
      b. neurobiotaxis.
      c. a severed nerve.
      d. graphomania.

_____10. The word psychosomatic refers to the
      a. body and the environment.
      b. mind and the environment.
      c. body and the mind.
      d. mind and mental illness.

_____11. A chart outlining the strength of the personality traits in an individual is called
      a. psychosomatics.
      b. a psychodrama.
      c. psychokinesia.
      d. a psychograph.

_____12. When a chorus does not sing on key and in unison, the result is
      a. euphony.
      b. audient.
      c. sonorous.
      d. cacophony.

_____13. If you suspect hearing trouble you should have a test on
      a. an audiometer.
      b. an auditorium.
      c. a phonasthenia.
      d. a unison.

_____14. A pathologist in a hospital would be responsible for
   a. performing autopsies.
   b. taking blood counts.
   c. physical therapy.
   d. cost accounting.

_____15. Myrtle was so telegenic that everyone urged her to make an immediate appointment with
   a. a ringmaster.
   b. a television producer.
   c. the telegraph company.
   d. a geneticist.

_____16. It was impossible to see the first men on the moon even if you looked through the most powerful
   a. telescope.
   b. telebarometer.
   c. telegrapher.
   d. telegony.

ANSWERS: 1—a; 2—b; 3—b; 4—d; 5—c; 6—d; 7—a; 8—d; 9—c; 10—c; 11—d; 12—d; 13—a; 14—a; 15—b; 16—a.

GENERAL POSTTEST

At the beginning of this book a pretest gave you an indication of your vocabulary ability. Now it is time for a posttest to show you how much you have learned. Compare your score on the pretest with your score on the posttest and see your improvement.

DIRECTIONS: In the space next to each number, write the letter that correctly completes the statement.

_____ 1. If a government were anxious to get rid of someone foreign-born it might consider
    a. deporting him.
    b. exporting him.
    c. importing him.
    d. supporting him.

_____ 2. If one person kills another he is guilty of
    a. homogeneity.
    b. homicide.
    c. honorifics.
    d. hominoids.

_____ 3. Jack's chronic illness would
    a. soon be over.
    b. respond to wonder drugs.
    c. surely last a long time.
    d. never have occurred if he'd been careful.

_____ 4. It was difficult to discredit Jim's version of the fight because he was ordinarily
    a. credible.
    b. a liar.
    c. accredited.
    d. a usurper.

_____ 5. Witches in stories often use
    a. motorcycles.
    b. benedictions.
    c. maledictions.
    d. narcosis.

_____ 6. Jack could easily read plans for assembling the TV set because he
    a. knew the nomenclature.
    b. was homogeneous.

c. knew the salesman.

d. acted forthright.

_____ 7. You would be most likely to arrange for an inscription on
a. an award plaque.
b. a valuable acre of city land.
c. the license plate of a new automobile.
d. a paperback novel.

_____ 8. A person with graphobia is likely to select a
job as
a. a typist.
b. a sign painter.
c. a lifeguard.
d. a magazine writer.

_____ 9. If you had claustrophobia, you would feel a
need to
a. stay out of small enclosures.
b. stay out of trouble.
c. sleep late every day.
d. walk a great deal every day.

_____ 10. Young children will be best entertained by a
a. colloquium.
b. ventriloquist.
c. soliloquist.
d. grandiloquence.

_____ 11. A telephoto lens would most probably be used
for
a. a studio portrait.
b. copying a painting in a museum.
c. spying on a military installation.
d. examining geologic specimens.

_____ 12. Some schools of psychology believe that a neurosis is less severe than a
a. psychometrist.
b. psychoanalyst.
c. psychosis.
d. psychogenesis.

_____ 13. The application of various forms of mental
treatment to nervous and mental disorders is
called.

    a. psychotherapy.
    b. psychopathic.
    c. psychodynamic.
    d. psychometric.

_____14. If someone has neuralgia he has
    a. nerve pain.
    b. mental illness.
    c. speech defect.
    d. headaches.

_____15. When a person can copy a question but cannot write the answer, even though he knows it, his condition is called
    a. agraphia.
    b. macrographia.
    c. dermographia.
    d. echographia.

_____16. Policemen frequently have use for a
    a. kymograph.
    b. ergograph.
    c. polygraph.
    d. opthalmograph.

_____17. A theomaniac would have an unnatural interest in
    a. sex.
    b. drugs.
    c. fires.
    d. religion.

_____18. Someone with kleptomania would be a great problem if he went
    a. to sleep.
    b. to a store.
    c. to a swim meet.
    d. to a nudist camp.

_____19. A malcontent can best be described as one who
    a. is unhappy about circumstances or conditions he finds himself in.
    b. regards apples as one of the healthiest fruits to eat.
    c. feels that seeing movies is more useful than reading books.
    d. is content to be a follower rather than a leader.

NAME:

_____20. One country does not ordinarily cede its ter-
ritory to another nation without cause because
it usually does not wish to
    a. increase the tariffs.
    b. change its customs.
    c. lose land, population, and industry.
    d. change its flag.

_____21. If you were moved to intercede during a
campus strike you were
    a. ignoring the situation.
    b. having all your grades lowered.
    c. attempting to solve the problems faced
       by both sides.
    d. turning around and going home.

_____22. Public service advertisements always recom-
mend a visit to the dentist
    a. biennally.
    b. annually.
    c. semiannually.
    d. quarterly.

_____23. You can amoritze the debt by
    a. regular payments.
    b. good looks.
    c. delving into the occult.
    d. hiring an amanuensis.

_____24. If you tell me what transpired at the meeting
    a. I will remain in ignorance.
    b. know that it was cancelled.
    c. know what happened during it.
    d. realize how everyone was sweating.

_____25. A person who has most likely made a system-
atic study of theology is
    a. a thespian.
    b. a minister.
    c. a theorist.
    d. a theme writer.

ANSWERS TO POSTTEST

1—a; 2—b; 3—c; 4—a; 5—c; 6—a; 7—a; 8—c; 9—a; 10—b; 11—c; 12—c;
13—a; 14—a; 15—d; 16—c; 17—d; 18—b; 19—a; 20—c; 21—c; 22—c; 23—a;
24—c; 25—b.